A Basic Guide for
VALUING
a Company

Second Edition

Wilbur M. Yegge

John Wiley & Sons, Inc.

This book is lovingly dedicated to my sons, Andrew
and Trevor, and my daughter, Denise. It is also dedicated to
all buyers and sellers whose objective is to strike *fair deals.*

Library of Congress Cataloging-in-Publication Data

Yegge, Wilbur M.
    A basic guide for valuing a company / Wilbur M. Yegge.—2nd ed.
      p. cm.
    Includes index.
    ISBN 0-471-15047-9 (pbk : alk. paper).
     1. Business enterprises—Valuation—Handbooks, manuals, etc. I. Title.

HF5681.V3 Y43 2001
658.15—dc21

                                    2001026546

Printed in the United States of America
10 9 8 7 6 5 4 3 2

Acknowledgments

So many individuals, over so many years, contributed "real-life" scenarios that form the essence of practice leading to writing this manuscript—far too many to name, but I deeply thank you all.

A few, however, made in-process contributions. I acknowledge the Honorable Richard Nass, B.S., M.B.A.—business associate, friend, and Maine House representative. To "wade" in the waters of any technical or grammatical beginning is a tenacious undertaking, but to wade in mine necessitates uncommon stamina. Dick, your countless hours of critique are deeply appreciated from the bottom of my heart.

Thomas Dobens, C.P.A.—once more you add technical "surefootedness" to my characterizations. To Robert Nadeau, Esq., my thanks go out for legal review and formative contribution to the issue of ethics. Mary Rich once again helped reduce the "cowboy" in some of my grammar.

Writers often feel the need to engage agents, and perhaps some do need agents, but Michael Hamilton, senior editor at Wiley, is ample encouragement to "go-it-alone." Throughout our dealings, you have been honest and fair (giving a hint to the backbone in my writing). Thank you for your invitation to produce this series, and for your unfailing help.

> *"Man has only been out of the jungle for 25,000 years . . . perhaps this is why we have not learned to deal with others as well as we should."*
>
> W.M.Y.

Contents

Introduction

We have seen strong growth in new business creation during the past 10 years. The trend is expected to continue, and is likely to accelerate, as downsizing intensifies at large companies and in swollen bureaucracies of government. The owners of a large number of small businesses started after World War II are on the verge of retirement or of transferring these businesses to family members or heirs. A report of the *Boston Business Journal* early in 1993 forecasted that the wealth being transferred during the next 15 years approximated $6.8 trillion. Technology is creating a need for new small businesses and for global marketplaces, which in turn fosters virgin opportunities for their future growth. Selling, buying, and family-business transfers will significantly increase as corporate jobs disappear, as World War II "bloomers" retire, and as the global market expands. There is an insufficient number of trained personnel to handle the volume of business valuations that currently exist, let alone those portended by the future. This book is written for buyers and sellers to assist in doing the transaction themselves.

In Search of Business Worth could easily have been an appropriate title to this book, because "search" is the real dilemma to overcome. Financial know-how is so well documented and available that it provides escape from inordinate learning by even novice attendees. However, that's not to say that trial and error are uninvited, because formulas alone are only nostrums for successful valuation. Variations in techniques no doubt cover the globe, because for every "accepted" formula there are practitioners who define what's accepted . . . and there are a large number of individuals who are, or consider themselves, the experts. In fact, practitioners themselves are a good part of the problem in this broadly defined field of business valuation. The task is not simply a numbers game, though many would have it so. Market research and analysis is the rascal portending the real search. Why? Because "bean counters" are not market researchers unless they make themselves thus, and the marketplace is where answers to the search for business value lie. Though the formulas are defined by an accounting process, the best practitioners are usually not accountants per se.

Perhaps the most widely revered expertise, because it is widely known and broadly advertised, comes from the membership in the American Society of Appraisers (ASA). In more recent years the Society has issued a specialized designation termed Business Valuator (BV). Thus the "expert" carries ASA-BV on his or her calling card. A major contributor to ASA-BV entry and continuing membership criteria is Dr. Shannon Pratt, whom I know to be eminently qualified in both the publicly traded and closely held valuation fields. But as you will see later in the text, I take issue with transforming *all* real estate appraisers into business valuation experts. Not that there is no parallel in these two sciences, because there is considerable parallel, but because real estate appraisal is much more a science than an art, particularly in the closely held arena. Don't misunderstand me; there certainly are some fine ASA-BV experts who have developed appropriate mind-sets for the task.

The family-owned and/or closely held business is the more difficult tiger to tame. Publicly traded companies seek to show bottom-line profit to satisfy "public owners," while closely held enterprises seek only to satisfy private interests, *before profit falls to the bottom line.* Thus the "documents" by which the *psychology of ownerships* are measured send out different messages in each. Very little of the "Captain, may I?" attitude common to public companies occurs in the private domain. Subsequently, since ownership and management of closely held enterprises are often one and the same, financial records are massaged for tax avoidance. In addition, private ownerships can, and sometimes do, play the game of chance by stretching the "gray" areas in law beyond the limits. All of this leads to difficult interpretations of what *really* goes on in these companies. When small-company owners have elected to step over the boundaries of law, and they sometimes do, the valuator must face moral issues and questions of "recognizing" marginal or illegal acts—presumably presented with supporting paper-trail facts—in his or her evaluations, or of denying their existence, to the extent of "reported" data. I will not touch upon "moral fiber" in this book because the targeted reader is unlikely to be an expert in valuation, and because each individual sets up his or her own parameters by which he or she judges what is, or is not, morally correct. For the cautionary benefit of buyers I will, however, simply spell out practices that I have seen. We all know the "games" that go on. We really do.

The heart of valuing the family-owned or closely held business is found through understanding the operating objectives of its owner/managers. For until objectives are defined, valuation assignments are unlikely to arrive at predictable *estimates of fair market values*. Determining specific operations and operating philosophies; "recasting-out" items unrelated to true business needs; determining values in "hard" assets; ascertaining overall economic conditions in the businesses, in the related industries, and in the national, regional, and local impacts on these businesses—all are included in the broad-based task we are about to cover. We will then tie these data into marketplace realities. However, before proceeding I must once violate my nolo contendere position on moral ethics: *To believe in claims unsupported by "visual" fact is an act of foolish courage!*

Business valuations for closely held small companies are either acts of exorcism, or acts of examination, or both. The long-overdue discussion between psychology and business valuation has begun. True examination of closely held enterprise compels exploration of the paradoxical human psyche (not presented in the complex terms of the psychologist). I trust we all know the terms "cause" and "effect." To study comparable sales (as appraisers coin market data) is to study *effect*. To study human psyche, however, is to study *cause*. Effect records yesterday's happenings, but cause allows us to look into tomorrow's events.

In this book I present a sample of some of the scientific techniques used to value 10 different types of businesses. I say "some" because I don't know them all, and because each practitioner employs "base formulas" in different ways, often modified by his or her own perceptions in formula use. Because of the "art form" necessary to conduct the closely held business valuation especially, the key to successful *estimating* rests in the "user," not the formula itself.

Causal behavior, sometimes subliminally, is interwoven throughout the book. It is my hope that the reader, who will most likely be a periodic practitioner, will benefit both through enhanced uses of the formulas and in practical applications for negotiating the small-company purchase and sale. In Appendix A, I conclude with my own answers to a practice exercise embodied within the text (one concerning a business that was sold at arm's length).

This book is a companion to *A Basic Guide for Buying and Selling a Company*. And as with its companion, that "rascal" *perception* must be equally handled. For nearly all that we do in life, perception, even of the facts, is still the name of the game. Thus, I repeat from the former *Yegge's scoring rules for success*.

As you read and/or complete your own exercise, please take caution not to "throw the baby out with the wash water." As you will learn, how small companies can be financed affects estimated prices. Beyond the art form, price estimates are also molded by their restricting terms.

The information technology era has brought about a need for a change in mind-set—not formulas—for valuation tactics. The breathless over-confidence of observers, investors, and founders alike led to mass failure for dot-com businesses. With all the brightest minds taking bows, as the curtain came down, the *talent issue*—none other—has proved to be the Achilles' heel. In Chapter 23, learn what we missed—how to avoid compounding the overvaluation practices of the past.

Wilbur M. Yegge
Naples, Florida
March 2001

"For to win one hundred victories in one hundred battles is not the acme of skill. To subdue the enemy without fighting is the acme of skill."

Sun Tzu, *The Art of War*

"True victory is not defeating an enemy. True victory gives love and changes the enemy's heart."

Morihel Ueshiba, founder of Aikido

1

Setting the Stage ... This Business of Valuing Small, Closely Held Companies

Mary said to me, "I got a deal! I bought 'X' and I paid 'Y' dollars for it!" *My perception* of her deal compelled me to say, "**You paid what?!**" As you already know, each person's observation of the same event can *normally* be counted upon to be quite different. This, of course, is true about value in small companies.

We must let go of old assumptions that we know how things work regarding price and value in small, closely held companies. We really don't. For one thing, the earmarks of entrepreneurs are their independence and nonconformance with traditional practices. Quite frequently, they will be found never agreeing on anything from the past. For another, they are not bound by the decisions passed down by a corporate board of directors.

The *model definition* of fair market value used by most professional appraisers tends to revolve around several connected definitions provided in *Black's Law Dictionary.* The terms "cash market value," "fair market value," "reasonable market value," and "fair cash market value" are substantially synonymous terms and *mean the highest price the property would bring free of encumbrances, at a fair and voluntary private sale for cash.* At first blush, this crisp and straightforward concept seems rather easy to understand.

I'd now like you to read this same definition with its inherent conceptual fallacy exposed ... and, also, present it in the light of the small-company transaction.

> 'Fair market value' (FMV) is not designed with any particular individual in mind, nor the 'real' transaction for that matter. FMV is a hypothetical value for the 'model' transaction. The governing conditions in this ideal concept are *full knowledge* and *freedom to act.* But in reality, these ideal conditions are rarely present. Emotional

and subjective elements often override rational considerations, and *full knowledge is something rarely attained by the arm's-length potential buyer* who previously has not been involved in the business. Thus, the necessary conclusion is that few buy/sell transactions involving closely held small businesses are done at so-called fair market values. (Summarized from comments of T. S. Tony Leung, C.P.A.)

When my editor at John Wiley & Sons, Inc., Mike Hamilton, asked me to do a book on valuation, I was left with two choices: to write strictly as a technician and be similar to most competing works, or to reach into people-driven factors of how deals *really* go together as far as pricing is concerned. You will soon learn that this was not really an option for me. And, subsequently, the work of this book is akin to the preceding description by Mr. Leung.

However, the "stage" for inclusive discussion will be less than complete until we bring some of the more commonly found *myths* surrounding business valuation and pricing into view. I make no attempt to rank these in any particular order or to set precedence in how buyers and sellers might emphasize them during their negotiating processes. All are covered thoroughly in this book, including how these myths can and do creep in to complicate a reasonable and fair settlement on price between the principals in deals.

MYTHS COMMONLY ASSOCIATED WITH BUSINESS VALUE

Myth #1: The value of a closely held company is based on its "future" earnings.

There is absolutely no question that intrinsic decisions reached by buyers are deeply steeped in the prospects for earning livings beyond the dates of their purchases. But the fact is also that buyers expect to pay no more than the "present value" of those earnings on the dates of those transactions.

Discounted cash flow (DCF) methodologies are developed to analyze values in light of a business's future earnings. Simply described, these formulas consider business earnings for a number of forecasted years into the future; quite often, 10 years are used. Earnings are then "discounted" back to "present" value (value of future earnings stated in today's dollars). I have absolutely no qualms about the basic principle in this formula, and, as evidence of its goodness, it is frequently the method of choice in valuing publicly traded companies. Its use in valuing closely held companies, however, gives me more than moderate anxiety.

General Motors booked over $15 million of sales per *clock hour* in 1994. Even if sales sputter and are off by a million or so per hour, there is still a whopping annual sales volume left over. According to my studies of recent years, it is estimated that 74% of small, closely held companies in America realize under $1 million of sales *per year*. Most of these businesses struggle year after year just to make ends meet. For the most part, in valuing small companies, I cannot subscribe to methods that project values based on future earnings for businesses that breathe a sigh of relief when just *meeting* last year's sales! And I assure you, neither do most buyers. Bear in mind that regardless of what product, service, or entity we sell, ultimately it is the *consumer who will decide* whether we survive or fold. That consumer of the smaller company's goods and services is quite likely to be inordinately "attached" to the personality and characteristics of a past owner. Detach him or her from the business and what the replacement owner inherits may not be a suitable match in terms of today's value.

Regardless of the benefits I have received from formal education in psychology, accounting, industrial science, and mathematics, I still puzzle occasionally about the use of financial tables, as many expert technicians also do. Formulas, like languages, if not used daily can cause even the competent mind to wander and fail periodically. Try reading the 846 pages in *Handbook of Financial Mathematics, Formulas and Tables* by Robert P. Vichas (Prentice-Hall), if you doubt my concerns over formula usage! My point: Mastering DCF methodology is beyond the reach of the vast majority of periodic users. Unless the processor routinely and repetitively uses DCF, it is unlikely he or she will be able to collect and consider all the "character" and market variables in the proper light. Future earnings, discounted or not, belong to the owners taking the business into those future events. Thus, the message for sellers is simple—if you want future values, stay with your businesses, make the future happen, and depart when you've reached the target value of choice. The message for buyers is also simple—don't pay prices today that are based solely on future earnings. By the same token, don't buy a business that cannot foresee earnings in the future.

Myth #2: Real property and other hard asset values are always "add-ons" to business cash flow values.

Business "facilities" in the context of enterprise are no different per se from other required operational hard assets in terms of cash flow. In other words, the business "value" treats real estate, owned or leased, in the same way as furniture, fixtures, and equipment for the purposes of the valuation assignment, because facilities are as necessary to the operational function as are equipment and other hard assets. However, one should always appraise real estate as a stand-alone value, because it can often be sold with or without the business and because real estate ownership usually comprises the most valuable of business assets. It can also be the asset least affected in its value under the "hammer" of liquidation and can be the most viable asset pledged as collateral in terms of financing or refinancing the business as a whole. But real estate values *are not* add-ons to business values predicted through cash flow analysis. Cash flow value determinants predict what "can" be paid for the real estate, but not "what" the real estate is worth in market terms.

Market values of real estate and other hard assets collectively can enhance or negate the values of the business as a whole. When cash flows will not support the purchase of hard assets, including real estate purchase or lease, the prospect is strong that there is no remaining business value to discuss. Thus, we might have no more than an "asset" sale . . . and no real business to sell. The purchase of hard assets that are "excessively" supported by cash flows (cash flow inclusive of debt service *and* a new owner salary and profit), however, will enhance business values in the nature of both purchase price and financing terms. You'll see this more clearly as we move through several exercises later.

Myth #3: You should always press for all-cash deals.

Granted, this might be desirable, but the fact remains that better than 70% of all closely held transactions contain some element of seller financing. Thus, wanting and getting may not be an option for most, and "pressing" too hard and too long for cash-out may translate into no deal at all.

Structuring "installment" sales has tax benefits that should not be overlooked. As long as constructive receipt is divided into at least two tax years, capital gains tax may be less under present laws. Considering present legislative discussions, capital gains and depreciation treatments may even get better. The key to safety in private financing arrangements is to "know" player histories well and to recognize the strengths and weaknesses proposed in the deals themselves.

An all-cash requirement lowers purchase price. Financing, private or institutional, can assist or raise havoc with the price. Some sellers are willing to substantially discount business values for all cash, but many more will not be so willing. The statistics are against "getting your cake and eating it" at closing—concurrent with a price that may be all that your business is truthfully worth.

Myth #4: The darker "their" sunglasses, the more you'll receive.

Keeping a serious buyer in the dark about the reality in available cash flow, value, price, and terms sets the stage for personal disasters for both seller and buyer. Disproportionate outlooks will grow unmanageably through unchecked perceptions, and if the courts don't give a blow to the head, the ultimate settlement structure might. If you want to enjoy or walk away from a deal without looking back, the only safe assurance is in keeping the match open and on equal footing. Everybody has problems of one sort or the other. Share them . . . after all, one of you is selling, the other buying, and sharing may represent all the help you need to do your deal with safety. Dark conventional sunglasses keep out light, but they won't protect you from dangerous ultraviolet rays. Keeping secrets about the business's prognosis will rarely sweeten the pot permanently.

Myth #5: If I set the price high, I can always drop it.

Yes, you can, but can you do so soon enough to capture a sale? Pricing in its relationship to a marketable time frame is an issue in business valuation. Too low on the price, and a business sells too quickly in relationship to value. Too high, and it sells too slowly or not at all. Ever notice how shelved products get "ratty" and dusty when they move too slowly? They fail to be appealing when they get into this condition, and either they must be heavily discounted to be moved, or they can't be sold at all. Believe it or not, the same thing happens to small businesses. A price must be kept in line with the specific marketplace for that value to perform outside of wish-list expectations. Pricing, timed appropriately to the market, *protects* maximum value achieved.

Myth #6: If I make a low-ball offer, I can always go up.

Yes, you can, but the "sledding" from an undignified low-balling position is never easy. Everybody wants to buy low and sell high, and some do, but the overall problem with this concept is that *everybody* wants to do it. Low-ball offers tick people off! They also set them into fortified trenches. Emulate lost cooperation, and you'll likely lose out on the deal. Make a reasonable offer, or pass.

Myth #7: Third-party evidence calls the shots.

Don't you believe it! Buyers and sellers have their own private agendas, and valuation specialists are no more or less acceptable to the players than are accountants and lawyers. The closely held arena is *filled* with I-want-to-gain motivations (often quite rigid individual motivations of both buyers and sellers), and third-party advice is frequently considered no more valuable in negotiations than the contents of a baby's messy diaper. What it adds is the starting point for discussions—but you can count on negotiations being steeped deeply in "I-want-to-gain."

Myth #8: Choices for small-company buyers and sellers are like picking stones from the ground.

It is estimated that more than a million businesses are for sale on the U.S. market annually. Nice numbers. But take a hard look at the numbers. About 300,000 companies actually sell, and about 255,000 that do sell are very small businesses. We can draw some conclusions from these estimates—although sellers are aplenty and buyers are abundant, four out of five businesses do not sell. Of those that do not sell, 52.1% pass into bankruptcy or fade into oblivion. Something is wildly wrong with an 80% failure rate (four out of five not selling). Is it stubbornness in pricing? Is it unreal objectives of buyers? Is it undesirability of the businesses themselves? What is it that causes this failure of buyers and sellers to complete transactions? My best guess is that someone's *value system* is on the blink . . . at least four out of five times.

The acts of buying, selling, and pricing the small company are laced with many myths that serve no good to anyone. In many respects, these myths are rooted in the same market capitalism of bigger business, but in the smaller realm they are dominated by profit-driven *private* firms and *private* consumers. Instability, insecurity, and excess are inherent. Sellers overpromise and generate distrust in buyers. Buyers over- or underestimate their capacity and generate this same distrust in sellers. People who buy and sell small companies often indeed find the process itself inadequate.

The Small Business Administration's (SBA) at-or-under-500-employee model for small business fails to reach down to the needs of the approximately 89% of all American businesses that employ 20 and fewer people. Until 1978, when Babson College, in Wellesley, Massachusetts, developed the smaller entrepreneurial teaching model (now cloned to some greater or lesser degree in nearly 400 colleges and universities nationwide), our educational system taught us the ways of big corporate America. Learning about smaller business was left to the classroom of hard knocks. Yet we have been expected to overlay all the teachings of big business onto a very small arena that doesn't follow these corporate rules. No wonder myths developed. You might want to take a good look at my other two books as well: *A Basic Guide for Buying and Selling a Company* and *Self-Defense Finance for Small Businesses.* You *can* correct the myths and do your deals!

"Small—*If you think you are too small to be effective, you have never been to bed with a mosquito.*"

Betty Reese

2

Dispelling Perceptions about Value

(Because It's a Rascal We Can't Really Ignore)

Value. What is value? Is value a one-way street? And who sees *what* as value?

Let's say you have the good fortune of purchasing an automobile for $10,000; then you learn that your neighbor buys an identical car for $10,300 . . . what, then, is the value? Both you and your neighbor seem content with the prices paid—unless, of course, he or she learns what *you* paid. Then up goes the "cheat" flag for your neighbor, and a "confirmed value" flag for you.

Now let's see value as perceived in its more complex state. I drive a 10-year-old Mercedes (bought it new in my other life). Granted, the car is impeccably maintained, without a speck of rust—no dents. I know how little there is in my bank account, but I can't believe how others look at me in awe. No one, absolutely no one, accepts that I'm not rolling in dough. It's the darn Mercedes! If my car was even a 10-year-old Cadillac or Lincoln, people might be more prone to accept the real pecking order of things in my pocketbook. It's all perception! And to "deny" realities in another's perception is often only an invitation for his or her further disbelief.

Both of the preceding stories end on notes of *individual perception*. The first is confirmed by one single fact while the second, because of subliminal "suspicion," may *never* be confirmed at all. To this degree, perception is the *truth* in all value. Not one person will see the same value in any person, place, or thing. It's life . . . it's nature's way . . . it's human. It's one of the costumes always worn by our individual value systems. Thus it might follow that the only truth about truth is true fallacy in the eyes of another.

Business value is no more or less susceptible to perception than all other things. Two separate buyers will not see the same business as having the same value. Sellers will not see the values of their businesses in the same way as buyers. Bankers, accountants, lawyers will all have different perceptions of value as well.

Not all appraisers will agree, but some do so without knowing they do, that the *small-company appraisal process begins with evaluating human behavior* through the antics of their buyers and sellers. Not nearly true for publicly held business evaluations. This represents the first of many issues that the business appraiser must resolve during the process of estimating closely held company value. The smaller the business, the more evident is this problem. However, the evaluation of human behavior is much more complex than it seems. As an appraiser, the tool used is "behavior common to all buyers and sellers," aptly termed *comparable* practice; in other words, average indicators of behavior as it "affected" past practice. The difficulty presented here is simply that individuals acting on their own behalf cannot be counted upon to behave according to average standards in future actions. Therefore, the appraiser must have firsthand knowledge about how (cause) *specific* buyers and sellers might individually react to value over specific businesses.

Unfortunately, most appraisers are so busy doing evaluations that they do not frequently "test the water" running between "average" and firsthand players. This sets the plot for another, and sometimes critical, perception variable: the appraiser's own perception of value. Now I know that the appraisal industry argues, under the guise of using *comparable sale* data, that an appraiser's perception won't be an issue in evaluation. In the case of home, machinery, furniture, and many other appraised items, this is certainly a valid defense in an upswinging economy. However, homes, machines, furniture, and so on are *abundantly traded* and have distinct stand-alone values that are more determined by "wear and tear" than by the mind-sets of the people who live in or run them. Business value depends on the *effective* employment of capital, manpower, machine, and material to produce profits; therefore, "business" value depends on the skills that vary widely among individuals. *Time, Inc., Newsweek,* and many other fine business magazines report how much the fulcrum has shifted from the once higher business costs for machine and material to those of *human expense.* Real property and fixturing values in businesses can be reasonably ascertained in conventional fashion; however, the human element, especially in closely held companies, is much more complex and not really comparable from company to company. Small-company owners are the most independent, nonconforming individuals on earth. They can be counted on for one thing . . . never agreeing on anything. Entrepreneurs do not play the "Captain, May I?" game . . . they are the captain, and humanly different at that! No one human can be predicted even to run the same company the same way as another would. Where, then, is comparability?

Comparable value is an appraisal term, and I maintain that business valuators are not really a part of that fine organization called the appraisal society. True, business valuators can certainly be appraisers and do most often use selected appraisal tools, but they must also be something quite different—behavioral scientists. Yes, my belief is contested, but the more than 1,200 valuation assignments behind me, 300 of which were for and predicted within 10% of "sold" prices, are my convincing evidence for these beliefs. Defended in its behavioral context, I have not lost footholds in value through expert testimony in civil and criminal court cases. Comparability evaluation of "hard" assets is a valuable determinant for business's housing, raw material, and equipment and fixturing, but not for its "intangible" portions.

In its more theoretical definition, intangible value could be termed a condition of cash flow that *exceeds* supporting payments for the purchase of hard assets. Since cash flow is affected principally by the man or woman in control, intangible value is weighted heavily on the attributes of the individual and also·will be quite separate from the issue of tangible asset values. When cash flow fails to accommodate the purchase of hard assets at fair market value, there is simply no intangible element to value. Stated another way, there are only assets to sell—no real business, and no real business value. In defense of this argument, the Internal Revenue Service (IRS) broadly defines goodwill (intangible) as any amount paid for a business that exceeds the fair market value of hard assets.

A common misconception among sellers is that the value of their business has something to do with outstanding debt owed, and/or a relationship to what they originally paid for this business 1, 5, 10, or more years ago. This myth needs to be dispelled. *Present* business value has nothing to do with these two issues established from the *past!* In no small regard, the *intensity* in a small company's value *lives on a sliding scale* and is made up of its present-day and mercurial components. Folks, it's worth only what it's worth in today's terms.

Many texts say that business value is essentially made up of two elements: *tangible* (hard) assets, which are the facilities, furniture, fixtures, equipment, inventories, supplies, and so on, and *intangible* assets, which cover a plethora of things, including *predictable* cash flows, and the "enduring mark" that each particular business (or owner) leaves on its affected community of employees, customers, and suppliers. I have no argument with these summary theories, but in cases of closely held companies, the concept for values must be carried out to include tangible assets, intangible assets, *and perception*. I maintain that many scientific techniques do not appropriately recognize perceptions of the human being, and subsequently the human influence on value, particularly as it relates to the closely held arena. I'll explain why momentarily, but first let's examine forces setting closely held enterprises apart from publicly traded enterprises. A common saying is that a picture is worth a thousand words; thus, I'll diagram and then talk about the differences. For brevity, I will use overall, generic references for both types of companies, because the various levels of stock trades and forms of ownerships only complicate the rather simple point I will make. Focus is also limited to owners and managements, not the reasons why certain companies exist.

PUBLICLY TRADED COMPANIES

Stockholders (includes people from all walks of life, male and female, college and noncollege educated, rich and of modest means, children's college funds, institutional holders, etc.)

Company Management (may also be stockholders as well, and for the purpose of our diagram, let's assume none are major stockholders)

Profit or loss affects value of stock as well as perceived value of future returns.

Management's role is to *efficiently* operate the company for the benefit of *returns to stockholders*. In fact, job "continuation" for top executives is frequently based upon how "stock" performs in the market.

The purchase and sale of stock of the public company could loosely be termed a game of poker, where stock certificates essentially represent the "ante," and the game is played purely for *money*. The company itself may have very little, if anything, to do with the "game" played around its stock. Some publicly traded companies have hundreds of thousands of stockholders, and unless a few hold "controlling" interests by owning large numbers of shares, it will generally take "class-action" efforts to exert much influence on the nonowner (relative) management of the company itself. For example General Motors, as of its March 1995 proxy, had 693,000 employees and 860,000 stockholders. Officers and directors owned 1% of its stock.

When a publicly traded company performs well, stock prices tend to rise and stockholders become satisfied. The reverse is often true when the company performs not so well. For the purpose of my discussion—stock ownership and trading are much more complex than this simplified example—stock ownership in the public company is, for the average purchaser, an investment (one of purely making money) and an acquisition unrelated to running the company. *For all practical purposes, the average stockholder is "impersonal" with regard to the company itself . . . he or she just wants to see the stock prices rise and the company to pay dividends.*

Management's job is to run the publicly traded company in such a fashion that it *maximizes returns* to the bottom line for stockholders. Many top executive jobs hinge on that fact! They are hired for that purpose, and they can be, and usually are, fired if it's not achieved. Make no mistake about it, stockholders (joined collectively or as major holders) can be a very powerful lobbying influence on what, when, where, and how a publicly traded company survives. But, in a general sense, the name of the game for owners is "make a buck," not make a product or service. Reduced to its simplest terms, management is not ownership, and ownership is not management; maximized returns to the bottom line is the game, and ownership interests are not commonly shared.

"Value" in the publicly traded company gets fragmented at this point. Company operations do influence but rarely exert "actual control" over their stock prices. Stock prices and earning ratios influence company values, but the values of public companies are not always in direct relationship to stock prices. All this sounds confusing and complex, and it certainly is . . . and that's why the valuation of publicly traded companies is a subject unto its own. This book is not about valuing public companies, so we'll leave this element with my points summarized in the preceding paragraphs. However, one final and important point remains—how taxes on income are treated. Since ownerships are in the form of stock, not company assets, shareholders of the publicly traded company are forced into capital gains treatment on their stock and the higher than ordinary income level of "dividend" taxation on stock earnings. Any tax "sheltering" effect must normally come from resources *other* than the company itself.

Closely Held (Privately Owned) Companies

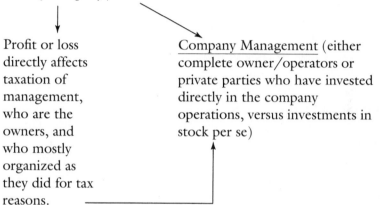

Stockholders (Stock is wholly owned by company managers and/or private investors who share the goals of company managers. We'll reference ownership by the generic term *stockholder,* but forms of actual organization could be sole proprietor, partnership, "C" or "S" corporation, limited liability company.)

Profit or loss directly affects taxation of management, who are the owners, and who mostly organized as they did for tax reasons.

Company Management (either complete owner/operators or private parties who have invested directly in the company operations, versus investments in stock per se)

The purchase and sale of the closely held company might also be likened to the game of poker in public companies; however, the "ante" in a closely held company *is the company itself.* The stock held in the closely held enterprise is virtually immaterial to estimates of its value—and values are values regardless of whether stock or asset transactions are on the table. Now I know that some of you may "technically" find reason to disagree with this statement . . . specifically when small companies acquire other small businesses, both reacting as entities. But this transaction is rare in the arena where most small-company transfers occur. *Stock of the closely held company has no "free-floating" or market value that is detached from the value of tangible and intangible assets held by the company itself.*

Management and/or private investors, since their objectives are to *make a buck solely from the company's performance itself,* organize their companies along lines that best "shelter" incomes and/or reduce exposures to personal liabilities. Because management controls most or all of the stock, their positions as stockholders and management share a duality of interest to *minimize* bottom lines. Stated simply, the income from the company goes essentially into the "same pockets," *but net income* could be altered by the way that it is taken out of the company by owners. Internal Revenue laws do not distinguish between stock owned in public or private firms . . . stock is stock. Income paid to a shareholder who is frequently also the sole manager/owner will be taxed at the level of dividend or capital gain versus ordinary income, if he or she is not careful of how cash flows are diverted from bottom lines. Salaries paid to management are controllable by the management themselves because they are the owners and, subsequently, become major sources for bottom-line diversion of corporate incomes into personal, ordinary income status. And, of course, when organized as C corporations, income that drops to bottom lines is taxed at corporate rates and may represent "double taxation" to the closely held, small-company owners.

We need get no more complex in our discussion than this, because regardless of whether the small company is organized as a sole proprietorship, partnership, limited liability company, or corporation, closely held owner objectives are the same: Minimize the "marbles" Uncle Sam has to count . . . "take out" any and all income in the least taxable form. Because they are "controlling" owners of these companies, they can also make free-wheeling decisions and take *independent* actions that directly influence where, when, and how income generated from the business flows through the IRS tax network. As mentioned earlier, the most notable control is exerted through flexibility in payment of salaries to owner/managers—increase salaries and, obviously, less income flows to the company's bottom line. Increase salaries enough in the C corporation format, and no profit flows down; because there are no corporate or dividend taxable proceeds, corporate income is thus diverted into the ordinary income of salaries paid. Avoidance of higher levels of taxation in this example sounds simple, but of course the IRS (wouldn't you know it) has its own set of "brakes" on the entrepreneur—salaries being paid must *not* exceed levels paid by others for comparable work . . . the ol' salary survey test of sorts.

SUMMARY DIFFERENCES AS THEY RELATE TO BUSINESS VALUE

1. The *obligated* task of management in the publicly traded company is to maximize bottom-line profits, whereas the *elective* task in the closely held company is to minimize profits that can be taxed.

2. Stockholders of the publicly traded company are principally investors in the *stock market* rather than the company itself; closely held
investors "bet" their bucks and returns on the *assets* of the company
itself.

3. Although company performance influences stock market performance of the public company's trade prices, *individual* stockholders
tend to have *little or no direct say* in *how the company is run*. Stockholders of the closely held company have *all* the say in how the
company is run, because individuals are quite regularly one and the
same as management and because they often are *the* company.

4. Stocks of the public company can fall separately under the influence
of supply and demand, titillated and interwoven with other company stock offerings, and broadly influenced by general market
economies—perhaps involving many issues that are unrelated to a
specific company's performance. Stocks of the closely held company
have virtually no stock market value and serve only the interests and
whims of the investor(s) in the company's assets. Not their stocks
but the value of businesses themselves is subjected more to industry
and local market economies.

FOCUS OF PERCEPTIONS

Undoubtedly, stock traders in the public domain consider various company performances, but investment decisions are *based on broad stock market perceptions*. How one stock's performance stacks up against others is
the *cause* for trades, and the specifics of a company's operations—marketing, sales promotion, production, customer and employee relations,
and so on—take a back seat to the specific shuffle in turning a buck into
more bucks. *Focused perceptions in the closely held enterprise zero in on the
employment of its assets to make and increase that same kind of buck.* In
some respects, business valuation of the publicly traded company is made
inordinately complex because stock values do not necessarily relate closely
to the asset values in the company proper. Yet stock trading prices bear
heavily on the perception of what price an actual company might bring
when sold to another public company. There's a bit of "churning" going
on through the sale of one public company to another, because consoli-
dations can increase stock prices of both, and since public companies tend
frequently to own "treasury stock" (corporately owned stock), these pools

form war chests that increase proportionately and can enhance the acquirer's balance sheet.

The overview between public and private companies is important because business schools tend to concentrate on the ways in public arenas and represent where many buyers are taught. However, it's time for us to move on to this book's purpose—closely held business valuation.

AN OVERVIEW OF THE TASK OF ESTIMATING VALUES IN SMALL COMPANIES

From the foregoing discussion, we should be able to conclude that *perceptions of value* in the closely held company are *individually swayed* and factually weighted by *productivity of company assets employed*. In other words, each component of business value, including any reference to facts, might change through the personal perceptions of individual buyers and sellers. Thus we most likely have a paradox on our hands that refutes one possible ironclad value. To solve for the paradox, we must examine the following: (a) general market conditions; (b) specific business conditions; and (c) individual buyer and seller perceptions.

We start by flipping our "tassels" over to become scientists in the next chapter.

> *"Everything has been thought of before, but the problem is to think of it again."*
>
> Johann W. von Goethe

> *"How do you become an expert? Well, I can only suggest what has worked for me. Write a book about it."*
>
> Robert G. Allen, *Creating Wealth*

3

Intangible Values

In the last chapter I touched upon possible sliding-scale effects caused between tangible values and intangible values. Here I will demonstrate how they truly interact with each other to portray overall estimated values in closely held small companies.

The concepts in determining tangible asset values have been bandied about for years and are quite well refined. With possible exceptions to varying levels of skills offered through appraisers themselves, I cannot quarrel with the techniques used.

However, intangible business value is a highly judgmental aspect of business valuation and requires conscientious attention. As mentioned, the IRS roughly defines intangible value, or goodwill, as that amount paid for a business in excess of the market value of hard assets. Numerous rating schemes have been developed through the years to determine intangible value. Many provide logic to the rationale and assist in developing more *defendable* values for the parties involved. In the final analysis, however, technical competence and experienced financial judgment must win out. The final value judgment must meet tests of cash flow analysis; when it does not, rating schemes are not worth the paper printed on.

Professional service organizations, such as those for physicians, lawyers, accountants, consultants, and so on, are among the more difficult types of businesses for which to establish an intangible value. Practitioner characteristics, personalities, and *reputation* play heavily into the generation of cash streams. Take the specific practitioner out of the business, and the cash stream will quite often suffer considerably. Therefore, a fundamental question is: How much business value is directly attributable to a "person," and how much of that value will remain if he or she leaves? To the unwary, this can present the classic dilemma of "getting lost in the numbers." Subsequently, the purchase of a "sole practitioner" business can be much more risky than the purchase of a business with multiple practitioners who remain after the purchase. These "people" or owner-restrictive elements can be present in all types of businesses and, with safety in mind, cannot be overlooked. A "business continuation" risk tends to decrease with increasing size of staff and, when the present owner is more separated from *practice work*, by the demands of administrative duty.

Service businesses in general, unless cash flow is quite substantial, tend rarely to command in-line prices equivalent to their hard-asset but equally cash-productive counterparts. While cash may be king in the world of users, tangible hard assets call the shots in terms of "leveraged" or financed deals. Since service businesses tend to be skinny in these *touchable* fixed assets, either the war chests of King Cash get depleted or prices are lowered.

On the far side of the spectrum, we might find "asset-intense" businesses, such as motels, manufacturers, and other operations where significant investments in physical plants, machinery, and equipment are present. Businesses such as these may frequently sell to customers who tend to be less "attached" to the small-company owners. Bear in mind also that hard assets will comprise most of the financing collateral for loans and that "market value" is substantially influenced by *prevailing economies*. **An existing bank "climate" will affect market value.** Additional cash and/or attractive seller financing strategies will generally be required to make up any differences when purchase prices above market values of hard assets are contemplated.

Banks, though they *won't* finance without it, just do not place much credence in financing what they can't see and touch. Thus, a typical dilemma of service businesses is to obtain top prices irrespective of strong cash flows. But this dilemma can place pricing restrictions on asset-intense businesses as well. When cash flows in businesses exceed that necessary to retire debt and pay appropriate salaries and profits to owners, and when pricing extends into excesses, the remainders of pricing must come from buyer's cash reserves, through seller financing, or both.

From this discussion it could be alluded that a higher hard-asset value might sometimes translate into a lower intangible value. In the reverse, a low asset value might then bring a higher intangible value into play. Quite often this turns out to be the case. However, the elements of cash flow, frequently reasons for purchase, are possibly ignored by these assumptions when taken alone. Subsequently, one must clearly decide what part of value is tangible (hard assets) and what part of value is intangible (goodwill, as defined by the IRS). While touchable assets connote rather straightforward values, intangible values by their namesakes are less easily discerned. This is where quasi scientific formulas come into play.

In one respect we could say that all cash flow equals *total* value as its essence. The "physical" portion of these total values might then be revealed in the cash streams. When reversed out of the equation, the remainder then equals "intangible" value. This, of course, is as the IRS would have us see it. Fortunately, laws allow "goodwill" to be apportioned to such items as employment and noncompete contracts, trademarks, patents, copyrights, customer lists, and so on, which are handled in negotiations over the "attribution" schedule. Set in this light, some part of the streams pays for human and physical assets in the form of outflows to cover business expenses, including debt service and returns to owners. What's remaining as "excess" or flows over and above these costs might therefore be viewed as cash flows leading to assignments of intangible values. Applying this logic, little or no excess subsequently equals little or no intangible values and vice versa. Every business with an operating history has some intangible or goodwill value. Sometimes this intangible value is equal to the value of hard assets, and sometimes it is greater or less than the value of hard assets. Discerning a difference is key in establishing intangible value—one that can be "sold" at arm's length and outside of the definition laid down by the IRS. Thinking along this line led to scientific methodologies called "excess earnings formulas," and their sometimes close cousins "net multipliers," which will be covered later.

Internal and External Forces Being Exerted on Intangible Values

Up to this point we have been discussing intangible value in its broadest concept. We know that we can allocate various items permitted by law, and that pricing or values beyond the values in hard assets can be termed intangible values. This is the "effect" that intangible plays on the overall value or price of a business, which, of course, is normally adequate for buyers and sellers to do their deals. However, the business appraiser (valuator) must understand the effects that *cause* has on streams of cash produced. While business evaluation processes all hinge on how well or how poorly closely held operations have performed, "operating performance" can be measured by *internal* and *external* forces exerted upon it. The internal quotient results from the specific company's effective or ineffective employment of manpower, money, and machines—all being subject to the "discretions" in the owner's operating philosophies. External conditions such as industry trends and general economic forces that influence operations may rarely be within the control of management (see Chapter 4). Thus, both internal and external forces are the composition of "intangibles' " relative cause. We measure internal conditions by the application of ratios and other financial tools (to some degree, we thus measure internal and external forces). Again, this is a scientific process but one that is conspicuously absent in a large number of real estate appraiser's kits.

The discussions could theoretically conclude at this point; however, we would be failing to recognize the *entrepreneurial spirit* afforded through closely held ownerships. We've all heard the term "niche." Only a few industries fade into oblivion; they usually evolve into new or modified something or others. Recognizing and implementing combatant processes set some small-company owners apart as true entrepreneurs, while others will just "cry in their beer" so to speak. The discretion of ownership affords opportunities of planning and navigating the maze common to smaller companies. This is to say that sailors of old, and small-company owners of new, could have navigated better with compasses or business plans. Unfortunately, both were or are prone to navigate by the "seat of their pants."

On occasion we must give credit in assigning intangible values for the hook or niche that an entrepreneur has developed . . . but not too far beyond the extent of established cash flows. This has too frequently been the argument for valuations based on "future" earnings. It's okay to recognize the niche built by a retiring owner, but one must balance this portending niche value in light of any displacements to success that may be caused by those retiring owners. What they have done is done, but will it stay done when these owners leave their small businesses? What can't be replicated in their wake falls out of equations of value. This element is nearly impossible to measure scientifically in the closely held small company, but one method, called the "discounted cash flow," is rather frequently used in attempts to do so. This method is a common method of choice of many valuation experts. Applied to General Motor's over $15 million of sales *per hour,* it works wonders. But with the smaller company I question its applicable merit. The formula is simple enough for anyone to learn, but I'm afraid there may be only a handful of small-business evaluators who can effectively transpose the formula into valuing companies who struggle year after year just to make ends meet.

The charts on page 21 (Figure 3.1) may provoke insight and provide guidance. For nearly 30 years I have wrestled with the question: What is business value? And to this day, assignment of intangible value in small

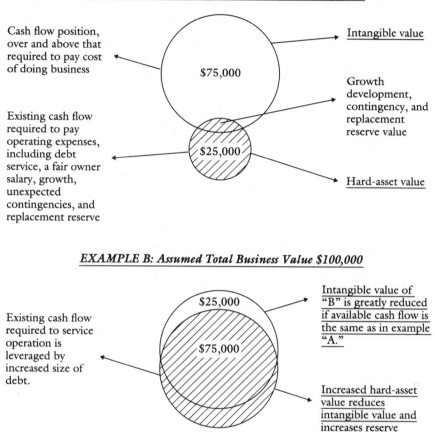

EXAMPLE A: Assumed Total Business Value $100,000

Cash flow position, over and above that required to pay cost of doing business → Intangible value

$75,000

Growth development, contingency, and replacement reserve value

Existing cash flow required to pay operating expenses, including debt service, a fair owner salary, growth, unexpected contingencies, and replacement reserve ← $25,000

Hard-asset value

EXAMPLE B: Assumed Total Business Value $100,000

$25,000

Intangible value of "B" is greatly reduced if available cash flow is the same as in example "A."

Existing cash flow required to service operation is leveraged by increased size of debt.

$75,000

Increased hard-asset value reduces intangible value and increases reserve requirement for contingency and replacement.

If the profits in example B were substantially increased, the "rings" might more resemble those presented in example A and total business value might increase proportionately. A lesser cash flow in example B might present little or no room for intangible value and might in fact present inadequate returns for more than a "net asset sale" or in other terms, insufficient cash flow provided to appropriately cover the cost/value of hard assets.

Figure 3.1. High/low hard-asset effect on intangible business value when the cash stream is equal.

business remains the more perplexing task. There simply is no "pat" answer or formula. My way is neither right nor wrong, and the task is not really made easier with experience. If I have learned one common essential, it is to *exercise caution* in assigning intangible value and throughout the whole process. There will always be reams of theory and flames of discussion, because scientific formulas developed for intangible value can do no more than "attempt" to measure the art form of human enterprise. Please note that the charts reflect "service" and "asset-intense" businesses, respectively. For purposes of demonstration, both businesses are assumed to have "equal" value.

Discovery of intangible values might arouse in some buyers and sellers the words of John Powell, S.J., bestselling author of *Why Am I Afraid to Tell You Who I Am?*, "But if I tell you who I am, you may not like who I am, and it is all that I have." *Arguments, discussions, or negotiations over settlement prices generally focus around the element in price that is elusive to definition—the intangible values or add-on pricing to values more readily established between parties for the hard assets.* I'll leave this chapter with the words of Powell, "all that I *have*," and the words of Henry M. Boettinger, author of *Moving Mountains*, "People seldom buy an idea without buying its author in the process." Intangible values in *smaller businesses* have a great deal to do with what their owners *have* done.

4

Industry and Economic Forces

To the equation of small-business valuation we must also add the watchwords of audacious big businesses, "globalization" and "technology." What is global economy but that of technology driving us indelibly into foreign lands? What is technology but that of driving us into "downsizing" methodology? And what is technology but that of exacerbating and/or stimulating small-business growth?

For all practical purposes, small business is an outgrowth from the Industrial Revolution. Because from that point on, we no longer owed our "souls to the Company store." But upon closer examination of the early evolution of small businesses, we learn that their *existence* was primarily based on concepts in "rural economies," and their owners were content to limit growth to the rural community's essential needs. In these economies, land values, as one measure of growth, were held constant by populations for the purpose of *farm* yields. In time, small businesses migrated into "urban economies" and were forced to compete in the same sense that urban land values must compete to meet investor expectations for *sustained growth*. In one sense we could call these phases one and two of small-business evolution.

"Independent" may be a small-business term lost in some phase between then and now. The independent pharmacy is nearly gone, and franchising has changed the face of how a plethora of other businesses operate. Starbucks and other companies like Green Mountain (company-owned outlets versus large-scale franchising) have nearly put uniquely local coffeehouses out of business. Blunt though the message might be: Independent small businesses must use big business wherewithal to survive.

Thus the "economist" in business valuators must surface, and although real estate appraisers may use economic tools on local-level assignments, because realty values are very locally determined, they rarely will be much more than a catch-22 in an overall global sense. The valuation exercise must thoroughly examine industry trends and *gross* economic forces affecting the closely held business. Doing well today does not forecast doing well tomorrow, or for that matter at all.

America is still as much a "land of milk and honey" as it ever was, but more than ever in our past, small-company owners must put their "eggs into baskets that can be watched." Irrespective of owner wishes and desires, the faces of small business are being changed whether we like it or not. What's here today that remains tomorrow will not be the same, and those conducting business valuations cannot afford to ignore the overall scene. In some respects, we might view some of these happenings where bigs gobble up smalls as a "Wal-Mart elimination theory."

INDUSTRY

Industry happenings have a great tendency to foretell *evolutions* in services and products handled by small companies. Because of advancing technology, things change quickly. Comparable data, including rule-of-thumb ratios, tell only of past occurrences. Where change is slow or static, that is acceptable information; however, given the pace of change we now endure, I wonder how long the past can be counted upon to forecast the present and, more importantly, the future.

Information supplied by industry spokespersons, because they use the same standards they pass out to the public, may not be nearly enough to go on. Quite often underfunded when memberships are shrinking, they may not always be the watchdogs for change. There is no replacement for reading about, listening to, and overtly examining what's being reported in the news with regard to pressures on industries and small companies alike.

If you are considering a small grocery store, call your local independent merchants association and/or distributor . . . then visit the nearest giant superstore. Unless you can find a "niche" for long-term operations, the small business you are considering may eventually be gobbled up. Where's the value in cash flows that may be strong now but could be waning in the near future?

If the small business you're considering is in the path of a technological advance, call the industry to determine what "insurance" for growth can be had. By all means, check what developmental explorations are on the horizon that could make your company's short-term advantage obsolete over the longer haul. When outlooks portend retrofitting operations to survive long term, what might be the cost to reorganize, and what values do current cash streams play in the process? No doubt that intangible values might subsequently shrink, but what about values in tangible assets that may become obsolete, or with those required to be purchased new?

In this tumultuous period of international change, you've got to really think hard about what might prevent the small company from staying around. By the same token, small companies that are likely to "hang tight" merit real attention and might justify conditions of future-oriented values. The vast majority of small companies, however, will be somewhere in the middle, and you won't be able to tell future existence through industry sources for sure. What's been printed may be obsolete, and answers may lie between the lines . . . quite possibly, forever to be found between the lines.

Bear in mind that the expense of dues prevents many small businesses from joining trade associations. And there are, of course, a plethora of other reasons that small-company owners do not join associations or trade groups. Your own accountant or banker may be able to fill in the gaps left at the end of your research . . . or in some instances they may be able to supply all that you want to know. Some minimal questions that should be asked of industry representatives are as follows:

1. How many members does the industry association have?
2. Is the membership growing?
3. Describe a "typical" member firm.
4. Does your group "lobby" in Washington, D.C., for the benefit of your members?
5. What are the major issues confronting your industry today?
6. What are members in general doing about these issues?
7. What is the industry association doing?
8. What services do you provide to member firms?
9. Do you collect, consolidate, and analyze operating histories on member firms? If so, what must I do to obtain a copy?
10. What do you forecast as the longer-term outlook for the industry and member firms?
11. What specific advice do you give to member companies about long-term survival?
12. Do you offer seminars and/or training sessions to your membership for increased efficiency to their operations?

13. What are the names of trade and news publications commonly read by industry members?

14. Do you publish an industry newsletter, and if so, how can I get copies of the last few issues?

Be particularly attentive to the "tone" in the answers being given. Answers also lead to asking other questions on your mind. Industry representatives are not always open to nonmember questioning; therefore, "how" you present your case while seeking information is important.

To obtain industry "typical" or average operating financial information, one can always turn to various compilation services such as Robert Morris Associates in Philadelphia, or Financial Research Associates in Winter Haven, Florida. There are also a plethora of business information services such as the Institute of Business Appraisers, Inc. (IBA) in Boynton Beach, Florida. The International Business Brokers Association (IBBA) in Reston, Virginia, might add greatly to your search as well.

Local, Regional, and National Economic Forces

As the economic telescope widens in scope, quite naturally so does the complexity in discerning value at the local level. For example, just a few years ago we would never have thought a 44,000-square-foot grocery superstore would locate in my hometown of 8,000 people (I brought it here). Beyond first imaginations, this store is now number two in sales for its state of operations.

Wal-Marts popping up in small communities are a common problem for small competitors. Local economies do not foretell the embryonic regional or national toils of big business. You've got to go to the heart of what causes big companies to strike near home base. Some answers are found through demographic information readily available from U.S. Census centers in each state. When added to expatriate populations that may swing in and out of communities, one begins to unfold scant bits of their rationale leading to selection of specific sites. Giants do not make their moves accidentally, and certainly not without due regard to profits. There must be both need and volume in these communities for bigs to come in. However, one does not need to dig too far into statistics to gain valuable answers.

Sometimes the review of local telephone "yellow pages" can magnify potential local invasions by bigs. Set in "have" and "have-not" columns, one begins to get the big picture locally. Existing migratory shopping patterns of local populations foretell changes in patterns likely to be caused by lower prices and availability offered mostly through being big. Thus a small company's present value (attached quite tightly to long-term survival) can be highly dependent upon the high or low prospect of being invaded by future competition.

Local and regional outlooks are broadcast on local TV . . . and are usually followed up with the national news. Locally tuned "suspicion" can often be fit into the regional and national perspective by just one or several one-hour TV news sessions. A call to a local or regional business-news reporter can greatly enhance the bigger picture for your small company locally. Newspapers keep reported stories of current or forecasted business events and trends on microfiche or in computers. And, of course, you can once again ask your accountant or banker for his or her views and outlooks. You might be surprised at how professionals collect and analyze economic data being brought to bear on local environments. Local professionals have not entirely escaped the effects of the bigs themselves.

National economic trends can forecast regional and local economies in advance. For example, national increases in interest rates forecast reduced sales of homes on a local level. The current national automobile market is flooded with excess inventory and suggests a good time to deal for a new or used car locally. A national shortage of widget A says buy now because new inventories are likely to be priced higher.

The "economy" is blamed for all sorts of things that might rightly have been our fault. The "weight" that economic influences put on small-business values (and formulas) is hard to measure until they translate into higher interest rates paid on the monies borrowed to operate or purchase small businesses. But with some degree of indicator application, we can see the "red flags" in their clouds hanging over the nation, the region, and locally. There will never be the "perfect" economic time to buy or sell a small company, but there may be a perfect time *not* to buy or sell.

SUMMARY

Banking a business's value solely on current operating results is risky business to say the least. By my yardstick, coined years ago, a business's professed value is "guilty until proven innocent" by covering all the short- and long-term influential factors indicating its value. And then value will only be as *value does* to the players who perceive that value.

One last comment/question of economic interest: Pay increases have been dipping further below the levels in costs of living for some time, and national indices warn that production costs are increasingly difficult to pass on to consumers. Is there a subtle message here about smaller-business values forecast on the far side? However, don't forgo consideration of "values added" for businesses that may have settled into niches predicting survival. Survival of the fittest may be quite necessary to satisfy customer demand long term, and bigs, though they have deep pockets, cannot be all things to all people.

> *" The theory of economics does not furnish a body of settled conclusions immediately applicable to policy. It is a method rather than a doctrine, an apparatus of the mind, a technique of thinking, which helps its possessor to draw correct conclusions."*
>
> John Maynard Keynes

> *" Montgomery Ward, in the late World War II and early postwar environment, lived under the policy guidance of a top management which erroneously assessed the basic course of the aggregate economy. As a consequence the company was dominated by the view that cash balances must be conserved, and not used actively for normal business purposes. The compulsion to maximum liquidity almost cost the company its existence and did destroy its relative competitive position."*
>
> Maurice W. Lee

5

The "Four Steeds" in Business Valuation

Up to now we've been mostly discussing scientific ritual leading up to establishing values in closely held businesses. But there are legions of opposition to contend with: namely, human intuition and a close cousin "I-don't-believe." This chapter is not intended as either a research treatise or an encyclopedia. Instead, the objective is a concise statement of the main problems growing out of the instinctively human relationship as it plays out in business valuation. The stress will be upon controversy, argument, and joinder of issues at all levels of analysis. To make discussion a bit more interesting, let's call these the "Four Steeds" who attempt to gallop through business valuation.

Argument is the steed of "war." It is human nature to argue, but it is also human nature to agree and to forgive. Regardless of scientific formulas being used, and regardless of the facts presented, arrayed, and analyzed, there will be contest between observers. Given this knowledge, the value processor must analyze situations in advance so that one is never blindsided. The essential conditions of business valuation are past, present, and predictable future cash flows, positions in the marketplace, established values in hard assets, financing economies, supply and demand, and logic of purpose for exercises. The situations for analysis are thus outlined. However, the variableness in human perception is where the steed rides aloft to commit acts of argument. Buyers and sellers both expect to *gain* through establishment of prices (values). The motivations of argument (war) are nearly always to gain.

For the benefit of both buyers and sellers who are conducting their own valuation tasks or looking over the shoulders of others doing the work, one must separate "oppositions" into two categories: inflexible participants and unwilling participants. *Inflexible attitude,* of course, is the war itself and unlikely to be won without incredible costs. *Unwilling attitudes,* however, are but battles within the war zone and might be won with convincing strategies.

Inflexible people are those guys and gals who live in "negative" worlds *day to day.* They blame everything that happens to them on other people and consistently live from a platform where they dictate all the rules that other people are expected to live by. They disrespect fair play and will not come up to level ground in negotiations because they simply don't want to do so. To play their game you must step down to their level, and let's be frank, you cannot win in the "because-I-want-it" field of play. To them, business value is never as business valuation does.

Unwilling people, however, are individuals who have a cause they'd *like* to achieve. They live in a positive world for the most part and comprise the vast majority of populations. They can be swayed by compelling arguments based in fact. With them, negotiations over business value rarely turn into arguments; negotiations are more like disagreements where "evidence" will gradually sink in to change their perception of that value.

Thus, to eliminate the steed of war in business valuation, one must eliminate discussions based in inflexible perception. In spite of factual evidence, inflexible participants will choose only their "rigid" contentions of value; therefore, the equation will remain lopsided in opinions of value. Unwilling riders will leave their steeds of war and shuck their armor when safely convinced that there is no more war.

Controversy is the steed of "conquest." Controversy, if not addressed each time its ugly head appears during various stages of negotiation over price, will trample business valuation proceedings. We humans digest information slowly, particularly if that information is contrary to our own prevailing beliefs. When asked to accept overwhelming contradiction in one fell swoop, we can easily turn aggressor and attempt to become conqueror. Thus the steed of conquest must be unsaddled slowly and "leaked" information bit by bit. Buyer's and seller's *need* is nearly always different, and, consequently, controversy can be expected. The motivations of controversy tend to be exhibited in personal need.

Joinder is the steed of "pestilence." Ganging together in cohorts to commit acts of "conviction" on opponents can assail the objectives of cooperation. On one hand, it connotes unsureness in your position, and, on the other, it suggests undue pressure. The better way to get cooperative agreement is to go one-on-one, and then seek third-party consultation to both, in the form of mediation if need be. Bear in mind that it is quite normal for presumed values in closely held enterprise to elicit initial disagreement in one form or the other, because even with the best technical guidance, they are still estimates. More often, the questionings that surround estimates of value are rooted in "learning" about how one arrived at stated opinions. To assume that questions will lead to discrediting these opinions is a mistake. Though questions can turn into disagreements, unruffled give-and-take conversation can go a long way toward gaining agreement. Solving puzzles and making deals around value are often products of identifying and meeting buyer and seller *desire*. The motivation of desire is a personal issue that is not shared well with outsiders.

The fourth steed, *the steed of "death,"* has no place in the business valuation process. Either one or both factions are inflexible, and no agreement will be reached. When a processor has substantiated evidence of portending value, and evidence is overtly rejected, only one additional process can prove or disprove estimates of value—the business's actual sale. Buyers and sellers transacting, irrespective of conditions under which they effect sales, are the only real proof of value. The target value in all estimating scenarios is that "predictable" and overlapping point where both buyers and sellers *cooperatively* become "ready, willing, and able." Deal killing can be an outgrowth of the motivation embarrassment-not-to-have (keeping up with the Joneses). But embarrassment-not-to-have can also be a principal motivation of deal making. There will rarely be logic in this motivation, thus *logical* counterproposals do not work as well as some might expect.

As you might guess, the four steeds can be the nemesis to the necessary art form in estimating business value. Human involvements in the process cannot be measured, nor can they easily be counteracted scientifically. Personal objectives of buyers and sellers will normally be different, and the views or perceptions of an estimated value will be accorded the light of each person's personal needs. In *mathematics* we expect *absolutes* in answers. Business valuation employs the science of *statistics,* where we expect *deviation* in answers. Thus, mutual accord must always be negotiated, even if the processor is an expert business evaluator.

> *"Ancestral evolution has made us all warriors. . . ."*
> William James

> *"Mind is target."*
> Kanjuro Shibata

6

Nontraditional Valuation Practitioners

BUSINESS BROKERS AS BUSINESS VALUATORS

The pros and cons of being both salesperson and valuator can be examined as the meeting of two opposite disciplines. The best sales representatives are renowned as not usually being the best administrators or sales managers. Top sales experts are worth their weight in gold because they adapt to uniquely personal self-imposed goals, and because they get "a special rush" out of each new sale. Top professional salespeople are difficult to manage within bureaucratic corporate structures because they pursue the selling process with a vengeance of personal success criteria, and "numbers and schemes" are often considered in their way. In many instances, they see their territories as personal businesses but expect "corporate" to keep track of what they do. The natural characteristics of top selling professionals call upon attributes that are inconsistent with the finite detail and analysis necessary to perform business valuation tasks. However, they are the most in-touch persons with any given market action. They gain the most sensitivity to ultimate consumers, and, thus, they are substantially representative of this consumer "voice."

As we know, not all salespeople are top performers. Thus, as we dip down on the scale of productivity, we tend to find individuals who exhibit broader-based ambitions and even multiple skills. Larger companies tend to select their sales management from these ranks. They know about selling, plus they tend to possess ambitions for higher management. Consequently, they more readily accept paperwork, analysis, budgeting, and supervisory responsibilities that go along with any administrative job.

Business brokerage is principally a selling field. Though brokers may perform many other duties, they get paid from sales completed. To get paid they must concentrate on selling, but we know from experience that some do better than others. Rare is the "agency," large or small, that is filled with all top performers. Subsequently, some brokers commingle selling with other office tasks, including business valuation. In combination with appropriate skills of a broker-valuator, larger offices with a few top salespeople can be especially well suited to conduct valuation tasks. Within such "grouping" of brokers, excellent firsthand market data can be found; and assuming the value-processor has relative skills, the predicted values being rendered can be quite reliable, particularly in relationship to local markets.

However, trade-news reports indicate that the size of business broker-age offices is decreasing and that larger offices tend to be located in metropolitan areas. Also reported is that brokerage practices tend more often to provide "opinions of value" versus full-scale valuation services. Thus, one cannot predictably count on finding qualified business valuation specialists in brokerage firms.

Ostensibly, one might generally look upon the business brokerage office as an "intuit-to-value-service" rather than broad-scale expertise.

I would also be amiss by not offering what I call "The Wounded Knee Theory." Selling suggests we have "inventories" to sell from. In the brokerage trade, inventory refers to the number of "listings" booked into offices. The dilemma presented in my "theory" is that of "volume" played against *quality* in listings. Shoppers (buyers) like to "kick the tires" as they shop the row (wide selection) of listings. Thus, some listings are taken simply to fill out the selection (50% of listings actually sold for an office is considered quite good within the industry). Since sales are what keep offices and brokers going, and buyers are attracted to offices with larger selections, I have great difficulty envisioning any substantial focus by brokers on detailed business valuation assignments. Nevertheless, a few do.

To summarize, brokerage offices and brokers are prone to compile the best market information with regard to comparable "local" transactions. From their firsthand experiences with both buyers and sellers, they may also render the more accurate "opinions of value." However, it is less likely that they will possess all the variable skills required of the full-scale valuation assignment. A few that do can make great experts.

COMMERCIAL BANKERS, ACCOUNTANTS, AND LAWYERS AS BUSINESS VALUATORS

Commercial Bankers

I've selected commercial bankers first because their education, experience, and wherewithal vary so much more than the other two. To get the big picture, one must recognize that the commercial banker's job is that of evaluating case information (presented by a customer) in light of a "realistic" payback of loan amounts requested. Although business plans offer, or at least should offer, most of the essential factors in business valuation processes, the banker is not concerned with "business value" per se but with "collateral" being offered and with the level of cash flows to support repayments. Thus, valuation is rarely an effort required by their jobs. However, in the loan review process, bankers do conduct financial analyses, calculate operating ratios, and compare applicants with industry standard performances. Larger commercial banks have wonderfully arrayed comparable data banks, and, of course, they also have reams of internal case histories. Smaller banks are prone to include at least some of these data and will fill in missing gaps through their own trade associations.

Somewhat more fragmented than business brokers are, commercial bankers also have firsthand experience with local buyers and sellers. They are also more likely to have "the tools" for business valuation, although, as mentioned, much less likely to be called upon to use these tools in actual business valuation assignments. However, commercial bankers, because of the multiplicity in applicants and the frequency in reviews, can normally supply a resourceful commentary to the end products of estimated values.

Accountants

The traditional form of training that accountants receive makes them most proficient in the scientific elements of business valuation. However, their training is also traditionally void of marketing research and studies in human enterprise (psychology). Generally missing from their everyday practices are "repeating impressions" of the vital influences that buyers bring to bear on the equation of value in closely held enterprise. Thus the general practitioner tends only to scientifically measure the value of hard assets in light of cash flows. More often, a general practice is so busy with traditional tax and accounting matters that they are shy to offer more than opinions of value to their clients. However, larger firms will often have specialized business valuation departments; in fact, the Association of Certified Public Accountants (ACPA) now offers the CPA-BV designation. Course work and examinations leading to this specialty are quite rigid, and I suspect eventually that good expertise will be available in even smaller firms. Once again, however, expertise in valuating the *closely held* enterprise is a keg of psychological worms unto its own. For the time being, this specialization seems more in tune with valuation of the publicly held sector business.

Lawyers

The traditional form of training that attorneys receive is excellent for negotiation and/or mediation, and while it emphasizes research and structure, the "ticket" alone does not provide much in the way of financial tools. However, attorneys must normally have completed undergraduate work prior to entering law schools. Political science or one of the wide-ranging social sciences seems to be the major concentration of choice in undergraduate studies for a great many. But some choose business and other routes that may be particularly applicable to business valuation practice. Business valuation, however, is quite inconsistent with the reasons that people customarily choose to become lawyers. There must be one or two out there, but personally, I've never met an attorney who is also a valuation expert. In my research for my companion books, I found that several lawyers had written works on buying and selling small businesses, but I did not find one who had written about business valuation. Educations and experiences of lawyers are traditionally inconsistent with educations and experiences of business valuation specialists. From the consulting practice point of view, clients of lawyers and judges are my own most frequent clients for business valuation.

SUMMARY

One could easily conclude from these overview descriptions that anyone who had combined unique professional educations and experiences, and specialized in business valuation practice, might also be the very best valuation expert . . . in fact, uniquely qualified. However, such a combination is not classically found. Therefore, valuation expertise is more likely to be discovered in the specialized profession where job loyalties serve no other purpose than that of estimating business values.

> *"Fame and Success. Don't confuse fame with success. Madonna is one and Helen Keller is the other."*
> Erma Bombeck

> *"Character. Be more concerned with your character than with your reputation. Your character is what you really are while your reputation is merely what others think you are."*
> John Wooden

7

The Data Collection Process

In many respects, the data necessary to the comprehensive business valuation task are quite similar to the information required by business plans. As such, many business owners may have already stockpiled much that will be needed.

PURPOSE

The purpose for conducting valuations should determine informational needs. In my consulting practice, buy/sell reasons account for less than 25% of valuation work. About 2% of these are conducted specifically for court litigation purposes. The lion's share of work is for organizational restructure (converting into corporate or LLC formats), partnership annual valuation, to add new owners or change ownership interests, for estate purposes, and "because I'd just like to know" reasons. Each purpose adds or deletes bits of information that may be important to the overall project. The conditions under which "reported values" might be contested via differing interests lend possible other structures to information that must be collected, analyzed, and included.

The following covers what might customarily be the range of data usually collected for valuation purposes. The reasons for assignments determine how the *emphasis* or outlooks on value shall be weighted, but the information required varies only slightly regardless of purpose; for example: (a) Purchase and sale between family members may forecast values different from values expected between nonfamily members (intrapartnership transfers might also fit this category); (b) litigation may create the need for unique defenses of values rendered; (c) estate may necessitate review of estimated values in light of IRS rules and laws to ensure adequate defense of values if contested in tax court and to maximize nontaxable proceeds to survivors; (d) key-person insurance may require estimated value reviews in light of "most likely" payouts in the events of owner(s) death(s). To assume there is only one correct estimate of value is a mistake, and as we know or will learn in the process, "right" is a matter of opinion. Thus, closely held business valuations should be balanced *between* two opposing forces for the *most reliable* estimates to hit their targets. The following list includes the minimal information that is necessary to conduct valuations.

1. Learn the basic company history. Bylaws and/or agreements between several owners may specify the "scheme" to be used in valuing specific companies or partnerships. Partnership buy/sell agreements (for the events of death or outright sale between principals) are notorious for "stipulated" valuation clauses. Constructed by lawyers, these clauses can describe off-the-shelf processes that may or may not be entirely germane to a specific company need. However, when formally agreed between principals, the choice for techniques being applied must follow the agreement or requires the full written consent by all principals to change. Bylaws and minutes from director meetings may describe the overview of company business, highlight particular problems encountered, and/or describe difficulties between owners. Although these can provide valuable insights, one must recognize that many smaller companies don't document meetings and may not even go through the process. Therefore, briefly described company histories by owners tend to be as reliable, if not more reliable, than corporate records. Nevertheless, these records should be examined for content.

2. Obtain other information relevant to subjective issues affecting possible present or future worth—details of past or pending lawsuits, occupationally related injuries, copyrights or patents, deeds or leases, past and present product/service pricing strategies, wholesale price catalogs, and so on (in other words, all legal and/or informal operating documents)—to include a picture of how the company functioned or functions from an *internal* point of view.

3. Have at least three to five years of formally prepared profit/loss and balance sheet information. These should be supplemented by *at least* a spot review of checkbook entries to fully understand the *patterns* of owners in business operations. A thorough review of six months or more of canceled checks and bank statements should also

be undertaken. The general guideline for review should be three to six months prior to and after each suspicious event in checkbooks and/or bank statements. Also include informal year-to-date data and reconcile against checkbook entries for authenticity of reported results.

4. Collect information and get a handle on the effects that competition has on the business. Visiting several competitors can be particularly helpful to fuller understandings. Examine price-quality-service factors in products/services of competitors in light of those prevailing in businesses being valued.

5. Compile lists and estimated values of furniture, fixtures, equipment, inventory, and other hard assets pertaining to the business. Determine whether outside "expert" opinions for these estimated values will be required.

6. Collect details of "owned" real estate to be included in the valuation task. Determine whether independent appraisals should be conducted.

7. Review data collected and conduct in-depth interviews with owners that are sufficient to:

   a. Fully understand how businesses have been operated, including specific problems encountered and solutions implemented.

   b. Determine "visions" of owners.

   c. Outline a "wished-I-had" statement of what was planned for the business but never achieved—including speculative reasons about why not. (Don't neglect conditions of inventory, equipment, facilities, etc.)

   d. Outline a "generic" resume of special skills and traits believed necessary to successfully operate the businesses.

   e. Agree on "missing" skills and traits that present owners might have used in past operations.

   f. Agree on an "open" perspective for completed values, and to determine *purpose* for the task and use of report.

8. Collect comparable market data on local, regional, and/or national levels.

We have now reached the stage of arraying, analyzing, questioning, reanalyzing, and, finally, estimating business values. On these we superimpose financing structures to determine how estimates might "fly" in a free-market economy; value estimates can't ignore pressures brought to bear by consumers (buyers), irrespective of the purposes outlined in the task.

"Management—*The worst rule of management is* if it ain't broke, don't fix it. *In today's economy, if it ain't broken, you might as well break it yourself, because it soon will be."*

D. Calloway, CEO of PepsiCo

8

Setting the Records Straight

We've been through the reasons that closely held financial records are consistently difficult to understand by outsiders of the companies being reviewed. Subsequently, we must recast or "reconstruct" *some* financial events to understand the true nature of cash flows available, and for analyzing the streams of cash in terms of business value.

RECONSTRUCTION AND WEIGHTING CASH FLOWS

The terms "reconstructed," "recast," and "weighted cash flow" may be foreign to many buyers and sellers, but they are terms you will hear frequently, especially in relationships with accountants, lawyers, and brokers. As previously explained, closely held ownerships afford some flexibility in how sales dollars drop down to profits or losses from a taxation point of view. This "camouflaging" of true cash streams, of course, dilutes ratio responses and other wisdoms leading to conventional interpretations of financial statements. Thus, the practice of reconstruction evolved. Reconstruction is no more than a "restaging" of operating events and owner decisions that otherwise "shelter" income from payments of taxes, and it resets the stage to reveal true operating income and expenses for further study. To a greater extent, loopholes in tax laws provide this flexibility (largely through salaries paid to owners, and the ongoing benefits of depreciation until a business is sold) for the small-business owner. However, valuation experts are aware that some owners push these gray areas in the laws to the hilt, and that some step over boundaries into uncharted waters of the law.

Before proceeding, I feel that I need to clarify my last sentence. Although I believe my statement is necessary for the benefit of unwary buyers, I also feel a need to present it in the proper light. The vast majority of sellers are honest, hardworking folks. From my own experience with literally thousands of potential sellers, less than 2% engaged in what appeared to be a tax-deceptive practice. And some of those few were actually naive in terms of tax laws. Small-business owners do not go into business because of great financial strength. They do so because of previously acquired skills in marketing or product and/or service knowledge . . . vis-à-vis, the "production" concept of bringing their ideas to the consumer table. I recently read in *Inc. Magazine* about a woman who started her own small business after 20 years as a practicing accountant. Her assessment of the company's growing but tough years that followed pinpointed that she had failed to apply her own education and experience as an accountant. You see, up to this point, she had judged that marketing was the necessary focus, not accounting and bookkeeping. In defense of responsible sellers, let's stop assuming that they are all underhanded. It's just not so of the majority! Having said this, however, the concentrated dilemma regularly faced is that sellers want to sell at high prices, just as much as buyers want to buy at low prices. But that alone does not allude to a fly in the ointment.

Tax laws do change from time to time, and "gray" areas in the laws may suggest different interpretation to different people. Your own assumptions are best verified through consultation with professional tax experts. All actions claimed should have "paper trails" to verify these claims. No paper trails equal little or no validity to claims . . . or at least that is how it ought to be if you want to stay whole in your estimates.

The following elements must typically be looked at as possibly holding items that merit exclusion.

Typical Items for Reconstruction (Remember, only *documented* paper trails verify claims!)

1. An owner's personal consumption of business products or services offered can affect *cost of goods sold, sales,* and *gross profits*. Although it is quite understandable that owners will take advantage of "wholesale" prices for goods they use personally, these goods must be minimally booked into sales at their wholesale price and appropriate federal, state, and/or local taxes paid as if the transactions were handled in the customary "business" sense—that's the law. However, practice does not always coincide with the law. Owners have been known to simply remove the goods, not reimburse their

companies, and not adjust inventory by booking these transactions into sales. This act, in terms of more significant goods removal, increases costs of goods sold, decreases gross profits, and misstates true levels of inventory on balance sheets. Upon finding these conditions, buyers must deal with their own beliefs in accepting or rejecting businesses offered under these conditions. On the other hand, sellers who follow the rules, and yet buy considerable product, may still set the equation askew. Goods purchased at wholesale, then booked into sales at wholesale, tend to distort the "message" being sent between sales and cost of goods sold to gross profit. Infrequent and smaller transactions may not cause enough change to bother, but when frequent and significant transactions have taken place, it's wise to remove the dollar amounts in both cost of goods and sales, then recalculate the gross profit as if no such transactions had taken place. Bear in mind, it's the dollars trickling down to gross profits by which small companies pay all other expenses, including owner salaries.

2. *Auto and travel expense* might be of trivial amounts or may contain significant expenditures for personal enjoyment. This expense item has a history of being notoriously misused. Auto and travel expenses are nondeductible under personal taxation but can be legitimate business expense in many instances. Obviously, what's not true business expense should be reconstructed out of expenses.

3. *Commissions paid to nonworking family members* can be another "catch basin" to drain bottom lines from taxable profits. Once again, this can be an illegal IRS dodge and, when found, should be reconstructed out of expenses.

4. *Insurance expense* sometimes contains payments of personal insurance bills. This one can be tricky, because an owner's key-person life and health care insurance could be acceptable costs that a new owner might expect to maintain (*the test is usual and customary*); however, home owner, personal auto, and so on, are no-nos and traditionally reconstructed out of expenses.

5. *Professional fees, repairs, maintenance, telephone, utility, and miscellaneous expenses* are also notorious for containing personally used items. Doctor and dentist bills, repairs and maintenance to personal homes, long-distance personal calls channeled to business phones, personal utility bills, and so on have been found within these expense categories. Thorough examination of expense *significance* must be made and a reconstruction included wherever

indicated. *"Director's" fees* have been known to reflect payments to family members, and though this may have been legal activity, the significance to buyers in this case is "hidden" operational cash, and perhaps merits reconstructing out of expenses.

6. *Owner's salaries and payroll taxes* are often the most significant variable to the bottom line in private companies. Frequently, salaries being paid to owners are based on profit versus any comparable market worth for the job of managing the company. These must be restated to comparable worth figures to examine the purchase cash-flow equation.

7. *Depreciation* is a product of *original* prices paid by owners. In a purchase/sale scenario, a new value for depreciable assets most likely will be clarified by the details of transaction, and new schedules for depreciation will be established. All depreciation expenses must be removed for reallocation at a later point in the valuation exercise. Bear in mind, however, that while depreciation seems like "funny money" to some operators, it is the IRS method of recognizing that assets do wear out with time. Therefore, in lieu of using depreciation per se, buyers should minimally consider a contingency reserve to recognize asset replacements that are likely to occur at one point or another.

8. *Interest expense* is a product of the present company's debt structure. In the purchase/sale scenario, mortgage and equipment financing will most likely change, and the new interest expense will be reflected in the final expense inserted. Reconstruct out the existing, and replace with the new, interest on debt being considered.

9. *Rent expense* must be thoroughly examined for conditions of business owner involvement. If the real property has been "arm's-length" leased from an unrelated third party, then the expense may require full inclusion. However, if the real property is owned by the specific business, or through ownership separate from the business but by the same owner, an assessment must be undertaken of comparable rental rates for the community where the business is operating, and those comparable findings must be used in lieu of "booked" rent expenses. When buyers are purchasing real estate with businesses, they should consult their accountants about the best personal tax-shelter scenarios and book appropriate amounts into expense columns accordingly.

10. *Property taxes* will occasionally include personal property taxes of owner's residences. Although nothing unattached to the business

itself is legitimate, personal taxes paid should be reconstructed out of expenses.

11. *Retirement plan expense* can often include "strange" conditions that are no more than owner perquisites. Chapter 19 in my *A Basic Guide for Buying and Selling a Company* covers a plethora of potential "benefit traps" that buyers can fall into. Pension plans need expert review for levels of funding and can represent major future liability to a new buyer if the plan is not appropriately acquired.

Please do not be misled by the limited number of potential areas for reconstruction. My years in small business lead me to believe that I've seen it all, but just when I say that, some new quirk seems inevitably to appear. Reconstruction is the task of "looking under stones" to see what is hidden for tax reasons, and what might really be available for a new buyer's use. Please don't accept claims on face value; require that claims be proven by documented evidence. If there is no evidence, *discount the claim* entirely from your examination process leading to the offers or value.

Weighting the Cash Streams

Numerous schemes have been developed to make a bevy of years look like one typical and reasonable year's performance; that's all weighting the cash streams is about. They all seem to do the job, but I'm hooked on the following because it's simple and works well.

Hypothetical Example

Reconstructed profit from 1998 ($150,000)	(1)*	=	$ 150,000
Reconstructed profit from 1999 (153,000)	(2)	=	306,000
Reconstructed profit from 2000 (147,000)	(3)	=	441,000
Reconstructed profit from 2001 (163,000)	(4)	=	652,000
	10*		$1,549,000

*Indicates that oldest year receives lowest weight and that the total of the years is ten.

$1,549,000 divided by ten years equals an annual weighted cash stream of $154,900. The next test is "eyeballing" the weighted stream to see whether it makes sense in terms of what the four years produced. In this case, the weighted number is between 2000 and 2001 and seems to be about right. 2000 was down below the prior years, but 2001 was above all four years. Only the facts of the case can tell us whether 2001 was a "quirk" year or if the business was taking off. My companion book, *A Basic Guide for Buying and Selling a Company*, does go into technical detail for those of you who want more information.

You cannot move a 200-ton stone with a wee stick. If a wee stick is all that you have, you must find a smaller rock to move . . . if you want to move at all. Keep your perspective in line with your tools and you'll all do better deals.

"Our greatest weariness comes from work not done."
Eric Hoffer

"Very flawed messengers become angels because they deliver messages we wouldn't have heard otherwise."
Bill Moyers

9

Valuation Techniques

As mentioned earlier, there are no doubt as many formulas and approaches as there are valuation practitioners. Some are complex, deserve to remain in the abodes of experts, and do not fit the periodic buyer's and seller's use. Formulas need be no more difficult in everyday use than to estimate risk in four basic elements:

1. *Business risk*—Will the companies that you are buying or selling experience hard times, or even go under? Will competition put asunder well-laid plans?
2. *Market risk*—Will changes in the economy cause these businesses to gain or lose value?
3. *Interest-rate risk*—Will interest rates go up, causing the market values of your companies to decline? If you plan to hold companies for longer periods, will dropping rates eventually allow you to refinance debt?
4. *Liquidity risk*—When you want to sell businesses, will there be ready markets for them?

In one respect, buying and selling a closely held enterprise is really no different than how one might consider investments in a stock market. Principles of sound investment are very important considerations, but I'm not convinced that the average small-company buyer or seller views purchase and sale in that manner. Many formulas attempt to measure these investment criteria along with the businesses themselves; however, it seems evident that is less the case with participants per se.

Estimating business value is both elusive and theoretical in concept. Theoretical in that value is not *real* until a transaction between ready, willing, and able buyers and sellers is completed. Elusive in that the task in business valuation is to estimate, within broad general market indices and predictable buyer and seller actions, the point at which ready, willing, and able players *are likely* to do their deal. Thus the concept of value reads, "Any price is fair so long as the business can pay for itself out of earnings within a *reasonable* period of time and provide a *reasonable* return to the investor." What is reasonable is left to the imaginations in the case and/ or the judgments of experts.

However, my experience has been that buyers, and some sellers, will carry this definition of value into the realm of practicality on personal levels. It has also been my experience that the calipers for examination are set for instant gratification rather than the long market haul. When it all boils down to purchase, buyers have been primarily concerned with paying for debt, and earning wages. This may not be good enough in the long term, but it's quite frequently the "value determinant" on personal levels. Recalling Leung's more realistic definition of fair market value from Chapter 1, emotional and subjective elements often override rational considerations. Subsequently, the following formula (not in any textbook I've seen) tends to prevail. I call it the "forget the scientist, this is what counts" method. Preceding it is a simple hypothetical case for use in practice sessions later on.

Hypothetical Case: Last year's reconstructed cash flow available is $75,000 before debt service, depreciation, and owner withdrawal. Hard (tangible) assets amount to $60,000 fair market value. Institutional financing is available on just $35,000 of these assets. The offering price is $250,000. The buyer has $50,000 for down payment.

FORGET THE SCIENTIST, THIS IS WHAT COUNTS METHOD

Offering Price	$250,000
Less: Down Payment	− 50,000
Less: Bank Financing	− 35,000
"Uncovered" Debt	$165,000

Let's assume that the seller is willing to "cover" the $165,000 by seller-financed paper. Terms are 9% interest, 20 years, with a balloon at the end of the fifth year. Bank debt is 10%, for 15 years. The first completed year under a new buyer might end as follows:

Cash Flow	$ 75,000
Less: Bank Principal/Interest	−4,513
Less: Seller Principal/Interest	−17,815
Cash Flow Free of Debt	$ 52,672

In many instances, the buyer's examination of the purchasing price might stop here. To his or her simpler way of reckoning, the $50,000 down payment could be returned in just one year of operating the business. Some may carry this process into return on investments such as the following:

Cash Flow Free of Debt	$ 52,672
Less: Ownership Salary	− 35,000
Cash Flow for Investment Return	$ 17,672

Return on Investment:

$$\frac{\$\,75,000}{\$250,000} \;=\; 30\%$$

Return on Pretax Equity:

$$\frac{\$\,17,672}{\$\,50,000} \;=\; 35\%$$

Not a bad deal you say? On the surface, it does look like a pretty good deal for the buyer. Returns are better than the general market, including most venture capital investor returns.

Unfortunately, it's a snapshot of just one year's cash flow. For additional consideration by the buyer, it might be wise to calculate the new equation of debt and salary into several past years' actual cash flow. Are several past years' performances adequately consistent with the sample year used, and has there been adequate cash to accommodate any down year? What's the prognosis for future years, and will a pretty good deal still be good then?

In addition, this snapshot does not address a potentially serious purchasing problem, the seller's five-year balloon payment. Hard-asset value is $60,000 (bank will only finance $35,000), but the seller's balloon payment at the end of the fifth year will be $147,851 in our example. Where is this money going to come from? What havoc will the balloon structure cause for calculated returns? Is the price really so good under these longer-term conditions? Obviously, we can't answer these questions without more information, but we can be highly suspicious that the balloon payment might make today's $250,000 price unreasonable at the end of the fifth year.

All other conditions being equally attractive, removal of the seller's "balloon" entirely suggests that the purchase price could be quite good. But to assume that average small businesses would, in five short years, accumulate sufficient hard assets over the $60,000 that a bank might lend $147,851 against is ludicrous to say the least. The balloon payment will come from the personal estate of the buyer, if it can be made at all.

What Then Might Be an Appropriate Purchase Price?

Let's assume three things for purposes of discussion: (a) the value of hard assets remains $60,000 at the end of the fifth year; (b) a balloon payment will be necessary to get the deal completed; and (c) cash flow of $75,000 remained the same in forecasts to year five. Bank debt at purchase equaled $35,000. By the end of the fifth year, this bank loan would have amortized down to $28,837, or would provide an equity position of just $6,163—assuming no additional principal payments are made. Thus, total debt at the end of the fifth year is $176,688 ($147,851 + $28,837). Let's also make our example tight as a drum—the buyer has no further assets to create additional equity for collateral (which reflects a whole lot of purchase situations). But he or she does have "excess" cash flows above a reasonable and market-comparable salary. Reasonable salary ($35,000) you say? Think on this a minute: How practical is it to expect that *anyone* could receive $35,000 per year on an investment of $50,000 (down payment)? That's a 70% return *per annum!* Granted, you've got to work for it, but you've also purchased *job insurance.* It's therefore practical to say that the salaried return is reasonable, at least in the context of money invested. In this light we may decide that the $17,672 is "excess" for the purpose of valuation. The buyer will need *contingency and working capital reserves,* so let's assign $5,672 for those annual purposes. This leaves us with $12,000 per year, times five years, or $60,000 of discretionary cash to assimilate into the equation of business value.

Cash Flow Free of Debt	$ 52,672
Less: Ownership Salary	− 35,000
Cash Flow for Investment Return	$ 17,672
Less: Contingency/Working Capital	− 5,672
Annual Discretionary Cash	$ 12,000
Times Five Years	×5
Accumulative End of Fifth Year	$ 60,000

The question now becomes, "What price could be paid initially such that this specific buyer could purchase under the same terms outlined in the original proposal and still not worry about business interruption beyond the fifth year?"

Down Payment Amount	$ 50,000
"Excess" Earnings (5 years)	60,000
Bank Debt	35,000
Seller-Financed Debt	
(amount that will exhaust principal completely	
by the end of the fifth year through payment	
of the same $1,485 monthly payment)	71,537
Purchase Price	$216,537

In this conditionally "rigid," hypothetical case example, the buyer could not pay more than $216,537. Thus the seller might have to seek a new buyer entirely or restructure payout conditions such that the "excess" earnings, when coupled with his or her financing, build up closer to the anticipated price . . . *without a balloon.*

Let's take a look at what happens in a seven-year scenario under the same frozen parameters.

Down Payment Amount	$ 50,000
"Excess" Earnings (7 years)	84,000
Bank Debt	35,000
Seller-Financed Debt	
(amount that will exhaust principal completely	
by the end of the seventh year by paying	
the same $1,485 monthly payment)	92,299
Purchase Price	$261,299

In both examples, the buyer will have completely retired seller-financed debt but will have lost the use of $12,000 cash flow per year times five or seven years. When this goes down in purchase-and-sale agreements, it usually shows up as additional annual principal payments, which, of course, makes calculations of rates of returns mighty hard. And, of course, sellers also have the option to structure sales under less permissive rates of returns than in our example.

I elected to go through this rather "strained" example of business valuation because it is similar to what's being so frequently used by small-business buyers and sellers directly. For basic practical reasons, buyers just want to see whether they can survive the tariff asked of them by sellers. And, after all, when the deal is on the table, we're not talking about estimating value . . . we're talking about negotiating the actual price. Let's now take our situation back to when no buyer had yet appeared (same hypothetical case).

To conduct several of the following methods, we need to review a current balance sheet on our hypothetical company. Let's therefore assume the following very simple example:

Assets	
Cash	$ 1,000
Inventory	4,000
Accounts Receivable	5,000
Fixed Assets	
Equipment—Less Depreciation	$57,000
TOTAL ASSETS	$67,000
Liabilities	
Accounts Payable	$ 4,000
Loans	3,000
Total Liabilities	$ 7,000
Owner Equity	$60,000
TOTAL LIABILITIES & EQUITY	$67,000

BOOK VALUE METHOD

The book value method, which does not recognize the fair market value of assets, considers all the variables of a company's balance sheet and can be as simple as total liabilities subtracted from total assets. However, book value does no more than form a "reference" to overall business value and provide some wherewithal as regards financing.

Total Assets at October 16, 2001	$67,000
Total Liabilities	7,000
Book Value at October 16, 2001	$60,000

Adjusted Book Value Method

(This method recognizes the fair market value of assets.)

Assets	Balance Sheet Cost	Fair Market Value
Cash	$ 1,000	$ 1,000
Inventory	4,000	4,000
Acct./Rec.	5,000	5,000
Equipment	57,000	60,000
TOTAL ASSETS	$67,000	$70,000
Total Liabilities	$ 7,000	$ 7,000
Business Book Value	$60,000	
Adjusted Book Value at 10/16/01		$63,000

Hybrid Method

Before one can complete this method, which considers the fair market value of assets *plus* cash flow and market investment principles, both earnings and market investments must be considered. The ways to establish applicable earnings multipliers can vary all over the lot. The following is just one approach that offers some logic in the process of constructing multipliers.

1 = High amount of dollars in assets and low-risk business venture

2 = Medium amount of dollars in assets and medium-risk business venture

3 = Low amount of dollars in assets and high-risk business venture

	1	2	3
Yield on Risk-Free Investments Such as Government Bonds[a] (often 6%–9%)	8.0%	8.0%	8.0%
Risk Premium on Nonmanagerial Investments[a] (corporate bonds, utility stocks)	4.5%	4.5%	4.5%
Risk Premium on Personal Management[a]	7.5%	14.5%	22.5%
Capitalization Rate[b]	20.0%	27.0%	35.0%
Earnings Multipliers	5	3.7	2.9

[a]These rates are stated purely as examples. Actual rates to be used vary with prevailing economic times and can be composed through the assistance of expert investment advisers if need be.
[b]Capitalization rates can be turned into simpler-to-use multiples by dividing the rate into 100 (100 divided by 20 equals 5, for example).

This particular version of a hybrid method tends to place 40% of business value in book values. Given these sample data, and recalling our $75,000 earnings condition, we could value our hypothetical business as follows. However, before we finalize the assignment, we need to reconcile the "gray" area in the preceding 1-2-3 asset/risk elements. Assets are low, but risk seems low to medium, except for the high risk presented by an inability to finance balloon payment. Subsequently, we might arbitrarily decide upon an *off-the-scale* multiplier of 2.5 or select category 3 at 2.9. In note of the word *arbitrarily*—one might say that much in business valuation could be termed arbitrary.

Book Value at 10/16/01	$ 60,000	
Add: Appreciation in Assets	3,000	
Book Value as Adjusted	$ 63,000	
Weight to Adjusted Book Value	40%	$ 25,200
Reconstructed Net Income	$ 75,000	
Times Multiplier	×2.9	$217,500
Total Business Value		$242,700

OR

Total Business Value under a 2.5 Multiplier	$212,700
(to recognize the fifth-year balloon problem)	

This hybrid method is in many respects no different from the **capitalization of earnings method** outlined in many accounting texts. The "regular method," which uses three or more years net income, divided by the number of years used, and then taken times the earnings multiple considered is rather too commonly used. A variation called the "moving average method" weights each year with the oldest year getting the lowest weight, then divided by the sum total of weights, and this result taken times the earnings multiple considered. This variation, of course, gives greater benefit to the most recent years of performance. In that respect, it is more representative of present-day business status.

During the forget the scientist method, we talked about **excess earnings** as a possible condition of valuation and pricing. The following method makes use of the features of the hybrid but, importantly, adds the conditions under which a business might be financed. I prefer methods such as this in the closely held enterprise because value estimates are driven to be *proven* in light of marketplace economies then prevailing. They make the value processor *think* about more than formula-derived estimates. They make the value processor *examine* tax implications, market conditions between buyers and sellers, and reality financing structures. As with any other formula, there is just criticism of the excess earnings methodology. For one, it hinges largely on historical earnings . . . but then, so does the method called discounted cash flow, since forecasted future earnings must be based in some historical fact. And another, "Who *really* has excess earnings to begin with?" Nevertheless, I believe that in the hands of experienced processors, the excess earnings method is exceptionally useful when valuing the closely held enterprise. In addition, periodic users can successfully apply, with a small bit of trial and error, the formula themselves. It is the primary method I depend upon in the real case histories that follow later.

EXCESS EARNINGS METHOD

(This method considers cash flow and values in hard assets, estimates intangible values, and superimposes tax considerations and financing structures to prove the most-likely equation.)

Reconstructed Cash Flow	$ 75,000
Less: Comparable Salary	− 35,000
Less: Contingency Reserve	− 5,405
Net Cash Stream to Be Valued	$ 34,595
Cost of Money	
Market Value of Tangible Assets	$ 60,000
Times: Applied Lending Rate	×10%
Annual Cost of Money	$ 6,000
Excess of Cost of Earnings	
Return Net Cash Stream to Be Valued	$ 34,595
Less: Annual Cost of Money	− 6,000
Excess of Cost of Earnings	$ 28,595
Intangible Business Value	
Excess of Cost of Earnings	$ 28,595
Times: Intangible Net Multiplier Assigned	× 5.0
Intangible Business Value	$142,975
Add: Tangible Asset Value	60,000
TOTAL BUSINESS VALUE (Prior to Proof)	$202,975
	(Say $205,000)

(Please note Figure 9.1 at the end of section for guidance in muliplier selection.)

Financing Rationale

Total Investment	$205,000
Less: Down Payment	− 50,000
Balance to Be Financed	$155,000

Bank (10% × 15 years)

Amount	$ 35,000
Annual Principal/Interest Payment	− 4,513

Seller (9% × 5 years)

Amount	$120,000
Annual Principal/Interest Payment	− 29,892

Testing Estimated Business Value

Return: Net Cash Stream to Be Valued	$ 34,595
Less: Annual Bank Debt Service (P&I)	− 4,513
Less: Annual Seller Debt Service (P&I)	− 29,892
Pretax Cash Flow	$ 190
Add: Principal Reduction	24,000*
Pretax Equity Income	$ 24,190
Less: Estimated Depreciation (Let's Assume)	− 8,571
Less: Estimated Income Taxes (Let's Assume)	− 550
Net Operating Income (NOI)	$ 15,069

*Debt service includes an average $24,000 annual principal payment that is traditionally recorded on the balance sheet as a reduction in debt owed. This feature recognizes that the "owned equity" in the business increases by this average amount each year.

Return on Equity:

$$\frac{\text{Pretax Equity Income}}{\text{Down Payment}} = \frac{\$\ 24{,}190}{\$\ 50{,}000} = 48.4\%$$

Return on Total Investment:

$$\frac{\text{Net Operating Income}}{\text{Total Investment}} = \frac{\$\ 15{,}069}{\$205{,}000} = 7.4\%$$

While return on total investment is abysmally low in relation to conventionally expected investment returns, the return on equity is attractively high. Bear also in mind that an average of $24,000 is returned into equity each of five years, at the end of which, $120,000 of debt is retired. This type of "leverage" in the closely held purchase and sale can be especially attractive to getting any deal done. Assuming that the buyer at least held the line and made no improvements to cash flow during the five years, the following might be the buyer's annual return.

Basic Salary	$ 35,000
Gain of Principal	24,000
Effective Income in Each of 5 Years	$ 59,000*

*There is also the matter of $5,405 annually into the contingency and replacement reserve that would be at the discretion of the owner if not required for emergencies or asset replacements. At the end of the fifth year, principal and interest payments of $29,892 would cease and become available for additional salary or whatever.

Seller's Potential Cash Benefit	
Cash Down Payment	$ 50,000
Bank Financing Receipts	35,000
Gross Cash at Closing	$ 85,000*

*From which must be deducted capital gains and other taxes. Structured appropriately, the deal qualifies as an "installment" sale with the tax on proceeds from seller financing put off until later periods.

Projected Cash to Seller by End of Fifth Year	
Gross Cash at Closing	$ 85,000
Add: Principal Payment	120,000
Add: Interest Payment	29,460
Pretax Five-Year Proceeds	$234,460

The end result is not the $250,000 expected by the seller, but quite likely the seller has a much safer assurance of being paid in full . . . and walking away from the deal and never looking back. The seller could increase interest returns to $48,770 by extending his or her note to eight years. An eight-year term payout, and playing around with the valuation scenario again, might permit an increase in selling price and, therefore, an increase in principal and interest somewhat as well. *Restrictive financing decreases values.*

The chart on page 57 (Figure 9.1) is suggested only as a guide to selecting net multipliers as they relate to this specific excess earnings method for valuation. They are not likely to be germane in any other context.

As often mentioned in my books, I am not a strong believer in using the discounted cash flow (DCF) method for valuing the closely held, small enterprise. Nevertheless, in the hands of expert processors, the DCF and its close cousin, the discounted future earnings (DFE) method, can be conceptually excellent methods of choice. However, these processes take continued practice that the periodic user may not get. To illustrate, I will include the process for our hypothetical case but will not always exhibit DCF methods in the real case studies that follow later.

Typical Businesses	*Net Multiplier*	One or More Considerations

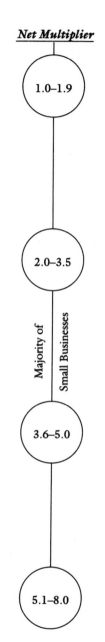

Typical Businesses

<u>Professional services</u>, i.e., physician, dentist, attorney, accountant, optometrist, architect, engineer, chiropractor, veterinarian, real estate, insurance, etc.

1.0–1.9

- Earnings relatively flat
- Dependent upon skill of owner
- Fierce competition
- Labor versus capital intense
- Low hard assets
- Start-up requires minimum capital outlay

<u>Other services</u>, i.e , advertising, funeral, entertainment, laundry, transportation hauling, printing, restaurant, janitorial, beauty salon, travel, employment agency, leasing services, etc.
<u>Contractors</u>, i e., general, electrical, plumbing and A/C, painting, masonry, etc.
<u>Retail</u>, i.e., computer, equipment, fuel oil, gift, video, stereo and TV, apparel, office supply, drug, general merchandise, food/beverage, liquor, florists, jewelry, sporting goods, floor covering, hardware, auto, etc.
<u>Wholesale</u>, i.e., building materials and supplies, food/beverage, auto supplies, electrical and plumbing supplies, etc.
<u>Manufacturing</u>, leased facilities and modest equipment investment

2.0–3.5

Majority of Small Businesses

- Average growth of earnings
- Skill of owner important but replaceable with short-term training
- Expected amount of competition
- Labor/capital intenseness mixed
- Modest investment in hard assets in relationship to cash stream
- Start-up requires larger cash position and larger amounts of working capital

3.6–5.0

- Significant growth of earnings
- Skill factor more removed in administrative versus "hands-on," high degree of transferability
- Virtually no competition
- Asset base high, requiring large initial cash outlay
- Start-up costly in terms of up-front costs

<u>Services</u>, i.e., motel, nursing home, parent bank, parent insurance, hospital, etc.
<u>Retail and manufacturing</u> owned real estate and large inventory and/or equipment investment

5.1–8.0

- Predictable growth or stability of earnings
- Operating skills transferable with education and/or minimal training
- Expected degree of competition
- Real estate and capital equipment intense
- Start-up almost cost prohibitive

Figure 9.1 Guide to selecting net multipliers.

Discounted Cash Flow of Future Earnings (The theory is that the value of a business depends on the future benefits [earnings] it will provide to owners. Traditionally, earnings are forecast from an historical performance base in some number of future years [usually five to ten years] and then discounted back to present using present value tables.)

For the sake of discussion, earnings are expected to grow annually at the rate of 10% per year. Let's use just four years and now, for the sake of argument, let's also assume Net Operating Income (NOI) is the $35,000 salary plus $2,000 out of the $5,405 contingency not required in the business, or NOI of $37,000 tax sheltered.

Base	Forecast Earnings			
Year	1	2	3	4
$37,000	$40,700	$44,770	$49,247	$54,172

Establishing Expected Rate of Return (The rate expected as a return on invested capital) For the loss of liquidity and venture rate of returns in the range up to 25%, let's assume 20% as a level of return on risk associated with small-business ownership. We'll also assume the earnings plateau in the fifth year at $55,000.

Value of Hypothetical Company:

$$\text{Forecast Year 1} \quad \frac{\$40,700}{(1 + .20)} \quad = \quad \$\ 33,917*$$

$$\text{Forecast Year 2} \quad \frac{\$44,770}{(1 + .20)^2} \quad = \quad \$\ 31,090*$$

$$\text{Forecast Year 3} \quad \frac{\$49,247}{(1 + .20)^3} \quad = \quad \$\ 28,499*$$

$$\text{Forecast Year 4} \quad \frac{\$54,172}{(1 + .20)^4} \quad = \quad \$\ 26,125*$$

$$\text{Plus} \quad \frac{(\$55,000 \text{ divided by } .20)}{(1 + .20)^4} \quad = \quad \$132,620*$$

Total Business Value   **$252,251***

*Earnings discounted to present value. *Handbook of Financial Mathematics, Formulas and Tables,* Robert P. Vichas, Prentice-Hall

On the basis of the discounting method, we might choose to negotiate the purchase of our hypothetical business for a price of $252,251 or less.

As you can see, DCF or DFE methods are quite complex and necessitate a great deal of accuracy in forecasting earnings into future years. Traditionally, value processors will complete high, low, and most-likely probability columns to refine their estimates. Unfortunately, small-company earnings are not reliable to forecast because, if for no other reason, the loss of present owners and the replacement by new and unknown owners create uncertainties in earnings under best conditions.

SUMMARY

In this chapter I have attempted to provide a range of formulas from quite simple to complex in nature. The sample included does not represent any particular cross section of choices but merely shows some of the formulas available. I've included the discounted method because business brokers can get hung up on using this process and thus many buyers and sellers may confront this method of pricing in working their deals.

My method of choice is the excess earnings process presented earlier. Understand that the "formula" is *never* an absolute. It's the *process of massaging* information such that debt outlined in negotiations, reasonable salaries, and other related expenses can be paid out of cash flow—within the time allotted through prevailing market and economic conditions. Play around with the process a bit; if your indicated total business value cannot meet the financing test, then you need to go back up to the value-estimating portion, massage that, then return once again to the financing portion, and so on. Pay particular attention to asset financing—make sure that bank portions fit within commercial lending criteria or the process simply won't balance the equation to value. In the next chapter we will do some experimenting in order that you might practice further in the use of this process if you choose.

Last, valuation schemes all tend to employ nondiscounted rules of thumb such as plowback, putback, and/or payback methods. Plowback, of course, restricts the equation to the *internal* availability of funds. Putback is on equal footing with the plowback method and entails *shelving* funds for emergencies arising elsewhere. Payback focuses on how long it will take to *recover* investment outlays. Therefore, one might theoretically look at plowback as a concept that says, "the estimated business value is appropriate when internal funding justifies the price." In this same light, putback suggests carving out a contingency fund from earnings prior to the valuation of cash streams. And payback is the measurement criteria for value and pricing overall. Having completed our hypothetical case exercise, it's time to move on to examining the trial and error that is used in one variation of the excess earnings formulas.

"Quality control is achieved most efficiently, of course, not by the inspection operation itself, but by getting at causes."

Dodge and Romig

10

Practicing with an Excess Earnings Method

We will use the same hypothetical case for ease of reference in this chapter. However, before delving into the practice work, I need to talk more about an ever-present environment surrounding the valuation task that must not be ignored. It is so easy for even some experts to slip into believing that business valuation is a precise science. It's not! It never can be, because people will never let it be that. You can count on the motivations for gain and need to rise frequently in individuals to complicate even what might otherwise look to be the simplest of business valuation assignments. Value in the small, closely held company is value as the participants to a deal would *have* value done. Proof, however, is "putting value where the mouth is," because saying it is so is not so until a deal *has* been done. As mentioned in the last chapter, value is both elusive and theoretical until price has been established by actual transactions. The goal in valuation, then, is to "estimate" *all* the various conditions that market economies might bring to bear on a "price" that would be most likely to *cause* transactions between buyers and sellers to occur. Regardless of the *purpose* of the task, this causation issue must be the focused target in valuing the small company. The parameters of intended use can then adjust the findings to fit the needs of recipients. Intrafamily transfers might suggest downward value adjustments, and estate or other purposes may offer specific refinements for their particular use. Losing sight of market-based elements too early in the process turns the task into shooting arrows at moving targets that the archer may not be able to hit.

Thus for reliability, the value processor must understand commercial lending parameters as well as prevailing interest rates, understand the supply of available sellers in relation to the demand exhibited by available buyers, understand at least two-cents' worth of human psychology, understand general investment principles, understand basic accounting and finance, understand forecasting models, be willing to doubt his or her own veracity, and, above all, keep a sense of humor. And humor is hard to do for the scientific-minded. Who, besides the incredibly, incredibly rich, for example, would admit to having "excess" money? Yet we choose to call this formula the excess earnings method.

Do you know what might happen to business results when you replace the current owner with a new operator (forecasts are often based on current-owner results)? Do you know what bankers require in candidates for commercial loans? Do you know what the current rate of interest is for commercial loans? Do you know what human perception does to value? Have you conducted appropriate market research on buyer and seller action? Can you read and understand financial statements? Do you know yourself? Until you can answer yes to all these questions, you are not nearly ready for the task. The method will do no more than *guide* what you already know. It will also guide you into the archer's moving target with what you don't know.

Hypothetical Case: Last year's reconstructed cash flow available is $75,000 before debt service, depreciation, and owner withdrawal. Hard (tangible) assets amount to $60,000 fair market value. Institutional financing is available on just $35,000 of these assets. The offering price is $250,000. The buyer has $50,000 for down payment.

In this chapter we are going to demonstrate how one might "massage" information to arrive at responsible judgments of business value. The first example is merely a repeat of last chapter's scenario and once again provided under simple circumstances. In Example 2, we will set up the task as if we had not previously completed Example 1, and then "back into" the method to arrive at value.

EXAMPLE 1

Excess Earnings Method

(This method considers cash flow and value in hard assets, estimates intangible values, and superimposes tax considerations and financing structures to prove the most-likely equation.)

Reconstructed Cash Flow	$ 75,000
Less: Comparable Salary	− 35,000
Less: Contingency Reserve	− 5,405
Net Cash Stream to Be Valued	$ 34,595

Example 1   **63**

Cost of Money

Market Value of Tangible Assets	$ 60,000
Times: Applied Lending Rate	×10%
Annual Cost of Money	$ 6,000

Excess of Cost of Earnings

Return Net Cash Stream to Be Valued	$ 34,595
Less: Annual Cost of Money	− 6,000
Excess of Cost of Earnings	$ 28,595

Intangible Business Value

Excess of Cost of Earnings	$ 28,595
Times: Intangible Net Multiplier Assigned	×5.0
Intangible Business Value	$142,975
Add: Tangible Asset Value	60,000
TOTAL BUSINESS VALUE (Prior to Proof)	$202,975
	(Say $205,000)

Financing Rationale

Total Investment	$205,000
Less: Down Payment	− 50,000
Balance to Be Financed	$155,000

Bank Financing (10% × 15 years)

Amount	$ 35,000
Annual Principal/Interest Payment	4,513

Seller Financing (9% × 5 years)

Amount	$120,000
Annual Principal/Interest Payment	29,892

Testing Estimated Business Value

Return: Net Cash Stream to Be Valued	$ 34,595
Less: Annual Bank Debt Service (P&I)	− 4,513
Less: Annual Seller Debt Service (P&I)	− 29,892
Pretax Cash Flow	$ 190
Add: Principal Reduction	24,000*
Pretax Equity Income	$ 24,190
Less: Estimated Depreciation (Let's Assume)	− 8,571
Less: Estimated Income Taxes (Let's Assume)	− 550
Net Operating Income (NOI)	$ 15,069

*Debt service includes an average $24,000 annual principal payment that is traditionally recorded on the balance sheet as a reduction in debt owed. This feature recognizes that the "owned equity" in the business increases by this average amount each year.

Return on Equity:

$$\frac{\text{Pretax Equity Income}}{\text{Down Payment}} = \frac{\$ 24,190}{\$ 50,000} = 48.4\%$$

$$\text{Return on Total Investment:}$$

$$\frac{\text{Net Operating Income}}{\text{Total Investment}} = \frac{\$ \ 15,069}{\$205,000} = 7.4\%$$

EXAMPLE 2

Assume that we have just been given the information provided in the hypothetical case. We need to determine whether $250,000 is an "affordable" price. (Boldface type highlights changes from Example 1.)

Reconstructed Cash Flow	$ 75,000
Less: Comparable Salary	− 35,000
Less: Contingency Reserve	− 5,405
Net Cash Stream to Be Valued	$ 34,595
Cost of Money	
Market Value of Tangible Assets	$ 60,000
Times: Applied Lending Rate	×10%
Annual Cost of Money	$ 6,000
Excess of Cost of Earnings	
Return Net Cash Stream to Be Valued	$ 34,595
Less: Annual Cost of Money	− 6,000
Excess of Cost of Earnings	$ 28,595
Intangible Business Value	
Excess of Cost of Earnings	$ 28,595
Times: Intangible Net Multiplier Assigned	×6.6[1]
Intangible Business Value	**$188,727**
Add: Tangible Asset Value	60,000
TOTAL BUSINESS VALUE (Prior to Proof)	**$248,727**
	(Say **$250,000**)

[1] Most frequently made error in using this process. Processors fail to understand "power" in a multiplier's ability to give false impressions of business *strengths* in the marketplace. The usual tendency is a compulsion to "overrate," thus, overvalue.

Financing Rationale	
Total Investment	**$250,000**
Less: Down Payment	− 50,000
Balance to Be Financed	**$200,000**
Bank Financing (10% × 15 years)	
Amount	$ 35,000
Annual Principal/Interest Payment	4,513

Example 2   **65**

Seller Financing (9% × **15** years)

Amount	**$165,000**
Annual Principal/Interest Payment	20,082

Balloon at end of 5th year $133,786

Testing Estimated Business Value

Return: Net Cash Stream to Be Valued	$ 34,595
Less: Annual Bank Debt Service (P&I)	− 4,513
Less: Annual Seller Debt Service (P&I)	− 20,082
Pretax Cash Flow	$ 10,000
Add: Principal Reduction	6,200*
Pretax Equity Income	$ 16,200
Less: Estimated Depreciation (Let's Assume)	− 8,571
Less: Estimated Income Taxes (Let's Assume)	− 550
Net Operating Income (NOI)	$ 7,079

*Debt service includes an average $6,200 annual principal payment that is traditionally recorded on the balance sheet as a reduction in debt owed. This feature recognizes that the "owned equity" in the business increases by this average amount each year.

Return on Equity:

$$\frac{\text{Pretax Equity Income}}{\text{Down Payment}} = \frac{\$ 16,200}{\$ 50,000} = 32.4\%$$

Return on Total Investment:

$$\frac{\text{Net Operating Income}}{\text{Total Investment}} = \frac{\$ 7,079}{\$250,000} = 2.8\%$$

Well, you say, it doesn't look too bad after all. Return on equity is still quite healthy and we pretty much threw the return on total investment out the window in Example 1 anyway. But tell me, what are you going to do about the balloon of $133,786 at the end of the fifth year? The buyer doesn't have it, and the bank won't finance it because the business is undercollateralized. Besides, there is still debt of $28,837 remaining on the original bank loan at the end of five years. Taken together, we must find $162,623 by the end of the fifth year.

By comparing the bold entries in Example 2 to those of Example 1, you'll be able to partially see what must be done to arrive at a price under the restrictive conditions presented in our case. We put the brakes on the multiplier in Example 1, thus reducing "estimated" total business value, but there's an unrecognized factor in the method that lets us factor in the balloon condition. It's not on the paper! It requires a "business finance calculator" or loan rate table to perform (or a visit to your friendly banker, broker, or accountant for use of theirs). The unknown that we are attempting to solve involves: (a) available business cash flow and (b) the seller's financed portion of debt. Our question: How much seller debt can "excess" cash flow support?

Reconstructed Cash Flow	$ 75,000
Less: Comparable Salary	− 35,000
Less: Contingency Reserve	− 5,405
Less: Bank P & I Payments	− 4,513
Available Cash Flow (Excess)	**$ 30,082**

Thirty thousand eighty-two dollars per year, or $2,506 per month in principal *and interest* payments will support about $120,000 of seller debt spread over a five-year period. How did I arrive at this? If you take an "equal monthly loan amortization payment" table, locate the page containing 9% and five years, we find that it takes $2.08 per month to amortize $100 dollars over the five years. $2,506 divided by $2.08 times $100 equals $120,481. Most rate tables commonly end on amounts up to $20,000 of debt, but, if you find a table that goes up into the hundreds of thousands, of course you needn't do the arithmetic. Simply find the five-year column under 9% and follow it down until you reach monthly payments near to $2,506—and read the bold dollars under the term/ amount column for the answer. Following shortly is an example of such a table (available inexpensively in bookstores).

Persons who have the business calculator either know how to perform the calculation or can look up the process in their operation manual for their particular machine. Bear in mind that the seller in this case imposed the five-year condition. The processor must complete estimates under the given set of circumstances or provide alternatives for consideration by the players to the deal. If players have not established a catch-basin framework, then the processor must use market indices and may still be advised to provide alternative choices for selection. Processors do not set values in the vacuum of their own minds unless, of course, they are also players in the deal. And we know that processors who are also players can become overrun by human emotions that make their value estimates questionable.

Example 2   67

Monthly Payment Necessary to Amortize a Loan (at 9%)

Term Amount	5 Years	6 Years	7 Years	8 Years	9 Years
$ 100	2.08	1.81	1.61	1.47	1.36
200	4.16	3.61	3.22	2.94	2.71
300	6.23	5.41	4.83	4.40	
400	8.31	7.22	6.44		
500	10.38	9.02			
600	12.46				

Two thousand five hundred and six dollars divided by 2.08 (italics) times $100 equals $120,481, or the maximum debt that can be supported if the seller insists on a five-year payout. A friend of mine once accused me of "donkey math" in using this simple approach. Perhaps so, but an amortization table for $120,481 at 9% for five years reveals the monthly principal and interest payment to be $2,500.99. Close enough in a system that overall is known to be somewhat arbitrary to begin with.

Thus, we can now return to the upper portion of the method, labeled Intangible Business Value. Our question now becomes: What multiplier, when taken times $28,595, will produce the proper total business value?

Intangible Business Value	
Excess of Cost of Earnings	$ 28,595
Times: Intangible Net Multiplier Assigned	×5.0
Intangible Business Value	$142,975
Add: Tangible Asset Value	60,000
TOTAL BUSINESS VALUE (Prior to Proof)	$202,975
	(Say $205,000)

This question is rather simply answered because we know that $60,000 of total value is assigned to tangible assets. We also know that $35,000 is provided through bank financing, that $50,000 is provided by down payment, and that $120,000 of seller debt is what the freight will bear. Thus, $35,000 plus $50,000 plus $120,000 equals $205,000. $205,000 minus $60,000 equals $145,000 divided by $28,595 equals an approximate 5.0 multiplier. Rather a neat check on initial judgment over multiplier selection, wouldn't you say? At this point, one simply redoes the process through to the end.

Methods, formulas—they are nothing more than fragile structures within which, through trial and error, the facts fit into narrow windows portending value.

> *"ALL YOUR LIFE you have been studying geometry informally, for all your life you have been studying the sizes and shapes of things. That is what geometry is—the accurate study of size and shape. Now you are ready to organize your ideas of geometry into a logical system of thought."*
>
> Unknown author

Prelude to Case Examples of Small-Business Valuation

All valuation examples in this book are taken from real case histories. My present consulting practice ranges to an approximate 1,800-mile radius from our primary office; thus, case examples have been selected from several different states and are not particularly reflective of Maine. To preserve specific anonymity, only information essential to valuation is supplied. However, each chapter begins with an overview of the particular industry and/or unique characteristics of that valuation assignment. Therefore, readers might want to review other pertinent chapters prior to conducting their own business valuations.

As we all know, learning is best achieved through repetition. By the same token, repetition can be boring unless the major points are restated through changing dialogue. I wish I could say that this has been achieved in my text, but it hasn't, for several reasons:

1. Shifting attention between formulas and dialogue causes most people to lose their train of thought.

2. Interpreting ratio and formula outcome takes practice and repetitive use.

3. Reproduction of the same formula and supporting dialogue, which I have done, allows readers to focus on practice and a reasonable mastery.

In this same vein of repetition aiding useful learning, I focus on four basic ways of looking at small-business value.

1. *Book Value.* Only a rare few small businesses will actually sell at the price this method offers. It is included to encourage readers to recognize the role hard assets play in the valuation assignment.

2. *Adjusted Book Value.* A very few more small businesses might sell under the pricing this method offers. This formula, in combination with "appraised" value of hard assets, translates book value into the more relevant fair market value of hard assets.

3. *Hybrid* (a variation of the capitalization method). This particular version provides structure as to how capitalizing or earnings multiples are formed using general investment criteria. In that respect, it favors the consumer or buyer . . . and forecasts a motivational trigger exciting them to relocate funds from "safer" investments to that of small-business purchase. While these multipliers may resemble "rule-of-thumb" ratios, they are not such. Hybrid formulas forecast "generic" and overall references to value, whereas rule-of-thumb methods are derived from historic transactions completed within specific industries.

4. *Excess Earnings.* At first more difficult to grasp, this method examines hard-asset purchase in light of available cash flow. It also examines small-business purchase in view of "financing" requirements essential to fulfill transaction prices. In that respect, some "proof" of value is offered. When this method is well understood, it offers a great deal of flexibility to buyers and sellers during negotiations, in that counteroffers can be factored back into the formula at any stage of calculation.

Several other methods or processes are sprinkled through various chapters, but the preceding four are used primarily.

No formula or method evaluates the training, education, personality, or characteristics of buyers and sellers. No formula or method guarantees the "correct" or "right" price. And even the most refined valuation expert cannot achieve this for you. Small-business valuation is no more, or less, than a *structured benchmark* for the participant's use during the negotiating process or for other general uses by small-business owners. In the buying and selling of small businesses, however, it is a qualifying process to ward off underpricing or overpayment, when all other factors are being fully considered. Don't expect more!

11

Professional-Practice Valuation

KEY FEATURES IN PROFESSIONAL-PRACTICE VALUATIONS

Professional practices include the wide medical and mental health fields and could include accounting, legal, engineering, veterinarian, chiropractic, optometric, some forms of consulting, and so on.

Similarities and differences between small businesses, in general, and professional practices must be understood. The following attributes, though some are distinguished by fine lines, are the essential characteristics to bear in mind.

1. Professional practices are primarily service businesses where incomes are generated by people themselves versus the employment of hard assets.

2. In relationships of *trust,* patients or clients, because they are only nominally capable of understanding or evaluating services rendered, must place great reliance on the professionals delivering those services.

3. Professional practices rely mainly on *referral* sources for new business because, for trust reasons, patients and clients gain comfort by word-of-mouth reference.

4. Professional practice generally entails specialized college degrees for practitioners, and thus practices have virtually no value to other than similarly degreed individuals.

5. Licensing by government bodies or certification by recognized professional organizations, which examine education, training, and rep-

utation to some greater or lesser degree, is also required for most professionals to practice.

Some professionals, as with many other small businesses, engage in tax-deferral practices not authorized by the IRS—that is, maximizing expenses and holding back checks and cash deposits near year-end to set off income into the new tax years. Professional practices often use the cash versus accrual system of accounting, which recognizes income when cash is received; therefore, no accounts receivable is traditionally booked to balance sheets. However, quite regularly there will be "receivables" to the firm. Subsequently, these amounts must be obtained through "internal" record-keeping sources, examined for age outstanding, and assessed for their practical collectibility. Some professionals tend not to keep "clean" or clearly understood information on receivables and tend also not to write off uncollectibles until prodded to do so. Many professionals require "advances" against future work. These also may not appear on the balance sheet and may be accounted for on informal documents that are maintained separately from customary bookkeeping established for reporting purposes. Frequently, these data will be housed in professional computer software that is uniquely dedicated to specific professions. Valuation processors should obtain a "hard copy" of all informal records along with various tax returns to ascertain the complete picture of operations.

Unbilled work in process, particularly in CPA, consulting, legal, and engineering firms, can be difficult to gather in larger firms. Most often, the individual practitioner keeps track of his or her own work in process until periodic submission for central billing to clients. However, time records are usually being maintained and professionals can usually estimate quite reliably unbilled work in process as well as estimated values upon completion. In larger practices, this may necessitate interviewing each individual practitioner to complete the large picture of work in process.

Inventory of supplies, though often quite small, can vary considerably, depending on the type of practice. Medical and dental practices will have good inventory details for controlled substances, syringes, and other related items, but, like other types of office environments, may not keep detailed accounting for other supplies. A review of one or two years' annual supply purchases, coupled with eyeballing what's there, can usually suffice whenever the professional cannot estimate supplies on hand.

Equipment, furniture, and fixturing can vary widely from professional to professional. Dentists will have considerably more valuable equipment but may not have the levels of investment in furniture that, say, lawyers or accountants may have. Most professionals keep a pretty good tab on these items and can reliably estimate their values.

Some professionals, particularly medical and dental practices, incur high insurance expenses. Insurance is normally prepaid in advance, as is rent. Therefore, for short periods, prepaid expenses might be a "declining" asset carried on balance sheets until attributed to expenses on income statements. Small practices not completing interim statements may not "decline" the asset but once per year when tax filing is due. Malpractice insurance for certain medical specialties can be inordinately high, and infrequent financial statement preparations can distort the true attribution from balance sheets to income statements. When this expenditure is significant, one should adjust for timing and allocate according to actual practice.

Leasehold improvements can be considerable in some practices, especially in urban settings where "first impressions" are frequently considered essential to doing business. Well-maintained improvements can successfully outlive their useful life in comparison to how one might write them off through depreciation for tax purposes. Therefore, an adjustment to fair market values may be appropriate for the purposes of practice valuation.

Leasing, rather than owning, the occupied real estate can be an important consideration in valuing the practice. Copies of leases should be examined for future rent escalation clauses, durations, and other features that may affect profits in future years. Attractive rates tied into long-term prospects can be valuable assets to professional practices. On the other hand, short-term leases or leases about to expire may have little value and could trigger added expenses that may dilute future profits.

Accrued or deferred liabilities (noted on balance sheets) could contain elements to be allocated to income statements. For example, payroll and payroll taxes accrue on balance sheets during pay periods until paychecks are delivered to employees, when in one fell swoop this accrual is delivered to income statements. The effect, of course, is a reduction of balance sheet liability and an increased expense to income statements. Deferred liabilities would be deferred revenues, expenses, and taxes. Many professional practices collect large fees in advance of performance, that is, retainers or full payments. These fees represent commitments to do work that entails revenue assets and expense and tax liabilities. Some professionals maintain "informal" records with regard to advance fees that necessitate the evaluator's examination. Accrued and deferred balance sheet accounts should be thoroughly reviewed for time/effect impacts on balance sheets and income statements, particularly as these events play into forecasts being used in valuation procedures.

Contingent liabilities relate to *unproven* events that may or may not create true liabilities. In professional practices, these tend to appear on balance sheets due to pending litigation claiming malpractice or disputed billing. Though exceedingly rare, unproven events might also appear as contingent assets in cases where professionals are plaintiffs for recovery of damages. The word *contingent* appearing anywhere on financial statements should trigger deep exploration by valuation processors, and full assessments of potential impacts on business values.

WHEN TO VALUE

Professional practices might rarely be valued for estate reasons because upon the demise of the professional, cash streams most often dry up. Thus, values in facilities, furniture, fixtures, and equipment may represent the only *real* values left. Because of the element of "trust," patient or client lists may or may not hold continuing value beyond the demise of the professional. More often, professional practices will be valued due to buy/ sell (including the addition of partners) and, unfortunately, conditions precipitated through divorce.

Professional practices can be among the most difficult of all businesses to estimate in terms of value. This is particularly true for sole practitioners in the medical, dental, and mental health fields. Such practices are incredibly, in fact crucially, tied into trust between patient/client and provider. To greater or lesser degrees, all professional-practice values hinge largely on the "individual reputation" of each specific professional, and this individual contribution to value will dilute only gradually as the practice is multiplied by a number of other individual participants. Only when the professional relegates duties *entirely* to administration will his or her absence be likely not to materially diminish the practice's value. Thus, focus on the task of this business valuation must be weighted heavily on examining value provided by each individual's contribution. However, one should not omit consideration for the "transferability" that many professionals can provide a newcomer coming into his or her practice. Trust and loyalty can be successfully transferred between cooperating professionals to patients and/or clients. Bear in mind that trust and loyalty transference is accommodated by the respect the patient/client has for the professional's judgment. Thus his or her personal endorsement of the newcomer can be widely accepted by patients and/or clients. The professional's "long-term acceptance" is then dependent upon his or her retention of the transferred trust and loyalty from the entrenched professional. Retention of revenues in many instances of buyout situations can be quite significant—some don't skip a beat from their former professional.

Multiprofessional practices tend often to execute buy/sell agreements among partners. These documents normally contain binding agreements of value in the event of death among partners and will spell out specific payments due to the estates of the decedents. They will also condition the structure for selling out or for bringing on new partners. Valuation processors should not overlook examining buy/sell agreements when they exist.

THE VALUATION TASK

For all practical purposes, the elements of review by the professional-practice value processor will be quite similar to those in value estimating other types of businesses. Goodwill, by its intangible nature, will always be elusive at best, thus also impossible to cover adequately in any generic discussion. However, in valuing the professional practice, one might relate the individual's personal impact on value to that of the capacity of a manufacturer's production machine. Broken completely, slowing due to wear and tear or missing parts, one can estimate "future" capacity based on the present and *forecast* condition of the machine. Thus proper attention must be given to future capacity (in relationship to past capacity) in the professional valuation process—a not dissimilar element of all business valuation estimates. The following chart highlights predominant similarities and differences.

Professional Practice	General Business
Expected Income	
Effect caused by displaced individual contribution	Can be same but more emphasis on business's overall contribution
Source of Customers	
Word-of-mouth referral	Advertising, sales promotion, and direct sales
Customer Attachments	
Trust/loyalty tied to individual professional	Trust/loyalty tied mainly to products or services

Professional Practice	General Business

Deliverance Availability

Work habits of the professional	Conditioned heavily by customer response

Thwarting Competition

"Niche" based on professional's own reputation	"Niche" mostly impersonal and tied into product/service features

Location

Patient/Client	Customer
More dependent on ease/access than storefront availability	Storefront availability
	Owner
Provider	Strategic wideband population need and complexly affected by competition; ease of entry
Strategic narrowband population need and affected mostly by "unique" competition; difficult entry	

Product/Service Pricing

Fees charged affected by supply/demand, insurance, and influenced by government	Prices set mostly by supply/demand

Effect of Employees

Influence professional's reputation and delivery	May affect business performance but customers are mostly influenced by product or service reputation

Business Marketability

Dependent on transfer of professional criteria (narrow scope market, limited to education/ licensing)	Dependent on business performance, business "appeal" (wide scope market, open to qualified buyers)

Prevailing Transfer Practices

"Earn-in/earn-out" or buy-out/earn-out within professional ranks*	Institutional debt and up-front cash

Income

Not usually a reference to practice; earnings tend to be paid out as salaries and benefits as earned above expenses	Income reflected as sales, less cost of goods sold and expenses, including salaries

Accounting Practice

Usually cash system	Normally accrual system

*Terms (jargon) often used by accountants, lawyers, and acquisition specialists that essentially depict no up-front cash infused by the purchaser, and a portion of the buyer's personal salary being "escrowed" to the acquisition of the business. Ownership does not customarily transfer until the escrow account represents 50% or more of the contracted purchase price.

THE VALUATION SESSION

Our first example is a single practitioner of general dentistry. Located in a small community within a nonurban area, he has practiced at this location for the past several years and serves the needs of patients of all ages. Most come from within a radius of seven miles. Nine other dentists compete within his radius of practice, and fees being charged by this practitioner are competitive with these other practitioners. His fees are approved by all dental insurance plans in the area.

Reputation as a "gentle doc" has spread into the community and his office is mercury-free. Approximately 20% of the practice is preventive services performed by two hygienists. About 57% of the practice falls into operative services, crown and bridge procedures, and removable prosthodontics, which he performs with the aid of an assistant. The balance of his practice is mixed procedures.

As a person strongly committed to family values, this dentist has not offered evening or extended hours of care. The operative work schedule is based on about 17 days per month. Heavily booked into the future, the doctor is concerned about patient waiting delays and lost practice revenues. At present, he is only selectively accepting new patients. Based on present patient load and new-patient inquiries, he believes he must extend the practice hours by adding 28 to 32 hours per week to his office schedule. To do so, he would add an associate or partner, and thus, the purpose for business valuation.

Methods used in professional-practice valuation have heightened or waned through the years due to their validity in application or due to the complexity involved. Some techniques have survived but method applications may be widely different between value processors. Again, not so important is the "how," because it's the end product measured by the marketplace that counts. Thus, the following processes are my own techniques. They will not necessarily be representative of other valuation practices. In that respect, I prevail upon you to forget the scientist in you and ask that you concentrate on *process-flow* logic. In doing so, you may discover simpler or better ways for yourself. The following statements have been "reconstructed" from historical performances, and, for purposes of this exercise, you must assume that entries have been examined and/or adjusted in their appropriate ways.

Balance Sheet

Assets	
Cash	$ 1,044
Inventory	21,458
Accounts Receivable	38,507
Less: Allowance—Doubtful	– 4,636
Total Current	$ 56,373
Furn./Fix./Equip.	$ 20,700[1]
Total Fixed	$ 20,700
TOTAL ASSETS	$ 77,073
Liabilities	
Payroll Taxes Payable	$ –0–
Notes Payable	22,455
Note Payable—Owner	2,300
Total Liabilities	$ 24,755
Professional's Equity	$ 52,318
TOTAL LIABILITIES & OWNER EQUITY	$ 77,073

[1]Stated at "fair market value."

Income Statements—Sole Proprietorship Practice

	1999	2000	Estimated 2001
Revenues	$221,188	$265,426	$362,957[1]
Expenses			
Advertising	$ 2,507	$ 4,958	$ 690
Bad Debt	1,093	—	—
Wages	56,073	75,840	82,800
Emp. Benefits	1,754	2,099	1,840
Practice Ins.	4,101	5,001	5,435
Acct./Legal	2,735	3,861	3,450
Office Exp.	5,691	7,881	7,880
Leased Equip.	8,880	6,639	12,650
Repairs	1,793	6,784	2,809
Supplies	23,654	21,458	20,700
Tax/Licenses	12,399	5,710	7,130
Meals/Ent.	199	817	345
Utilities	9,144	4,832	5,750
Lab Fees	15,566	21,930	20,890
Bank Charges	5,372	12,360	690
Auto Exp.	1,810	600	690
Cont. Educ.	1,883	—	690
Rent	[2]	11,256	20,700

Condo Fees	—	5,311	6,462
Leasehold Imp.	—	6,442	1,380
Dues	1,214	—	2,192
Other	6,695	23,131	18,731
Total Expenses	$162,563	$226,910	$223,904
Recast Income	$ 58,625	$ 38,516	$139,053

[1]Through nine months year-to-date, "collections" amounted to $267,897, which represents 155 out of an available 210-day annual practice. Seen in the light of $1,728.37 per practice day, 210 days would represent $362,957 in collected practice income.

Services performed through the nine months equaled $284,218 or $1,833.66 per practice day. Translated into 210 days, services performed would be $385,069. Thus, one might assume that accounts receivable would be $22,112 at the end of 2001. Also to be assumed is that forecast $362,957 in revenues is practical.

In 2000 the doctor purchased a condominium office and moved his practice to these new quarters, thus income is down due to one-time costs associated with this move.

[2]Rent for 1999 is included in "Other."

THE TASK

The purpose of valuation for this practice is to admit a new practitioner for the expansion of practice hours. Since the new practitioner will likely become a partner, our task is to establish a baseline value for buy-in. The balance sheet, of course, provides a good picture of asset values but ignores the "trust buildup" essential to practice success. As a refresher from earlier remarks, professional practices grow mostly through word of mouth, and patients or clients can often be persuaded to transfer loyalties to newcomers when encouraged to do so by initial providers. Subsequently, valuations for the purpose of adding partners are really no different than those for other types of businesses. However, the emphasis on debt conditions affecting value can be much less pronounced than those I point out in later types of companies. The owner contemplating business restructure to a partnership form of organization is rarely inclined to allow his or her balance sheet to be leveraged by debt as a matter of adding a new partner. Typically, the newcomer is required to furnish cash at the outset or enters into one of a variety of arrangements for gradual buy-in to the firm. In any event, the intangible value afforded through cash flows (in excess of supporting hard-asset values) need not be hampered in the valuation task by any lack of collateral or provisions for institutional financing, as might be the case in a business's outright sale.

This particular case contemplates the addition of a dental practitioner with perhaps no more than two to four years of experience beyond formal education. Between lingering college debts and limited practice time for recovery, it would be unlikely that a candidate would have amassed significant cash to purchase into the partnership. Thus, the partnership would evolve over time through earnings contributed back to the firm. There are no divided rights being contested in the initial ownership. Weighted historical cash streams shall not be considered, since the practice has grown close to capacity under the present work configuration and because appointment bookings must now be screened carefully prior to acceptance of new patients. Thus, 2001 estimated data shall be the basis upon which the value in this practice is founded. Evidence from similar transactions supports this conclusion. I might also point out that professional practices, in terms of value, rarely dig into past earnings for bearings on present-day value. Perhaps some "bean counters" may think they should; however, that is just not what happens in the marketplace as these firms change hands. And marketplace "action" cannot be ignored by value processors as they adjust the feathers on the dart homing toward estimated values.

Hybrid Method

(This is a form of the capitalization method.)

1 = High amount of dollars in assets and low-risk business venture

2 = Medium amount of dollars in assets and medium-risk business venture

3 = Low amount of dollars in assets and high-risk business venture

	1	2	3
Yield on Risk-Free Investments Such as Government Bonds[a] (often 6%–9%)	8.0%	8.0%	8.0%
Risk Premium on Nonmanagerial Investments[a] (corporate bonds, utility stocks)	4.5%	4.5%	4.5%
Risk Premium on Personal Management[a]	14.5%	22.5%	52.5%
Capitalization Rate	*27.0%*	*35.0%*	*65.0%*
Earnings Multipliers	**3.7**	**2.9**	**1.5**

[a]These rates are established at varying times during the year or when dramatic economic shifts occur.

As previously explained, earnings multipliers are calculated by dividing the capitalization rate into 100% (100 divided by 20 equals 5, etc.).

This particular version of a hybrid method tends to place 40% of business value in book values.

Book Value at 6/30/01	$ 61,589	
Add: Appreciation in Assets	at book	
Book Value as Adjusted	$ 61,589	
Weight to Adjusted Book Value	40%	$ 24,636
Reconstructed Net Income	$139,053	
Times Multiplier	×1.5	$ 208,580[1]
Total Business Value		**$233,216**

[1]This 1.5 multiplier has been selected because the practice has one professional, and because a foothold in the market is not fully determined. Illness or death of the single practitioner puts 100% of revenue at risk.

Excess Earnings Method

(This method considers cash flow and values in hard assets, estimates intangible values, and superimposes tax considerations and financing structures to prove the most-likely equation.) You will note later that "Reconstructed Cash Flow" will often be the product of "weighting" cash streams of several years. In this professional's case, his practice is rather new and growing. Also, by preference, he operates fewer hours than many of his peers, and his schedule is filled to a point of turning some patients away. Thus, I elected to use the estimated 2001, rather than a weighted average of the two other years given.

Reconstructed Cash Flow	$ 139,053
Less: Contingency Reserve	− 15,000
Net Cash Stream to Be Valued	$ 124,053
Cost of Money	
Value of Tangible Assets	$ 77,073
Times: Applied Lending Rate	×10%
Annual Cost of Money	$ 7,707
Excess of Cost of Earnings	
Return Net Cash Stream to Be Valued	$ 124,053
Less: Annual Cost of Money	− 7,707
Excess of Cost of Earnings	$ 116,346

Intangible Business Value
Excess of Cost of Earnings $ 116,346
Times: Intangible Net Multiplier Assigned   ×1.5
    Intangible Business Value $ 174,519
        Add: Tangible Asset Value   77,073

    TOTAL BUSINESS VALUE $ 251,592

Return on Professional's Investment:

$$\frac{\text{Net Cash Stream}}{\text{Total Investment (Assets)}} = \frac{\$\ 124,053}{\$\ \ 77,073} = 161.0\%$$

RULE-OF-THUMB ESTIMATES

I worry about applying rule-of-thumb estimates for dental and medical practices because it is such a "closed society," even friend to friend. The various associations do collect information with regard to practitioner earnings by years in practice within specific fields. These can be fairly reliable indices in regard to practice success when valuation assignments pertain to litigated issues. However, they may not be of particular import when the assignment is simply that of taking on a partner in a solely owned rural practice. Furthermore, there has been continuing suspicion on the part of the Internal Revenue Service (IRS) that not all revenues are consistently reported. Income not reported to the IRS may likely not be reported to association data banks as well. I'm not at all suggesting that medical and dental professionals are any more prone to processing revenues outside IRS regulations than are other small businesses, but I am suggesting we might know even less than we should know about what *really* happens in particular professional practices. Another problem confronted is that many practices possess both "business" and "practitioner" goodwill. Multiple professionals in collective practice may have both; however, sole practitioners may have only developed the latter. Data collected on actual practice transfers may be just as misleading for many of these same reasons. Therefore, I am highly suspicious of values portended from rule-of-thumb ratios for medical or dental practices. However, when combined with other techniques, they may shed additional light on estimated practice values.

At times I am confused by the plethora of "rules" I've seen quoted. From Boston to Chicago to Los Angeles there seems to be inconsistency, and when you add rural utterances, another rule crops up. However, from a broad perspective the pattern seems to evolve as value equals the fair market value (FMV) of hard assets (excluding real property holdings) plus 20% to 40% of gross revenues, or 50% to 100% of doctor's earnings (salary). Thus in our case, rule-of-thumb value might be forecast as follows.

Let's use 30% of revenues plus FMV of assets:

($362,957) (30%) = $108,887 plus $77,073 or estimated value of $185,960

Or let's use 85% of available cash flow plus FMV of assets:

($139,053) (85%) = $118,195 plus $77,073 or estimated value of $195,268

If we used the high ranges in each of these rule-of-thumb forecasts, we would show products of $222,255 and $216,126.

Results

Book Value Method (from balance sheet)	$ 77,073
Hybrid (capitalization) Method	$233,216
Excess Earnings Method	$251,592
Rule-of-Thumb Method (average of high ranges)	$219,191

In my opinion, the value of this dental practice on the date of appraisal was:

TWO HUNDRED FIFTY THOUSAND and No/100 ($250,000.00)

Some Rule-of-Thumb Guidelines for Other Professional Practices

(Real property that might be also sold is not included in these ratios to value.)

Law Firms

Since legal ethics prohibit revealing actual client information, law practices may be prevented from selling more than their net asset values. However, it is not uncommon for departing practitioners to "merge" some of these confidences with clients and new attorneys entering the scene. In so doing, split-fee arrangements are traditionally made when clients consent to use the new practitioner. However, my experience has been that a good many clients will be more apt to find another legal firm to represent them when their previous attorney chooses to leave his or her firm. Beyond appraisal of hard assets, excluding client records, I have never encountered rule-of-thumb methods that are applicable to legal firms.

Medical Doctors

As discussed above for dental and medical practices, I do not have a good deal of confidence here beyond the supplemental-to-other-method use for rule of thumb. However, it has been my general experience that when these methods are used, medical practices sell in the range of 25% to 70% of the latest year's *gross* revenues for supplies, equipment, and practice goodwill. Bear in mind that "goodwill" in all medically related practices is akin to those revenues remaining after the exchange of professionals takes place.

Accounting, Consulting, and Insurance Firms

These practices have commonly sold for fair market value of assets plus a percentage of the latest year's revenues. However, the value in revenues is suspect as to the number of clients that may remain after a sale. Thus retention of clients is an important aspect of any sale. More often, "goodwill" in accounting, consulting, and insurance firms is sold over time such that the buyer can be assured that clients booked into the latest year revenues are retainable. Quite frequently a penalty will be associated with these values in goodwill, when clients leave during a customarily specified time of payout for this aspect of the sale. Over and above the value of hard assets, goodwill tends to equal 70% to 150% of revenues. It is not unusual to see five-year time frames associated with goodwill payouts.

Engineering-Related Firms

Although all engineering-related firms tend to have a few repeating clients, many more clients will be onetime service users. Subsequently, past revenues may or may not particularly indicate their value in goodwill. Thus, fair market value of assets plus 20% to 45% of the latest year's revenues might be used. Obviously, clients with repeat-use history bear heavily in the application of the higher-end ratio. For all practical purposes, rule-of-thumb ratios in these firms tend to produce less than satisfactory indications of value.

Veterinary Practices

These are unusual professional practices to value under any method. Educational facilities turning out veterinarians are sorely limited in the United

States, and it is inordinately difficult for aspiring candidates to get in. Subsequently, the nation does not have an abundance of practitioners. I'm more aware of this condition because my son was finally admitted after a five-year wait beyond undergraduate pre-vet. This process, I'm told, is not at all unusual. Undersupply and overdemand tend to forecast premium prices in the market. Moreover, veterinarian practices can predictably command 75% to 125% of the latest year's revenues quite regularly for supplies, equipment, and goodwill.

Medical Laboratories

These facilities, when they come up for sale, are not often purchased by individuals. Quite regularly they are acquired by either investment groups or publicly traded companies. Values range widely but a good majority can fit within a range of between 55% and 90% of the latest year's revenues for goodwill and fair market value of supplies and equipment. Laboratories dealing with human tissue and/or those setting medical standards can command particularly high values, and rule-of-thumb methods may not be at all appropriate.

Optometrists and/or Optometric Firms

Value processors must be particularly careful to discern the differences between these two types of firms. Pure optometric firms are essentially retail operations and can be valued in the same light as other retail businesses. More and more optometrists are engaging in both refractory and retail sales of eyewear. Pure optometric firms tend to sell in a range between 45% and 65% of the latest year's revenues for supplies, equipment, inventoried client prescriptions, and goodwill. We are left with an ill-fitting bag of rules for the hybrid optometrist practice. However, in some respects it is no different than dental practices, since equipment costs run about the same and because the retail portion is relatively limited by the number of patients being seen. Subsequently, ratios tend to range between 35% and 55% of the latest year's revenues for supplies, equipment, transferable patient records, and goodwill.

Chiropractic Firms

These practices tend to accumulate equipment in the value range of dental practices and, subsequently, may command prices in the range of 25% to 45% of revenues, plus fair market value of equipment, supplies, goodwill, and transferable patient records. A relatively large number of chiropractors engage in the sale of nutritional supplements, including herbs. These, of course, may raise the level of revenues and supplies, but bear in mind that revenues from the sale of these supplements are normally limited to the in-house patient load. Like most professional practices, much of their value hinges on the transferability of patients to the incoming practitioner.

Physical and Occupational Therapy

These practices hold mixed bags of value because some are owned by hospitals and others are independently operated. Hospitals tend not to sell such "departments" because they can be reasonably profitable and provide a needed in-house service to the hospital. Independently operated facilities tend often to be owned by a consortium of individuals whereby as one may pass out, another will slip in, thus perpetuating the group ownership. I have not been able to locate any rule-of-thumb method that I personally feel could add to this book as to rule-of-thumb ratios. The one sale I participated in was to a hospital that purchased only the assets plus provided a three-year tenured employment contract to the previous owners.

12

Small Manufacturer Valuation

(With Ratio Studies)

Every small business presents its own peculiarities of valuation. For example, inventories in manufacturing companies are always in a state of flux. Normally they are partially made up of raw materials, partially of work in process, and partially of finished goods. Quite regularly manufacturers will take customer deposits against future product deliveries, and these advances to sales may be represented by raw materials, work in progress, and/or finished goods inventory. Thus, one must look at the jobs-in-progress system to reconcile what stages inventories may be at or are committed to. Also, since equipment and machinery are more vital to sales performance in the small manufacturer, it is always wise to have professionals estimate their condition, useful remaining lives, and approximate values. Appraisal of these items is far outside the bailiwick of the majority of real estate and business valuation specialists.

The manufacturer's income statements are generally more complex than those of other businesses. As processes grow more complex, and the businesses larger, many manufacturers will separate direct plant production costs from "administrative" expenses for measurements of performance and cost control. These firms are more apt to engage complex job-order or process accounting cost-control systems than the typical retail, distribution, or service business. Thus the value processor's examination of the income and balance sheet is incomplete until reconciled with the various product work-flow documents that force-feed these snapshot-in-time records. Manufacturers are more inclined to develop "in-house" ratios as production benchmarks and will more regularly compare themselves with industry standards. In fact, it is not uncommon for manufacturers to set production measurement criteria directly in line with these industry standards. Thus, they are more apt to judge the "quality" of

their businesses in light of how well they stack up against national, regional, or internal norms.

We will step through some ratio work, but we will not delve into ad-
justing for the in-process aspect during this exercise. The necessary examinations vary widely from industry to industry. And besides, this book
is focused mainly on the valuation process itself. For those wishing more
detailed information leading up to formulating recast/reconstructed
statements, I refer you to my book *Self-Defense Finance for Small Businesses* (John Wiley & Sons, Inc., 1995).

THE COMPANY

This manufacturing corporation was founded 12 years ago and is housed
in a 10,000-square-foot building, with the title to the building held privately by the business owner. Measured by local market standards, the
$28,000 annual rent is considered in line with others for comparable
space. The present space provides for considerable expansion of the business, and a lease for 10 years with two 5-year options will be transferred
with the business. Real estate is not being sold.

The firm engages in structural urethane foam molding, a relatively new
processing technique brought from Europe to the United States in the
late 1960s (first U.S.-produced part made for the automobile industry in
1975). As defined by the *Modern Plastics Encyclopedia,* the process involves "simultaneous high-pressure in a small impingement mixing cham-
ber, followed by low pressure [50 pounds per square inch or under]
injection into a mold cavity." Further outlined are the processing advan-
tages (i.e., lower temperatures, lower pressures, lower equipment costs,
and greater design flexibility).

Current design and production in this particular business center around
business machine housings for the computer and electronics industry. The
business has developed a specific-need, low-volume "niche" in the
marketplace. It does not compete with high-pressure injection molding
or with the home computer market. The present owner has experimented
with a number of other products quite adaptable for production with this
process. High strength, low weight, dimensional stability, chemical resis-
tance, weatherability, and surface appearance make this process suitable
for numerous applications in office furniture components and the construction industry. An industry brochure shows product application to
tool handles, furniture components, bicycle seats, stair treads, beer barrel
covers, window frame parts, lawn tractor engine covers and body panels,

recreational vehicle body panels, solar panel frames, luggage components, plus a myriad of other applications. The outlook for future growth appears outstanding; however, beyond developing various prototype products, this business has not conducted serious market research toward expansion of its lines. The company employs 15 persons year-round.

Balance Sheet

PLASTICS MANUFACTURER
Recast Balance Sheet
(For Valuation Purpose)
June 30, 2001

Assets
  Current
Cash	$ 136,893
Accounts receivable	187,206
Prepaid Fed/State Income Taxes	2,417
Inventory [$22,736 Work in Process]	52,252
Total Current Assets	$ 378,768

  Plant & Equipment
Leasehold Improvements (completed June 15, 2001)	$ 87,895
Machinery and Equipment (appraised fair market value)	280,407
Office Equipment (appraised fair market value)	5,405
Total Plant & Equipment	$ 373,707

TOTAL ASSETS	$ 752,475

Liabilities
  Current
Accounts Payable	$ 67,099
Customer Deposits	16,330
Accrued Payroll and Payroll Taxes	100,103
Total Current Liabilities	$ 183,532
Stockholder Equity	$ 568,943
TOTAL LIABILITIES & STOCKHOLDER EQUITY	$ 752,475

PLASTICS MANUFACTURER
Recast Income Statements for Valuation

	1998	1999	2000	6 Months Y-T-D 2001	12-Month Forecast 2001
Sales	$803,430	$827,847	$923,487	$698,733	$1,000,000
Cost of Sales	374,709	377,810	422,034	310,214	452,800
Gross Profit	$428,721	$450,037	$501,453	$388,519	$ 547,200
% Gross Profit	53.4%	54.4%	54.3%	55.6%	54.7%
Expenses					
Adv./Promotion	2,695	225	1,202	196	2,500
Vehicle Exp.	1,318	2,383	1,939	1,274	5,000
Bad Debt	2,000	1,059	1,047	—	2,000
Cleaning	8,016	8,108	7,203	1,980	5,000
Dues/Subs.	651	243	262	272	250
Utilities	26,607	30,068	36,939	36,529	40,300
Miscellaneous	4,325	4,466	4,739	2,116	4,600
Freight	975	1,482	2,032	2,725	3,850
Insurance—Gp.	2,380	5,077	4,289	2,161	4,500
Insurance—Gen.	12,216	13,966	12,929	6,221	13,900
Prof. Fees	4,873	7,385	4,915	5,199	5,400
Contract Serv.	12,625	11,966	11,082	3,579	8,000
Office Exp.	364	448	523	279	600
Nondirect Labor	58,800	57,074	60,950	37,162	60,000
Off./Maint. Wages	28,253	28,679	34,169	28,366	36,000
Employment Taxes	21,862	20,671	24,934	19,335	24,518
Commissions	9,043	2,169	8,496	10,266	18,250
Rent	26,000	28,000	28,000	14,000	28,000
R&M—Building	560	99	647	2,085	2,100
R&M—Equipment	7,809	7,286	7,665	4,602	7,800
Small Tools	1,547	5,284	3,047	801	2,500
Supplies—Office	1,262	1,640	948	1,464	1,700
Supplies—Opers.	8,227	4,027	6,002	2,998	5,600
Supplies—Factory	5,688	9,399	8,127	5,396	8,700
Equip. Lease	11,611	8,314	7,929	8,286	8,300
Telephone	5,529	5,774	6,741	5,756	7,300
Travel/Ent.	8,721	6,270	8,957	7,584	9,000
Taxes—Other	561	342	1,101	3,505	4,100
Total Expenses	$274,518	$271,904	$296,814	$214,137	$ 319,768
Recast Income	$154,203	$178,133	$204,639	$174,382	$ 227,432
Recast Income as a Percent of Sales	19.2%	21.5%	22.2%	25.0%	22.7%

FINANCIAL ANALYSIS

Since our purpose for valuation is established as an "assets" versus a stock transaction, we need to be careful in drawing conclusions under the generally accepted parameters of ratio comparisons. Both industry and analytical services tend occasionally to produce "after-tax" comparisons, but close examinations of their study reports will normally reveal before-tax data as well. Also, the particular company we're about to value does not fit well within the "norms" of the general plastics manufacturer category, which is traditionally represented in many of these studies. Low p.s.i. mold injection means much lower tooling and equipment costs, thus the balance sheet in our sample company is unlikely to resemble those typically found with conventional high p.s.i. injection molding counterparts. Subsequently, the task necessitated locating "close-in" industry-compiled ratios, which are presented here.

A quick preview of the balance and income statements leaves little doubt that this company is well within the "healthy" segment of financial comparison. However, ratio work should not be ignored as a supplement to valuation tasks. The first step in any valuation assignment is to decide whether the business itself merits any comparative work at all.

Thus the nature of our task is to (a) analyze income statements for justification of further review; (b) determine what's being sold or offered in the way of assets; (c) determine a comparative merit standing within a range of businesses available; and (d) estimate the "price" most likely to be achieved when the business is exposed to a set marketing time frame (usually 6 to 12 months). In other words, if the business is being marketed assertively, it should "sell" at or near the estimated price within this time frame. Price estimating without target sale predictions attached frequently translate into "accidental," unpredictable, and/or no likelihood of sale.

"Eyeballing" the income statements reveals steady growth of sales, and the cost of sales and expenses under control. Setting the recast statements side by side as we have here allows for observances of developing positive or negative trends. Calculating percentage gross profits and recast income flows helps identify peaks and valleys and directs the eye where to look for additional exploration. As these percentages show, our sample company apparently has been managed exceedingly well from an internal point of view. Sales may not have grown substantially, but growth has been predictably steady. The balance sheet is also very strong. However, what we can't tell at this time is how it stacks up within its industry as a whole (competitive criteria). Ratio analysis can provide some insight.

Financial experts will not always agree as to which ratios are particularly germane to the small and privately owned enterprise. I feel that it is essential to examine the following (note—for brevity, some ratios calculated from balance sheet data are not included here):

$$\textbf{Ratio for Gross Margin} = \frac{\text{Gross Profit}}{\text{Sales}} \text{ or}$$

1998	1999	2000	6 Mo. 2001	Industry Median
53.4	54.4	54.3	55.6	42.9

This ratio measures the percentage of sales dollars left after cost of manufactured goods is deducted. The significant trend in our company is for efficiency of the manufacturing process; however, in calculating this ratio we need to assure ourselves that we included "apples" in our cost of goods comparable to "apples" in the cost of goods in surveyed samples. Thus we must explore the survey's definition of items included in cost of goods and perhaps even restructure the target company's statements to reflect same-case scenarios.

It should be noted that ratios for net profit, before and after taxes, can be most useful ratios. The fact that private owners frequently manage their business to "minimize" the bottom line often produces little meaningful information from these ratios. Therefore, they are not included.

$$\textbf{Current Ratio} = \frac{\text{Total Current Assets}}{\text{Total Current Liabilities}} \text{ or}$$

2001	Industry Median
2.1	1.5

The current ratio provides a rough indication of a company's ability to service its obligations due within one year. Progressively higher ratios signify increasing ability to service short-term obligations.

$$\textbf{Quick Ratio} = \frac{\text{Cash and Equivalents + Receivables}}{\text{Total Current Liabilities}} \text{ or}$$

2001	Industry Median
1.8	.8

The quick, or "acid test," ratio is a refinement of the current ratio and more thoroughly measures liquid assets of cash and accounts receivable in the sense of ability to pay off current obligations. Higher ratios indicate greater liquidity as a general rule.

$$\text{Sales/Receivable Ratio} = \frac{\text{(Income Statement)}}{\frac{\text{Sales}}{\text{Receivables}}} \quad \text{or}$$
$$\text{(Balance Sheet)}$$

1998	1999	2000	12 Mo. 2001	Industry Median
5.9	9.1	5.0	5.3	7.0

Note: Balance sheets for 1998 to 2000 have not been previously shown, but I've calculated them for general reference. This will be true for the following as well.

This is an important ratio and measures the number of times that receivables turn over during the year. Our target company seems to turn these over more slowly than the industry median. Significant to note, however, is the very small write-off of bad debt on their income statements. This should trigger a look-see at receivable "aging." Perhaps more needs to be written off, or agreements with customers might suggest this to be standard to the target company.

$$\text{Day's Receivable Ratio} = \frac{365}{\text{Sale/Receivable Ratio}} \quad \text{or}$$

1998	1999	2000	6 Mo. 2001	Industry Median
62	40	73	60	50 days

This highlights the average time in terms of days that receivables are outstanding. Generally, the longer that receivables are outstanding, the greater the chance that they may not be collectible. Slow-turnover accounts merit individual examination for conditions of cause.

$$\text{Cost of Sales/Payables Ratio} = \frac{\text{Cost of Sales}}{\text{Payables}} \quad \text{or}$$

1998	1999	2000	6 Mo. 2001	Industry Median
5.9	4.8	6.6	4.6	7.3

Generally, the higher their turnover rate, the shorter the time between purchase and payment. Higher turnover, which our target company appears to experience, supports income statement cash flow strengths to pay bills in spite of slower receivable collections. This practice may be somewhat misguided in light of investment principles whereby one normally attempts to match collections relatively close to payments so that more business income can be directed into the pockets of owners.

$$\text{Sales/Working Capital Ratio} \;=\; \frac{\text{Sales}}{\text{Working Capital}} \quad \text{or}$$

1998	1999	2000	6 Mo. 2001	Industry Median
4.4	4.6	2.9	4.2	6.9

Note: Current assets less current liabilities equals working capital.

A low ratio may indicate an inefficient use of working capital, whereas a very high ratio often signals a vulnerable position for creditors. Our target company has been below the median, and with exception for 2000, may be modestly inefficient in the use of its working capital.

To analyze how well inventory is being managed, the cost of sales to inventory ratio can identify important potential shortsightedness.

$$\text{Cost of Sales/Inventory Ratio} \;=\; \frac{\text{Cost of Sales}}{\text{Inventory}} \quad \text{or}$$

1998	1999	2000	6 Mo. 2001	Industry Median
5.3	5.9	8.1	5.9	4.7

A higher inventory turnover can signify a more liquid position and/or better skills at marketing, whereas a lower turnover of inventory may indicate shortages of merchandise for sale, overstocking, or obsolescence in inventory.

Conclusion

There are, of course, a number of other financial analyses we might conduct, but from visual inspection and brief ratio analysis, it can be reasonably concluded that our target company presents a solid base upon which to commence the valuation estimate. Perhaps there is a bit of wiggle room in management of collections and working capital, but I would see this weakness as a plus in the eyes of prudent buyers. The balance sheet is strong, sales and profits have been growing quite dependably, opportunities exist for product-line expansion, and the target company enjoys a "niche" market hold. Manufacturing companies in general hold the highest esteem in the eyes of buyers, and this particular company stacks up well within that perceptive esteem. Technology is repetitively applied and can be learned with relative ease by nontechnical prospective buyers. The founder and present owner has a degree in liberal arts. Thus we must weigh "sex appeal" into our mathematical equation because all of the right things are "right" to the discerning eyes of buyers . . . as long as the price is also right. What, then, is the right price?

THE VALUATION EXERCISE

The forget the scientist, this is what counts method is more traditionally a process employed by buyers, so we will put this one off until the end.

Book Value Method

Total Assets at June 30, 2001	$601,247*
Total Liabilities	183,532
Book Value at June 30, 2001	**$417,715**

*Includes deduction of $151,228 in accelerated depreciation. $752,475 − $151,228 = $601,247.

Adjusted Book Value Method

Assets	Balance Sheet Cost	Fair Market Value
Cash	$136,893	$ 36,790 **
Acct./Rec.	187,206	187,206
Inventory	52,252	52,252
Prepaid Taxes	2,417	2,417
Equipment, etc.	222,479	373,707 [1]
Total Assets	$601,247	$652,372

Total Liabilities	$183,532	$ 83,429 **
	$417,715	
Adjusted Book Value at 6/30/01 (relative to stockholder equity)		**$568,943**

[1]Stated at appraised and, thus, fair market value.
**Cash reduced by accrued payroll items of $100,103—obligation assumed paid.

Hybrid Method

(This is a form of the capitalization method.)

1 = High amount of dollars in assets and low-risk business venture
2 = Medium amount of dollars in assets and medium-risk business venture
3 = Low amount of dollars in assets and high-risk business venture

	1	2	3
Yield on Risk-Free Investments Such as Government Bonds[a] (often 6%–9%)	8.0%	8.0%	8.0%
Risk Premium on Nonmanagerial Investments[a] (corporate bonds, utility stocks)	4.5%	4.5%	4.5%
Risk Premium on Personal Management[a]	7.5%	14.5%	22.5%
Capitalization Rate	20.0%	27.0%	35.0%
Earnings Multipliers	5	3.7	2.9

[a]These rates are stated purely as examples. Actual rates to be used vary with prevailing economic times and can be composed through the assistance of expert investment advisers if need be.

This particular version of a hybrid method tends to place 40% of business value in book values. However, before we finalize the assignment, we need to reconcile the "gray" area in the 1-2-3 asset/risk elements above. Assets are high and risk seems low to medium due to the stability of cash flow in three previous years. The seller has declared that he or she *wants all cash at closing*. In this particular case there is no "asking price," because we have been assigned the task of estimating the *market entry* price. Subsequently, we must determine the "target" rather than prove or disprove validity in an asking price. Experience in working with this instrument teaches one *not* to be too bold in assigning multipliers. I have a saying in my firm that goes: "Only God gets a multiplier of much in excess of 5—and I've never been asked by him or her." The key to reducing labor hours in the assignment is to be conservative in determining multipliers.

Weighted Cash Streams

Prior to completing this and the excess earnings method, we must reconcile how we are going to treat earnings to ensure that we have a "single" stream of cash to use for reconstructed net income. I prefer the weighted average technique as follows:

	(a)	Assigned Weight	Weighted Product
1998	$154,204	(1)	$ 154,204
1999	178,133	(2)	356,266
2000	204,639	(3)	613,917
2001	227,432	(4)	909,728
Totals		(10)	$2,034,115
		Divided by:	10
Weighted Average Reconstructed			$ 203,412

Eyeballing column (a) we can conclude that the weighted average reconstructed income seems reasonably fair on the surface—the weighted is approximately equal to completed 2000. However, we must bear in mind that income between 1998 and 2000 has progressed consistently upward, and that there is *no* compelling evidence that this company could not complete the 2001 forecast of $227,432. *At this stage we need to be extra conservative because of the all-cash proposal.*

Book Value at 6/30/01	$417,715	
Add: Appreciation in Assets	151,228	
Book Value as Adjusted	$568,943	
Weight Assigned to Adjusted Book Value 40%		$227,577
Weighted/Reconstructed Net Income	$203,412	
Times Multiplier	×3.7	$ 752,624
Total Business Value		$ 980,201

OR

Total Business Value under a 3.7 Multiplier	$ 980,000
(to recognize the all-cash condition)	

Excess Earnings Method

(This method considers cash flow and values in hard assets, estimates intangible values, and superimposes tax considerations and financing structures to prove the most-likely equation.)

Weighted/Reconstructed Net Income	$ 203,412
Less: Comparable Salary	− 50,000
Less: Contingency Reserve	− 10,000
Net Cash Stream to Be Valued	$ 143,412
Cost of Money	
Market Value of Tangible Assets	$ 568,943
Times: Applied Lending Rate	×10%
Annual Cost of Money	$ 56,894
Excess of Cost of Earnings	
Return Net Cash Stream to Be Valued	$ 143,412
Less: Annual Cost of Money	− 56,894
Excess of Cost of Earnings	$ 86,518
Intangible Business Value	
Excess of Cost of Earnings	$ 86,518
Times: Intangible Net Multiplier Assigned	×5.0
Intangible Business Value	$ 432,590
Add: Market Value of Tangible Assets	568,943
TOTAL BUSINESS VALUE (Prior to Proof)	$1,001,533
	(Say **$1,000,000**)
Financing Rationale	
Total Investment	$1,000,000
Less: Down Payment (25%)	− 250,000
Balance to Be Financed	$ 750,000

At this point, we know that we have a serious problem with financing because total assets less liabilities equal $568,943, and we know that banks want "collateral" to make loans. We also know that $250,000 cash is a lot of money to expect from buyers in general, and as it is, this cash requirement already puts us into a category of finding perhaps no more than 3% to 5% of all buyers that will qualify to purchase this business. It's important to use a good deal of logic at this stage of valuation or you will waste a lot of time coming up with reliable estimates. One can set up the financing scenario any way appropriate to their local conditions, but my guess is that the following would be pretty close. (So as not to be confusing, equipment is listed on the balance sheet as $280,407 plus $5,405 or $285,812. When added to leasehold improvements of $87,895, we have fair market value of plant and equipment of $373,707. The reason

I've broken these down in this stage is that banks finance each item differently, if at all.)

Equipment ($285,812) at 70% of Appraised Value	$200,068
Inventory ($52,252) at 60% of Book Value	31,351
Leasehold Improvements ($87,895 and long-term	
lease conditions) at 40% of 2001 (new) Value	35,158
Receivables Minus Payables ($120,107) at 70%	84,075
Estimated Bank Financing	$350,652*
	(Say $350,000)

Bank (10% × 15 years)

Amount	$350,000
Annual Principal/Interest Payment	45,133

Testing Estimated Business Value

Return: Net Cash Stream to Be Valued	$143,412
Less: Annual Bank Debt Service (P&I)	− 45,133
Pretax Cash Flow	$ 98,279
Add: Principal Reduction	13,078*
Pretax Equity Income	$111,357
Less: Est. Dep. & Amortization (Let's Assume)	− 41,027
Less: Estimated Income Taxes (Let's Assume)	− 12,100
Net Operating Income (NOI)	$ 58,230

*Debt service includes an average $13,078 annual principal payment that is traditionally recorded on the balance sheet as a reduction in debt owed. This feature recognizes that the "owned equity" in the business increases by this average amount each year.

Return on Equity:

$$\frac{\text{Pretax Equity Income}}{\text{Down Payment}} = \frac{\$111,357}{\$250,000} = 44.5\%$$

Return on Total Investment:

$$\frac{\text{Net Operating Income}}{\text{Total Investment}} = \frac{\$ 58,230}{\$1,000,000} = 5.8\%$$

Although return on total investment is abysmally low in relationship to conventionally expected investment returns, the return on equity is attractively high and cash flow is strong.

Basic Salary	$ 50,000
Net Operating Income	58,230
Gain of Principal	13,078
Tax-Sheltered Income (Dep.)	41,027
Effective Income	$162,335*

*There is also the matter of $10,000 annually into the contingency and replacement reserve that would be at the discretion of the owner, if not required for emergencies or asset replacements.

At this time we have estimated business value . . . but have we estimated *the* estimated value? $250,000 cash down payment plus $350,000, or $600,000, leaves us with a $400,000 shortfall of the all-cash target specified by the seller. If we leave the price at $1,000,000, either the buyer has to make up the difference outside this business ($250,000 plus $400,000 equals $650,000 cash down payment), or the seller must become flexible toward providing $400,000 of seller financing, or find another buyer with more cash, or the estimated price must be "squeezed" to fit the conditions of this buyer. We need not muddy the field, but since this is a real case history, I can say unequivocally that the bank would not provide more than the $350,000 stated. The buyer had a net worth of well over $1.5 million, had more cash, but was adamant in not giving up more than $250,000 toward purchase. The seller wanted his million dollar price and was adamant in not providing partial financing—but still wanted to sell to this buyer. We had a dilemma . . . or so it would seem. *Key in this specific transaction was that both buyer and seller were bent on doing this deal.* How then might we resolve the discrepancy?

1. We know that we are $400,000 short of financing.

2. We know that we have an effective income stream of $149,257 ($162,335 minus noncash equity buildup $13,078)—a powerful stream in light of cash outlay at purchase.

3. We know that the seller is anxious to receive cash as quickly as possible.

4. Thus, one possible solution might be answered by the question: What effect would a five-year payout of $400,000 bring to bear on the buyer?

In attempting to solve for this question, we return to the point in the equation for Financing Rationale.

Financing Rationale	
Total Investment	$1,000,000
Less: Down Payment (25%)	− 250,000
Balance to Be Financed	$ 750,000
Bank (10% × 15 years)	
Amount	$350,000
Annual Principal/Interest Payment	45,133

Seller (10% × 5 years)

Amount	$400,000
Annual Principal/Interest Payment	101,986
Total Annual Principal/Interest Payment	$ 147,119

Testing Estimated Business Value

Return: Net Cash Stream to Be Valued	$ 143,412
Less: Annual Debt Service (P&I)	− 147,119
Pretax Cash Flow	$ − 3,707
Add: Principal Reduction	93,078*
Pretax Equity Income	$ 89,371
Less: Est. Dep. & Amortization (Let's Assume)	− 41,027
Less: Estimated Income Taxes (Let's Assume)	− 2,000*
Net Operating Income (NOI)	$ 46,344

*Debt service includes an average $93,078 annual principal payment that is traditionally recorded on the balance sheet as a reduction in debt owed. This feature recognizes that the "owned equity" in the business increases by this average amount each year. Tax obligations are reduced since interest expense is deductible from business cash flow.

Return on Equity:

$$\frac{\text{Pretax Equity Income}}{\text{Down Payment}} = \frac{\$ 89,371}{\$250,000} = 35.7\%$$

Return on Total Investment:

$$\frac{\text{Net Operating Income}}{\text{Total Investment}} = \frac{\$ 46,344}{\$1,000,000} = 4.6\%$$

Note that returns decrease somewhat but are still quite reasonable under our new scenario. This is because the average annual principal being returned to the balance sheet in the way of debt reduction has grown by $76,293 from $13,078 to $89,371. However, let's look at how the buyer might view this posture.

Buyer's Potential Cash Benefit

Forecast Annual Salary	$ 50,000
Pretax Cash Flow (contingency not considered)	− 3,707
Income Sheltered by Depreciation	41,027
Less: Provision for Taxes	− 2,000
Discretionary Cash	$ 85,320
Add: Equity Buildup	93,078
Discretionary and Nondiscretionary Cash	$178,398

Although the business's cash flow would be highly leveraged during the first five years, at the end of this period the buyer could have amassed ownership equity of $650,000 (down payment of $250,000 plus

$400,000 paid through the business itself). Depreciation-sheltered income seems more than adequate to live comfortably, the historical cash stream steadily growing, and the factor of risk greatly reduced after the fifth year. Not your traditional leveraged buyout but representative of the type of "leverage" sought by quite a few moneyed buyers.

Give and take between buyers and sellers is almost always necessary to do deals; therefore, give-and-take scenarios are also necessary even when estimating value for just one of the parties. In this case, we've taken something additional from the buyer in the way of strapping cash flows. Now it's time to seek something additional from the seller. Obviously, he or she has an option for rejecting this buyer, but if he or she wants to do this particular deal, something now has to give on their end—and we can assume that the only thing left is seller financing.

Seller's Potential Cash Benefit	
Cash Down Payment	$ 250,000
Bank Financing Receipts	350,000
Gross Cash at Closing	$ 600,000*

*From which must be deducted capital gains and other taxes. Structured appropriately, the deal qualifies as an "installment" sale with the proceeds in seller financing put off regarding taxes until later periods.

Projected Annual Principal/Interest Payments	$ 101,986
Projected Cash to Seller By End of Fifth Year	
Gross Cash At Closing	$ 600,000
Add: Principal Payment	400,000
Add: Interest Payment	109,929
Pretax Five-Year Proceeds	$1,109,929

This is not the all-cash deal expected by the seller but, based on the buyer's willingness, is all that the seller can get in this deal. Restrictive financing conditions decrease values. When push comes to shove, the buyer in our case might finally come up with a few more dollars or pledge personal assets to some degree, but probably not for the whole $400,000 shortfall. This being a real case from my files, I can tell you the answer. The seller ultimately relented on all cash at closing, financed $400,000, and stuck by his $1,000,000 price. Buyer and seller closed on their deal.

Forget the Scientist, This Is What Counts Method

Offering Price	$1,000,000
Less: Down Payment	− 250,000
Less: Financing	− 750,000
"Uncovered" Debt	− 0 −

Cash Flow (commonly used last completed year,
   assuming that conditions of the business
   warrant such) $ 204,639
Less: Principal/Interest   147,119
Cash Flow Free of Debt $ 57,520

It is **not** common for buyers to forthrightly consider the amortization of debt (building up of equity through mortgage payments) in their process, no more than it is routine for homeowners to consider this factor when buying the home. They hear about it, perhaps know about it, but it's not part of their purchasing rationale. In part, this is because equity builds up so slowly in the beginning of long-term loans. However, it's mostly to do with the fact that they "want" the business or home and also just want to know they can pay for it. Loans bearing heavy mortgage payments can be tolerated short term when the business can stand the freight and when equity buildups amount to significant dollars during the period.

In our real case, the buyer elected to proceed with his purchase because with the added seller financing, the business would *largely pay for itself* out of cash flow. And at the end of the fifth year would be a substantial relief from debt payments and the accumulation of an outstanding equity position. Bear in mind that this might not always be the fair market indicator for estimating value.

Business Is Fairly Priced If:

1. Asking price is not greater than 150% of net worth (except where reconstructed profits are 40% of asking price).
   a. Net worth $568,943 times 150% equals $853,415.
   b. Reconstructed profits $204,639 divided by asking price $1,000,000 equals 20.5%.
2. At least 10% sales growth per year is being realized.
   a. Growth is under 10% per year but steady. 1998 to 1999 was 3%; 1999 to 2000 was 11.6%; and 2000 to 2001 was 8.3%.
3. Down payment is approximately the amount of one year's reconstructed profits.
   a. $250,000 minus $204,639 or $45,361 (22.2%) more.
4. Terms of payment of balance of purchase price (including interest) should not exceed 40% of annual reconstructed profit.
   a. Debt service $147,119 divided by $204,639 equals 71.9%.

What does all this mean for estimated value? It means that in the eyes of buyers who have read from a multitude of publications whence this information was gleaned, this price could be viewed as just too much to pay. Thus it could be quite possible that the *most-likely* value to attract buyers in a wider net might be closer to $850,000. Subsequently, we might estimate value to a sole participant within the following range: (a) high of market value—$1,000,000; and (b) most-likely selling price— $850,000. The fact that this business actually sold for $1,000,000 had primarily to do with the flexibility of players, terms from the seller, and a risk-oriented buyer. Possibly, a somewhat rare find. Manufacturing businesses, however, sit on the high end of the desirability scale for all buyers in general.

RULE-OF-THUMB ESTIMATES

Well-established small manufacturing companies with strong evidence of good operating performances have been known to change hands in the range of 4 to as high as 6 times reconstructed earnings. Thus for this case, estimated value ranges from a low of $818,556 to a high of $1,227,834 could be expected in any given market. A million dollar price tag in our example translates into 4.9 times earnings. While I don't generally agree, I have seen rule-of-thumb estimates quoting 1.5 to 2.5 times net, including equipment, *plus* inventory.

Results

Book Value Method	$ 417,715
Adjusted Book Value Method	568,943
Hybrid (capitalization) Method	980,000
Excess Earnings Method	1,000,000
Forget the Scientist Method (a guess by author)	850,000

I traditionally calculate the book and adjusted book value scenarios, although I know that good operations will not change hands at these prices. Data from these, however, are an important consideration to the hybrid and excess earnings formulas. And some businesses have not produced cash flows strong enough to support values beyond these hard-asset values. Thus overall business values may not be greater than the values they hold in these hard assets.

We knew from initial review of the balance and income statements that this plastics manufacturer had an added overall intangible value that was greater than the value in its assets. What we didn't know at the time was how much more could be justified.

Our real business example changed hands for the selling price of $1,000,000. Thirty days of hard negotiations by the buyer convinced him that the seller would not budge from the price. During this same period, the seller became convinced that the buyer would not contribute more in cash. Both wanted to transact with each other. While never sharing my opinion with buyer or seller, I was convinced that this business was worth every penny of the one million dollar price. My thoughts became irrelevant because the buyer bought . . . the seller sold . . . and that's the value or price that counted.

Discounted Cash Flow of Future Earnings (Just for the Fun of It)

Rather than apply percentages to earnings forecasts, the following logic exhibits greater degrees of believability in the forecasting process. Of course, one would want to fully consider the plethora of potential events affecting longer-term forecasts. Along with greater sales might also come the purchase of new machinery that might severely dilute earnings during the years of purchase. Research and development of new products is costly and may restrict earnings as these new products are brought into the market. Needless to say, one cannot just arbitrarily predict greater earnings each future year. However, for the sake of this exercise, let's assume the following:

Year	Earnings	Earnings Difference
1998	$154,203	
1999	178,133	$23,930
2000	204,639	26,506
2001	227,432	22,793
Total		73,229
Divided by		3
Average growth		24,410

		Earnings Addition
2002	251,842	24,410
2003	276,252	24,410
2004	300,662	24,410
2005	325,072	24,410
2006	349,482	24,410

Assuming that we had considered all the variables, one certainly could not accuse us of being too optimistic by forecasting in this straightforward manner. To simplify, let's drop the formula portion and go straight to the answers. I don't recommend using this method but thought including the results might be helpful once again to show its wide variation.

Forecast Year	Discounted .20	Discounted .25	Discounted .30
2001	$ 189,527	$ 181,946	$ 174,948
2002	174,890	161,179	149,019
2003	159,868	141,443	125,741
2004	144,995	123,172	105,270
Plus	783,834	532,687	379,389
Estimated Value	$1,453,114	$1,140,427	$ 934,367

Although notably conservative in my forecasting, we can see that it still takes considerable discount of these future earnings to arrive at the transaction price for this business . . . in fact, between 25% and 30%. Quite regularly I find processors using the 20% discount rate in their calculations to estimate business values. Sellers are just not inclined to let buyers gain the higher returns through their sales. Thus, discounted methods, when used alone, tend frequently to overvalue the small, closely held enterprise. Even some of our nation's expert valuation specialists are hesitant to apply this formula, and many simply won't use it at all.

As Sigmund Freud so often said of his cigar, "A teddy bear is sometimes just a teddy bear!"

13

Valuation of a Restaurant

The aroma of good food is hard to beat. My uncle built a chain of 90 smorgasbord restaurants. Ray Kroc built McDonald's. Although both had formal educations only up to the eighth grade, their dedication gained them experience far beyond the reach of classrooms. Speaking with them, or doing business with them, you would not suspect either had not passed through the ivy league halls of Harvard.

The restaurant business in many respects is among the more complex of businesses to run. I can't tell you of the times I've shuddered in my thoughts when I heard someone say they wanted to go into this business because they had developed a whopping great menu. A good friend of mine owns and operates 17 fine-cuisine establishments. The smallest seats 240 persons. Average entree fare is $16.95. He never learned to cook . . . but he clearly understands how to bring industrial engineering to mass feeding. His thoughts: "I have hired some of the best chefs, but I have found only one that can function outside the kitchen. My head of operations happens to be an industrial engineer." My friend and his wife moved recently into their newly completed $2.5 million home.

What does this have to do with restaurant valuation? A lot! The failure rate in this industry is inordinately high. Of all the businesses that lending institutions review, restaurants fit into a portfolio of their own. And you can't get in there without a great deal of finesse. Why do restaurants fail so often, and why do banks resist granting loans? The answer to these questions can be found in the required skill of operators.

Think about the last time you went to a restaurant with a party of four. Did all of you order the same entree? Now back to your own kitchen at home . . . what is the preparation time for each of the entrees ordered? Now think about 10 other tables of four being served at about the same time. Would you think there's a scheduling problem here? Let's add another complexity—synchronizing delivery of all these different meals to the 11 tables of four, artfully warm!

What about the skill of the servers? Just because one may be able to handle only three tables efficiently while another functions well with four or five does not make a poor waitress or waiter. But improper station assignment does make for poor management. Think how tiring it is to the calves of your legs when you take an extra long walk. Some of this is caused by the shoes worn, and some by the surface being walked on. Extra soft surfaces severely exacerbate tiring of the legs. Soft carpet in a restaurant is great for the customer but poor for the employee. Fatigue can plague performance and profits.

What about the menu itself? Do you offer all things to all people, or do you pare it down for profit based on facility, kitchen, and server capability? Is the menu constructed such that entree preparation times can be synchronized with timely warm delivery to the table? Is the menu reasonably "memorizable" by servers? Will the offered menu save on waste in the kitchen, and, subsequently, what role will portion control play in menu planning?

I have a very specific reason for briefly digressing into restaurant operations. Borrowing against this type of small business is among the most difficult to achieve. Value processors must stay acutely aware that banks do not routinely like to participate in the financing of restaurants. Neither do many sellers, because they know, or should know, just how difficult it is making a buck in this industry. Inadequate financing depresses value. Thus, you as the processor must be pointedly concerned about where financing will come from before you insert "conditions" into your rationale. Do not assume; find out what the party or parties are willing to provide! Call local banks until you find one that might play along. Find out what their criteria are for approval.

THE VALUATION EXERCISE

The purpose: Periodic review for internal use between owners.

Balance Sheet (Reconstructed to Fair Market Value)

Assets	
Cash	$200,927
Inventory	4,000
Total Current Assets	$204,927

Property & Equipment

Land	$364,210
Buildings	193,200
Equipment	127,610
Vehicles	14,154
Total Property/Equipment	$699,174

Investments	$ 15,500
TOTAL ASSETS	$919,601

Liabilities

Sales Tax Payable	$ 13,865
Payroll Taxes Payable	1,590
Current Portion Long-Term Debt	18,283
Notes Payable	−2,423
Other Accrued Expenses	12,773
Total Current Liabilities	$ 44,088

Noncurrent Liabilities

Long-Term Debt Net of Current	$158,101
Note Payable—Officer	49,931
Total Noncurrent Liabilities	$208,032

Equity

Retained Earnings	$ 86,640
Net Income	116,752
Stockholder "A"	232,045
Stockholder "B"	232,044
Total Equity	$667,481

TOTAL LIABILITIES & EQUITY	$919,601

Income Statements (Reconstructed for Valuation)

Recast Income Statements for Valuation

	1998	1999	2000	9-Months Y-T-D 2001	12-Month Forecast 2001
Sales	$540,555	$776,412	$1,063,993	$1,104,305	$1,500,000
Cost of Sales	184,164	263,633	386,720	395,039	537,000
Gross Profit	$356,391	$512,779	$ 677,273	$ 709,266	$ 963,000
% Gross Profit	65.9%	66.0%	63.7%	64.2%	64.2%
Expenses					
Wages & Taxes	$ 93,624	$132,392	$ 216,104	$ 243,041	$ 315,000
Advertising	7,599	11,993	17,694	24,193	30,000
Auto Expense	7,966	7,864	606	3,290	4,392

Bank Ser. Charges	1,475	2,514	904	3,958	5,250
Contributions	590	300	710	1,521	2,000
Dues & Subs.	255	1,239	625	1,510	2,000
Emp. Benefits	475	—	2,559	2,818	4,800
Equipment Rental	—	—	—	11,529	17,172
Utilities	17,164	25,261	32,442	33,215	45,000
Insurance	27,735	35,106	35,881	47,747	52,592
Linen & Cleaning	547	671	968	816	1,050
Taxes/Licenses	25,166	50,412	52,393	16,426	73,500
Prof. Fees	3,075	3,841	4,800	200	6,000
Miscellaneous	—	—	—	632	500
Office Expense	2,529	4,267	7,503	5,225	7,500
Contract Services	6,671	8,055	13,827	14,302	19,500
Rent	4,550	4,575	4,650	375	5,000
Repair/Maint.	15,216	13,520	32,164	32,639	45,000
Supplies	18,062	33,585	41,931	26,352	37,500
Telephone	3,271	4,838	6,350	5,132	7,500
Trash Removal	2,364	3,415	3,992	3,284	4,500
Travel/Ent.	2,006	1,595	452	4,091	5,000
Total Expenses	$240,340	$345,443	$ 476,555	$ 482,296	$ 690,756
Recast Income	$116,051	$167,336	$ 200,718	$ 226,970	$ 272,244
Recast Income as a Percent of Sales	21.5%	21.6%	18.9%	20.6%	18.1%

When income statements are set side by side, and debt service, depreciation, and owner salaries removed, the picture becomes quite clear as to how the infrastructure of operations really works. Debt leverage, depreciation "funny money," and owner's salaries have little or nothing to do with operations per se, and, as we know by now, owners camouflage their profits from being taxed on the bottom line. Thus reconstruction of statements lets us see performance as it really is.

This restaurant business, owned by two brothers, is a fine example of a well-run operation. One brother is the chef, and the other is the business manager. Note how clustered, year to year, are the *percent* gross profits and recast incomes. Sales increased 43.6% between 1998 and 1999, 37% between 1999 and 2000, and, in nine months year-to-date in 2001, they have already exceeded all of 2000's performance. In this light, the $1.5 million 2001 forecast is hard to doubt.

Year		Sales	Increase
1998		$ 540,555	
1999		776,412	43.6%
2000		1,063,993	37.0%
2001	(forecast)	1,500,000	41.0%

Nine-month year-to-date recast income stands at 21% yield through actual performance, yet the 12-month forecast reduces this income to 18%. I don't know about you, but eyeballing these statements convinces me that the forecast for the 2001 completed year is quite believable. The forecast gross profit percentage and individual expenses track in line with the past year's performance. The balance sheet reveals exceptional liquidity and strong equity positions for the owners, and thus we must summarily conclude that there is growth and good management present in our valuation-targeted business. Knowing this business since its inception, I can assure you that it started out leveraged to the hilt and from a foreclosed property base. These statements represent over 11 years of hard, intelligent work. We might also guess that it could stand among the top 25% of the best-run companies in the industry. But we don't know that without comparisons.

	2001 Subject	Smaller Industry Sample A	Industry Sample B[1]
Sales	100.0%	100.0%	100.0%
Cost of Sales	35.8	37.0	41.2
Gross Profit	64.2	63.0	58.8
Labor Expense	21.3	29.8	—

Ratios		Upper Quartile	
Current	4.6	3.0	1.4
Current Assets/Total Assets	.223	.547	—
Debt/Worth (Safety)	.335	.911	.10
Fixed/Worth	1.0	—	1.2
Debt/Assets	.243	.790	.325
Sales/Total Assets	1.6	4.4	3.4
Sales/Net Worth	2.2	13.8	3.8
Land/Buildings as % Total Assets	.606	.650	—
Equipment as % of Total Assets	13.9	30.9	—

[1] 389 restaurants of all types other than franchised operations in similar sales-size comparison.

> *Current Ratio:* Generally, the higher the current ratio, the greater the company's ability to pay current obligations.

> *Current Assets over Total Assets:* Indicates the percentage of the company's total assets that are current—the lower the percentage the greater the liquidity.

Debt to Worth: Referred to as the safety ratio, this ratio determines the extent to which the owner's personal investment has been made in relationship to outside debt. The higher the ratio, the greater the risk that is being assumed by present and future lenders.

Fixed to Worth: Measures amount of owner's equity invested in facilities and equipment. A lower ratio suggests a better margin of safety to creditors in the event of liquidation.

Total Debt to Total Assets: Expressed as a percentage, this measures the leverage by long-term debt of all assets.

Sales to Total Assets: Provides an indication of how well assets are employed to produce sales—the higher the ratio, the better employed.

Sales to Net Worth: A higher ratio indicates that owner's funds are being turned more effectively to generate sales.

With these brief data, we can draw a general overall conclusion that this restaurant compares favorably to the 287 firms in the smaller sample A, and 389 mixed category firms in the upper quartile sample B. They may be somewhat heavy on assets in relation to sales, but growth could be precipitating this feature of operations. In fact, facilities and equipment were expanded by over $150,000 during the past two years alone to accommodate the five-year forecast for growth in sales. This operation fits nicely into the upper quartile of the top 25% of the sample average. Though I can do no more than guess at where they might fit into the national picture, their performance falls within the top 10% of restaurants in their local geographical region. With this in mind, we can now proceed with the valuation.

Book Value Method

Total Assets at September 30	$455,512[1]
Total Liabilities	252,120[1]
Book Value at June 30, 2001	$203,392[1]

[1]This will not reconcile with the previously shown balance sheet since that statement has been reconstructed to show a fair market value of assets. However, the owner's book value (in accounting terms) is as depicted by these numbers.

Adjusted Book Value Method

Assets	Balance Sheet Cost	Fair Market Value
Cash	$200,927	$200,927
Inventory	4,000	4,000
Property & Equipment	235,085	699,174[1]
Investments	15,500	15,500
Total Assets	$455,512	$919,601
Total Liabilities	$252,120	$252,120
	$203,392	
Adjusted Book Value at 6/30/01 (relative to stockholder equity)		$667,481

[1]Stated at appraised and thus, Fair Market Value.

Hybrid Method

(This is a form of the capitalization method.)

1 = High amount of dollars in assets and low-risk business venture

2 = Medium amount of dollars in assets and medium-risk business venture

3 = Low amount of dollars in assets and high-risk business venture

	1	2	3
Yield on Risk-Free Investments Such as Government Bonds[1] (often 6%–9%)	8.0%	8.0%	8.0%
Risk Premium on Nonmanagerial Investments[1] (corporate bonds, utility stocks)	4.5%	4.5%	4.5%
Risk Premium on Personal Management[1]	7.5%	14.5%	22.5%
Capitalization Rate	*20.0%*	*27.0%*	*35.0%*
Earnings Multipliers	**5**	**3.7**	**2.9**

[1]These rates are stated purely as examples. Actual rates to be used vary with prevailing economic times and can be composed through the assistance of expert investment advisers if need be.

Addendum to overall table: You'll note that this table changes from that used in the professional-practice valuation in the previous chapter. This is because capitalization rates and earnings multipliers change from business to business. This table, showing several rates in a range, is provided simply to give readers a scope of the judgmental conditions the value processor undergoes.

This particular version of a hybrid method tends to place 40% of business value in book values. However, before we finalize the assignment, we need to reconcile the "gray" area in the 1-2-3 asset/risk elements above. Assets are high and risk seems low to medium due to the stability of cash flow in three previous years, and the availability of a large amount of cash. Experience in working with this instrument teaches one *not* to be too bold in assigning multipliers. For the convenience of readers, I have a saying in my firm that goes: "Only God gets a multiplier of much in excess of 5—and, I've never been asked by him or her." The key to reducing labor hours in the assignment is to be conservative in determining multipliers.

Weighted Cash Streams

Prior to completing this and the excess earnings method, we must reconcile how we are going to treat earnings to ensure that we have a "single" stream of cash to use for reconstructed net income. I prefer the weighted average technique as follows:

	(a)	Assigned Weight	Weighted Product
1998	$116,051	(1)	$ 116,051
1999	167,336	(2)	334,672
2000	200,718	(3)	602,154
2001	272,244	(4)	1,088,976
Totals		(10)	$2,141,853
		Divided by:	10
Weighted Average Reconstructed			$ 214,185

Eyeballing column (a), we can conclude that the weighted average reconstructed income seems reasonably fair on the surface; the weighted is slightly higher than the completed 2000 but, based on the track record, may be somewhat inappropriate because the restaurant completed $226,970 during the first nine months of 2001. Furthermore, there is *no* compelling evidence that this operation could not complete the 2001 forecast of $272,224. *At this stage we need to be conservative because the formula will get us up to par in the end.* However, I have a leg up on you through experience; thus, I'm going to arbitrarily start with $250,000, in spite of what I've calculated as the weighted average cash flow.

Book Value at 6/30/01	$203,392	
Add: Appreciation in Assets	464,089	
Book Value as Adjusted	$667,481	
Weight Assigned to Adjusted Book Value	40%	$ 266,992
Reconstructed Net Income	$250,000	
Times Multiplier	×3.0	$ 750,000
Total Business Value		$1,016,992

Excess Earnings Method

(This method considers cash flow and value in hard assets, estimates intangible values, and superimposes tax considerations and financing structures to prove the most-likely equation.)

Reconstructed Cash Flow	$ 250,000
Less: Comparable Salary (Industry Composite)	− 80,000
Less: Contingency Reserve	− 15,000
Net Cash Stream to Be Valued	*$ 155,000*
Cost of Money	
Market Value of Tangible Assets	$ 699,174
Times: Applied Lending Rate	×10%
Annual Cost of Money	$ 69,917
Excess of Cost of Earnings	
Return Net Cash Stream to Be Valued	$ 155,000
Less: Annual Cost of Money	− 69,917
Excess of Cost of Earnings	$ 85,083
Intangible Business Value	
Excess of Cost of Earnings	$ 85,083
Times: Intangible Net Multiplier Assigned	×5.0
Intangible Business Value	$ 425,415
Add: Tangible Asset Value	699,174
TOTAL BUSINESS VALUE (Prior to Proof)	$1,124,589
	(Say $1,125,000)
Financing Rationale	
Total Investment	$1,125,000
Less: Down Payment (25%)	− 280,000
Balance to Be Financed	$ 845,000

At this point, we know that we have a serious problem with financing because total assets less liabilities equal $667,481, and we know that banks want "collateral" to make loans. We also know that banks don't like to finance restaurants. In addition, we know that $280,000 cash is a lot of money to expect from buyers in general; thus, as it is, this cash requirement already puts us into a category of finding perhaps no more than 3% to 5% of all buyers who will qualify to purchase this restaurant business. It's important to use a good deal of logic at this stage of valuation or you will waste a lot of time coming up with reliable estimates. One can set up the financing scenario any way appropriate to their local conditions, but my guess is that the following would be pretty close.

The business's ownership of real property is a key feature that makes this particular restaurant more inclined to locate financing. Combined with a Small Business Administration (SBA) loan, other assets may receive more attention, since banks can receive "guarantees" on substantial portions of their loans. Combine the strength of this operation with a buyer "experienced" at running a restaurant, and much of the stigma banks recount disappears. This business is no mom-and-pop venture, or at least it should not be; therefore, we might safely assume that a buyer *will* be experienced or not be *the* buyer. Also, the size of down payment cuts the chaff from the wheat and, more than likely, leaves us with a purposeful buyer intent on the restaurant business.

Equipment ($127,610) at 50% of Appraised Value	$ 63,805
Land/Buildings ($557,410) at 70% of Book Value	390,187
Leasehold Improvements	–0–*
	$453,992

(For good measure, say $460,000)

Leasehold improvements, traditionally painting, new flooring, etc., have a short life in restaurant operations. Subsequently, these are often "expensed" in years completed. Structural changes, new equipment, and furniture/fixtures are booked into their balance sheet categories, and thus, reflected there. Restaurant equipment holds a relatively low "hammer" value, due primarily to mass availability of used, functionally good replacements.

Bank (10% × 15 years)	
Amount	$460,000
Annual Principal/Interest Payment	– 59,318
Assume: Owner's Financing (8% x 20 years with a review toward "balloon" at the end of the fifth year [*not a balloon provision necessarily*])	
Amount	$385,000
Annual Principal/Interest Payment	– 38,643

Testing Estimated Business Value

Return: Net Cash Stream to Be Valued	$155,000
Less: Annual Debt Service (P&I)	– 97,961
Pretax Cash Flow	$ 57,039
Add: Principal Reduction	26,396*
Pretax Equity Income	$ 83,435
Less: Est. Dep. & Amortization (Let's Assume)	– 27,401
Less: Estimated Income Taxes (Let's Assume)	– 6,700
Net Operating Income (NOI)	$ 49,334

*Debt service includes an average $26,396 annual principal payment during the first few years that is traditionally recorded on the balance sheet as a reduction in debt owed. This feature recognizes that the "owned equity" in the business increases by this average amount each year during the early period of the loan.

Return on Equity:

$$\frac{\text{Pretax Equity Income}}{\text{Down Payment}} = \frac{\$\ 83,435}{\$280,000} = 29.8\%$$

Return on Total Investment:

$$\frac{\text{Net Operating Income}}{\text{Total Investment}} = \frac{\$\ 49,334}{\$1,125,000} = 4.4\%$$

Although return on total investment is abysmally low in relationship to conventionally expected investment returns, the return on equity is attractively better than most other optional uses of a buyer's cash. Cash flow is strong.

Basic Salary	$ 80,000
Net Operating Income	49,334
Gain of Principal	26,396
Tax-Sheltered Income (Dep.)	27,401
Effective Income	$183,131*

*There is also the matter of $15,000 annually into the contingency and replacement reserve that would be at the discretion of the owner if not required for emergencies or asset replacements.

At this time we have estimated business value . . . but have we estimated *the* estimated value? $280,000 cash down payment plus $460,000, or $740,000 leaves us with a $385,000 shortfall of the all-cash or cash-equivalent target that typifies the general definition of fair market value. If we leave the price at $1,125,000, either the buyer has to make up the difference outside this business, or the seller must become flexible toward providing $385,000 of seller financing, or find another buyer with more cash; or the estimated price must be "squeezed" to fit the conditions of available financing. We have a dilemma . . . or so it would seem. This business is not being valued for potential sale, and of course, it would be easy to "assume" that the owners would provide this financing. However, that would be an ill-founded assumption if taken alone. Thus we must explore the options and provide alternatives for choice. How then might we resolve the discrepancy?

1. We know that we are $385,000 short on conventional financing.
2. We know that we have an effective income stream of $156,735 ($183,131 minus non-cash equity buildup $26,396). A powerful stream in light of cash outlay at purchase.
3. We know that sellers in general are anxious to receive cash as quickly as possible.
4. We know that fair market value might be depressed to the amounts of down payment ($280,000) plus bank financing ($460,000) or the sum of $740,000. Of course, discounted thus, between the bank and a prospective buyer this estimated value might rise to $850,000 all said and done. This could be termed the fair market value of an all-cash deal.
5. Another possible alternative might be answered by the question: What effect would a five-year payout of $385,000 bring to bear on the buyer?

In attempting to solve for this alternative, we return to the point in the equation for Financing Rationale.

Financing Rationale	
Total Investment	$1,125,000
Less: Down Payment (25%)	− 280,000
Balance to Be Financed	$ 845,000
Bank (10% × 15 years)	
Amount	$350,000
Annual Principal/Interest Payment	45,133
Seller (8% × 5 years)	
Amount	$385,000
Annual Principal/Interest Payment	93,677
Total Annual Principal/Interest Payment	$ 138,810
Testing Estimated Business Value	
Return: Net Cash Stream to Be Valued	$ 155,000
Less: Annual Debt Service (P&I)	− 138,810
Pretax Cash Flow	$ 16,190
Add: Principal Reduction	94,188*

Pretax Equity Income	$ 110,378
Less: Est. Dep. & Amortization (Let's Assume)	− 27,401
Less: Estimated Income Taxes	–0–
Net Operating Income (NOI)	$ 82,977

*Debt service includes an average $94,188 annual principal payment that is traditionally recorded on the balance sheet as a reduction in debt owed. This feature recognizes that the "owned equity" in the business increases by this average amount each year. Tax obligations are reduced since interest expense is deductible from business cash flow.

Return on Equity:

$$\frac{\text{Pretax Equity Income}}{\text{Down Payment}} = \frac{\$110,378}{\$280,000} = 39.4\%$$

Return on Total Investment:

$$\frac{\text{Net Operating Income}}{\text{Total Investment}} = \frac{\$ 82,977}{\$1,125,000} = 7.4\%$$

Note that return on equity increased from 29.8% to 39.4%, and that return on total investment went from 4.4% to 7.4% under our new scenario. As we know, mortgage payments are normally comprised of both principal repayment and interest on debt. That portion of the payment designated as interest is lost to the gain of the financing party . . . and provides an "expense" to the income statement of the debtor. However, the principal portion is reconciled on a debtor's balance sheet as a reduction in debt owed and translates into an increase in owner's equity. It's similar to the mortgage with home ownership and paying off the loan. Granted, the debtor has no real control, nor can he or she make immediate use of this "principal" until the debt is paid or the business sold, but make no mistake, it nevertheless is income. In our case, annual debt service grew from the first instance of $97,961 to $138,810 in the last example. Along with these higher payments, the principal being returned to the balance sheet rose from $26,396 to $94,188. I'll admit that this feature is sometimes hard for the unwary to grasp. And I'll also admit that some accountants find it hard to admit this concept of "additional" income into valuation practice as I do. However, I maintain that it is a vital element for consideration in how a business "pays for itself" out of cash flow, although it may not always be how a prospective buyer might view the equation. So let's look at how a prospective buyer might view what we've presented.

Buyer's Potential Cash Benefit	
Forecast Annual Salary	$ 80,000

Pretax Cash Flow (Contingency not considered)	16,190
Income Sheltered by Depreciation	27,401
. . . Thus No Taxes	–0–
Discretionary Cash	$123,591
Add: Equity Buildup	94,188
Discretionary and Nondiscretionary Cash	$217,779

Under this scenario, the business's cash flow would not seem too highly leveraged during the first five years, and at the end of this period the buyer could have amassed ownership equity of $665,000 (down payment of $280,000, plus $385,000 paid through the business itself). In addition, $81,000 of equity would have built up during the five-year period in the bank loan. In the interim, discretionary income seems more than adequate to live comfortably. The historical cash stream has been growing steadily, and the factor of risk would be greatly reduced after the fifth year. Of course it's not the now-ancient 110% leveraged buyout, but it is representative of the type of "leverage" sought by quite a few moneyed buyers.

There's still a problem we've not addressed in this presentation. Don't be puzzled because I haven't told you about it yet; it is commonly ignored. This is the cost of expansion in business growth. This business has neared maximum capacity in its present facilities. Fortunately, however, the restaurant does have adequate land available for the building's expansion. How do we factor this in? We might not feel that it is necessary, because at the point of appraisal we have "momentary" value estimated and the cost of *future* value belongs to the party or parties then owning the business. In other words, if future cash flow belongs to future owners, so also does future expense. Accepting this concept, this is one area where inexperienced business appraisers get lost in the woods. Supply and demand economics generally dictate that the financing infrastructure accommodate reasonable growth. Our specific business may not present a problem in that regard. We allocated $15,000 to an annual contingency reserve at the outset of our assignment. Repair and maintenance expenses from past operating statements reveal hefty amounts plowed back into the facilities. $45,000 represents the estimated amount for 2001. Visual inspection of physical plant and equipment shows that much of this investment has been dedicated to accommodate the need caused by increasing business. In our case example, we have concluded that between contingency and repair and maintenance expenses there would be enough "squeeze" when set aside annually to fund reasonable growth. Cash flow beyond debt service might accommodate more financing so long as expansion were to provide additional collateral. As a side note, many businesses are not so fortunate.

Equipment and facilities needing short-term replacement must be factored into the valuation task.

For reasons outlined, I place small restaurants in the least-likely candidacy for application of discounted cash flow methods of valuation. My opinion, of course, but that's how I see it. I can't, however, ignore one other approach.

Forget the Scientist, This Is What Counts Method

Offering Price	$1,125,000
Less: Down Payment	− 280,000
Less: Bank Financing	− 460,000
"Uncovered" Debt	$ 385,000
? Owner Financing	− 385,000
Uncovered Debt	–0–
Cash Flow (commonly will use last completed year, 2000 in our case, assuming that conditions of the business warrant such)	$ 200,718
Less: Principal Interest (assumes both notes)	− 138,810
Cash Flow Free of Debt	$ 61,908

It is **not** common for buyers to forthrightly consider the amortization of debt (building up of equity through mortgage payments) in their processes, no more than it is routine for homeowners to consider this factor when buying the home. They hear about it, perhaps know about it, but it's not part of their purchasing rationale. In part, this is because equity builds up so slowly in the beginning of long-term loans. However, it's mostly to do with the fact that they "want" the business or home and also just want to know they can pay for it. Loans bearing heavy mortgage payments can be tolerated short term when the business can stand the freight and when equity buildups amount to significant dollars during the shorter period. The free cash flow of $61,908 presented in the forget the scientist method is a far cry from the estimated $96,190 in our valuation equation. Bear in mind that we used $250,000 rather than $200,718, as in the latter, and if you add the $49,282 to the $61,908, we come up with $111,190. In actual negotiations, value estimates will always be rendered a blow when opposing participants cannot agree on the stream of available cash under consideration.

Business Is Fairly Priced If:

1. Asking price is not greater than 150% of net worth (except where reconstructed profits are 40% of asking price)

    a. Net worth $667,481 times 150% equals $1,001,222.

    b. Reconstructed profits $200,718 divided by asking price $1,125,000 equals 17.8%.

2. At least 10% sales growth per year is being realized.

    a. Growth averaged 40.3% in the years 1998 through 2000. Forecast 2001 could be as high as 40%—9-month year-to-date has already topped 12-month 2000.

3. Down payment is approximately the amount of one year's reconstructed profits.

    a. $280,000 minus $200,718 or $79,282 (39.5%) more. Thus pressure to keep the down payment at $200,000 might be felt.

4. Terms of payment of balance of purchase price (including interest) should not exceed 40% of annual reconstructed profit.

    a. Debt service $138,810 divided by $200,718 equals 69.2%. This might form the basis for a buyer to attempt reducing the selling price.

What does all this mean for estimated value? It means that the price in the deal through the eyes of buyers, if they have read from a multitude of publications whence this information was gleaned, could be viewed as a bit too much to pay. Thus it could be quite possible that the *most-likely* value to attract buyers in a wider net might be closer to $950,000. Subsequently, we might estimate value to an owner within the following range: (a) high of market value—$1,125,000; and (b) most-likely selling price—$950,000. In a sale-oriented scenario, lack of substantial owner financing would likely depress the ultimate price to $800,000 to $850,000. This restaurant business has demonstrated very good growth and exhibits that it is under excellent management.

RULE-OF-THUMB ESTIMATES

Well-established small restaurants have rather traditionally considered their rough values to be slightly under one times gross sales. Restaurants with strong evidence in operating performances have been known to change hands in the range of net multipliers from 4 to as high as 8 times reconstructed earnings. Thus, for this restaurant, estimated rule-of-thumb values range from a low of $802,872 to a high of $1,605,744 as that which could be expected in any given market. $1,125,000 translates into

5.6 times earnings. Many restaurants, however, change hands at .25 to .5 times gross income, or 12 to 15 times earnings.

Results

Book Value Method	$ 203,392
Adjusted Book Value Method	667,401
Hybrid (capitalization) Method	1,016,992
Excess Earnings Method	
(a) Owner Financed $385,000 + / −	1,125,000
(b) No Owner Financing Provided	$800,000–$850,000
Forget the Scientist Method	950,000

It is my opinion that the value of our case example on the date of appraisal was as follows:

a. With adequate noninstitutional financing provisions:
ONE MILLION ONE HUNDRED TWENTY-FIVE THOUSAND and No/100 ($1,125,000.00)

b. Without adequate noninstitutional financing provisions:
EIGHT HUNDRED FIFTY THOUSAND and No/100 ($850,000.00).

    c. Most likely 6–12-month marketed selling price if offered out under a. above:
NINE HUNDRED FIFTY THOUSAND and No/100 ($950,000.00)

Internal Use

For the purposes of internal use, such as refinancing, ownership allocation, key-person insurance, and so on, I would recommend that the value $950,000 be considered.

14

Seventy Cents on the Dollar

Business valuation can be combined with marketing strategy to sell businesses out of bankruptcy proceedings. Although distressed purchase and sale should always be undertaken with great caution, appropriately skilled buyers can periodically locate fine turnaround candidates through court-appointed trustees. Quite often, because of sizable debt loads, these companies will need the protection of Chapter 11 to be sold in some semblance of a "going-concern" nature.

For the benefit of those unfamiliar with bankruptcy under Chapter 11, this provision essentially preserves the going-concern concept by temporarily sheltering a struggling business from unsecured creditors. Bear in mind, however, bankruptcy does not provide relief for the enterprise from its secured creditors (more often, commercial banks with secured loans outstanding). Simply stated, Chapter 11 requires the afflicted company to file a "work-out" plan with the court describing how it expects to recover and repay creditors. The judge and his or her staff decide on the merits of the case whether to accept or reject this plan. If the plan is rejected, the applicant will quite likely be forced into Chapter 7 (liquidation). The whole process can be quite complex and can entail substantial negotiation with both secured (hold security interests outside of bankruptcy protection) and unsecured creditors as well as court officers. Buyers or sellers considering this process are strongly advised to coordinate marketing or purchasing activity with experts who are both experienced in the "politics" and the laws of bankruptcy.

The case I'm about to describe might be a classic example of a small business that filed for "11" but due to very skinny assets and out-of-control spending was being forced into Chapter 7 (liquidation). The owner wanted to fight to preserve what had once been a thriving small and unique mail-order business. The task was to convince the court and creditors that the business had a reasonable chance of being sold as a going concern, thus the motivation to secure approval for Chapter 11. The owner accepted that there was little hope for personal salvation in the deal but was determined to preserve the "idea" and wanted to help recover what she could for well-meaning suppliers who had stood by her as long as each of them could. Appraised values of assets revealed that creditors might not get more than 10 cents on the dollar at auction. If they could raise the ante to creditors, we stood a chance of the judge reversing the opinion from Chapter 7 to Chapter 11 status.

As is often the case in distressed businesses, records were in shambles, as were the plethora of other elements commonly expected for completing "sane" valuation tasks. Subsequently, the following will not resemble the valuation processes outlined elsewhere in this text. And the not so obvious reason for inclusion is that this case may provide an additional defensive rationale to supplement the more conventional approaches to business value. The discussion also somewhat describes the conditions under which one might traditionally expect to find businesses once they have declared bankruptcy. We first entered the premises with the trustee under direct authority as court-appointed representatives of the court and trustee.

A BANKRUPTCY COURT PROPOSAL FOR DEBTOR PROTECTION UNDER CHAPTER 11

At the time of this report, the physical assets of the subject corporation are housed in an attached building at the personal residence and property of the owner. The attached building serves as a retail outlet as well as the catalog sales headquarters for the business. The operation had employees and was minimally functioning until the petition was filed. It is our understanding that employees were discharged, operations shut down, and the residential premises vacated on the day of filing. An inventory of physical assets was completed by us and witnessed by the court-appointed trustee. The status of inventory has been certified by the trustee and ourselves and a report has been submitted under separate cover to the court in accordance with the Bankruptcy Code.

The real property can be sold in the traditional foreclosed manner. In general, this property is in excellent shape for its age. It is located in a fair to average business area and should command sufficient capital to satisfy secured creditors. However, we recommend that the court appoint a local real estate agency to conduct marketing up to the point of auction. Two suggested agencies, along with the recommended listing price, are provided in our separate report.

In accordance with our directive from the trustee, the following represents an assessment of practical disposition of business property on behalf of the unsecured creditors.

Computer and Mailing List

During our inventory process, it was noted that the computer was still on and appeared fully operational. Data entry screens were viewing what appeared to be "dated" information. It is not known if a "hard copy" of the approximately 75,000 mailing-list names exists; therefore, caution should be exercised in dismantling the computer until at least such hard copy is produced and/or disk or tape records that contain such information are obtained and verified. Since the "list" can be sold to commercial mailing-list merchants, this is a valuable asset of the company and/or creditors. Upon directive of the trustee, we saved the screen, returned to the main menu, and shut down the computer. Since this machine is leased, we were advised not to produce duplicates or remove the tapes containing the mailing list and business records until directed by the court. According to the lease document, the owner is not personally cosigned, and the balance due on a five-year lease stands at $36,960. It is our opinion that this size of computer was an unnecessary extravagance at this stage of business development. We recommended pulling the list into hard copy, retaining the tapes in court files, and allowing the lessor to recover equipment.

During interviews with the business's founder, we were told that all names on the mailing list were productive during the course of a year. Approximately 30,000 were very productive to the catalog line. However, the founder feels that perhaps only 15,000, more or less, might be of significant value to even a catalog merchant with related lines. Trade practice is to cull mailing lists on the basis of repeat orders at least twice per year. Thus, mailing-list customers tend to become unique to each catalog company.

The founder made a regular practice of "renting" her customer names to commercial "list" merchants. In this business's last year of operation, slightly under $10,000 was received from these list rentals. Telephone conversations with two commercial houses support the following value conclusions.

Outright List Sale (75,000 names)

Top Repetitive Catalog Customers (15,000 @ $1.00)	$15,000
List Balance (60,000 @ $ .10)	6,000
Estimated List Value	$21,000

Sale to "Business" Purchaser (75,000 names)

30,000 @ $1.00	$30,000
45,000 @ $ .30	13,500
Estimated List Value	$43,500

We are informed by these two list-rental agencies that ongoing rentals will bring $.10 per name on a onetime use basis. Thirty cents is arbitrarily assigned to 45,000 names based on the following rationale:

1. Returns from this list will be greater to a user who is functionally operating this business.

2. The list will produce product sales for at least three uses without additional maintenance expense.

3. The repetitive buyer portion of the list is claimed to have been culled up until last month such that it is "doubly" productive; therefore, we assume that the remainder of the list has been at least reasonably maintained.

I recommend that this list be withheld from auction and vigorous attempts be made to sell it directly to a commercial list-rental agency where, without question, the yield will be higher. I recommend that the allocation to market value of this mailing list, when sold with the business as a going concern, be $43,500.

Furniture and Fixtures

Undepreciated book value of furniture and fixtures as of the last year-end balance sheet was $5,914. The figure for machinery and equipment was $2,681. No professional appraisal has been made or recommended, due to the cost in relationship to the probable or perceived value and visual inspection. One might reasonably assume that these asset values collectively would not be greater than $5,000 if sold individually. Under auction conditions, they will bring considerably less.

I recommend that the allocation to going-concern market value for these assets be $5,000.

Inventory

The value in these assets is clearly the more difficult to determine due to this business's struggle for some time. In attempting to do so, the following assumptions must be recognized:

1. The business has been in varying degrees of financial difficulty for two years—pronounced during the past six months.
2. The need to scurry for cash affords less time to study and research buying decisions. An increased incidence of poor product selection is usually evident under such pressure.
3. Since cash has been critically short during the last six months and the company has been unable to replenish stock, it is reasonably safe to assume that most of the higher turnover items have been depleted. Thus, what remains is likely to be slow-moving and/or distressed-sale merchandise. This is largely demonstrated in the dramatic drop in sales and increase in "unfilled" orders logged during the three-month period prior to shutdown. Catalog revenue dropped 36.6% and retail down by 59.5%. There is no local market evidence to support precipitous drop; and in fact, similar retail competitor sales have gained locally by about 18%. Book value of inventory decreased by $23,894 from the previous year as this business entered its selling season. One must necessarily assume that these assets have relatively small liquidity value at this time.

In attempting to *guess* with logic the value of these assets, I will use an old Missouri auctioneer's rule of thumb. You won't find this concept in your lexicon of terms, but in his day, his process of estimating "hammer" value was considered as accurate a forecast as money could buy.

Book Value at Current Value	$65,008
Less: Use Assumption Based on Visual/Ticket Sales	11,961
Assumed Remaining Inventory at Cost	$53,047
Marked Up to Customary Retail	$95,591
Therefore:	
30% @ 100% of retail	$28,677
30% @ 70% of retail	20,074
30% @ 10% of retail	2,868
10% @ no value	–0–
Assumed Retail Value	$51,619
Convert to Likely Current Book Value of Inventory	$28,645

This process assumes that remaining inventory would be marketed in traditional fashion in an ongoing operation. If the court wished to invest the time and money, and I don't recommend doing so, the mortality in inventory could be more accurately identified by use of the computer to target fast-moving, slow-moving, and virtually unsalable merchandise. It would be costly because of necessary correlations to physical count. Also, I'm not convinced we'd arrive ultimately at better information.

I, therefore, recommend that the fair market value allocation of inventory be $28,645. To ease the court's mind, we might consider this to be a base figure and, when under purchase agreement with a prospective buyer, take physical inventory and adjust to reflect actual count. Thus the buyer would shoulder most of the cost in the process. Under the hammer, I seriously doubt we might realize much over $5,000 to $10,000 from these assets.

Rationale for Marketing the Business as a Going Concern

The last accountant-prepared income statement (two years old) showed retail and catalog sales of $534,218 with an income to the owners of $43,387. Pro forma records from the accountant for the year prior to filing for bankruptcy revealed sales of $439,987 and owner's loss of $132,888. The loss was incurred primarily due to production of a color version of the company's catalog ($84,111 extra), and lease of the computer ($31,650). Bad debt and professional fees skyrocketed to make up most of the remainder. Both the accountant and I believe that the major factor precipitating this company's demise were the two outlandishly premature decisions on changing the catalog and leasing a computer at this stage of development. Through these proposed innovations, the owner also lost control of record keeping, and ultimately her business. It's my opinion that if we back out the computer and return to original catalog format (color failed miserably), we still appear to have a viable business for an appropriately skilled buyer.

Internal records reveal the following through the date of filing (10 months of fiscal year):

Gross Catalog Sales before Back Order	$235,603
Less: Back Order	− 18,645
Retail Sales	53,396
Less: Back Order	− 5,645
Sales Completed during 10 Months	$264,709

The Last Completed Year Revealed 55.48%

Cost of Goods Sold	146,861
Estimated Gross Profit (44.52%)	$117,848

According to the owner, she has been unable to fill 36.6% of catalog, and 54.4% of retail orders during this 10-month period. In addition, peak season retail stocking was limited to slow-moving inventory and/or what is considered "dead" merchandise. Most of the season was conducted at discount pricing; therefore, the preceding 44.52% gross profit is unlikely to be representative for this difficult period of sales. However, five years from inception and prior to the company's financial crisis, it did maintain gross profits near 45%. I can see no reason that an "unburdened" operator with fresh stock could not reproduce similar margins. The general economy and local selling season suggests that a business such as this should have moved up in sales like its counterparts did locally. Inordinate debt caused by poor business decisions brought this business to a standstill. If this business can be sold during the next six months, I am convinced it can be brought back to health. Based on the skinniness of assets, I am also convinced that creditor committee approval for marketing this business as a going concern will increase its yield well over the approximate $.10 on the $1 now represented.

In support of my argument I submit the following information to estimate how much greater yield:

Mailing List Names	75,000
5-year Average Sales per Catalog Mailed	$1.00
Projected Sales per Mailing	$ 75,000
Number of Mailings	×4
Gross Yearly Sales Forecast	$300,000
List Rental Revenue (annual)	15,000
Consolidated One-Location Retail Sales	27,000
Estimated Total Gross Sales	$342,000

Advertising in a major New York publication has been substantially productive to both sales and the addition of frequent-buyer names. Conversations with a number of mail-order company owners lead us to conclude that "street press" on this company is still intact. The trustee has held numerous conversations with back-order customers and concludes that most would prefer to receive products than to receive cash. The trustee also believes that customers would be thrilled to see this product line continue. However, it would be unrealistic to believe that interrupted operations will not negatively impact sales during the first year of any new operation. Applying probability theory, we can assume that operations might be impacted by 20% on the low side, 10% at the median, and we can assume zero impact at the high side. Since catalog operations are not dependent on location, the business can quite easily be moved without disruption. A large portion of retail sales has been conducted from a second location that was leased under attractive conditions. The lessor is willing to provide a one-year lease to a new owner under the same provisions. This frees the real property for disposition as the court so directs.

Estimated Reconstructed Profit and Loss for a New Operator at a New Location

Probability:	Low	Median	High
Gross Sales	$342,000	$342,000	$342,000
Less: Historical 1.8% Back Order	6,156	6,156	6,156
Less: Impact of Stopped Operation	68,400	34,200	–0–
Salvageable Sales	$267,444	$301,644	$335,844
Less: Cost of Goods Sold @ 55%	147,094	165,904	184,714
Estimated Gross Profit	$120,350	$135,740	$151,130
Probability:	Low	Median	High
Projected Operating Expenses (Based on Historical Experience)			
Contract Labor	$ 6,968	$ 6,968	$ 6,968
Supplies	2,350	2,350	2,350
Credit Card Discounts	3,450	3,450	3,450
Auto Expense	911	911	911
Insurance	1,100	1,100	1,100
Catalog Expense (4)	48,000	48,000	48,000
Professional Fees	1,000	1,000	1,000
Freight & Postage	13,289	13,289	13,289
Advertising	10,000	10,000	10,000
Telephone	1,096	1,096	1,096
Miscellaneous	1,772	1,772	1,772
Total Expense	$ 89,936	$ 89,936	$ 89,936
Available for Debt Service, Housing, and Owner Salary	$ 30,414	$ 45,804	$ 61,194

The available income for debt service, housing, and an owner salary is presented on a marginal line basis representing what we feel to be remaining in the aftershock. To the best of our knowledge the vast majority of previous customers are unaware of this company's difficulties. You will note that we began our premises on sales of $342,000, but also bear in mind that shortly less than one year ago, this company completed $534,218 of sales in spite of increasing financial difficulties. The year between then and now had generated sales of $439,987 when the "cupboards" must have been nearly bare.

Sales in this company have been driven by a uniquely hand-drawn black-and-white catalog. The attempt at a color version failed abysmally to pull anywhere near the returns generated by the last black-and-white sent just three months earlier. The color version modeled the company after its giant competitors and stole away its unique characteristics. The founder believes that an appropriately written letter in the body of the catalog previously used could actually be a great marketing tool while it covers the blunder of the color piece. The company had developed a solid repeat-buyer list of some 30,000 customers. Consistent repeats from this list averaged $1.00 of purchase per catalog mailed. Assuming these folks are still on the hook, and it appears that they are, $30,000 of revenue from this group alone per catalog might be expected. Four catalogs per year translates into $120,000 base sales. Prior to the demise of the company, retail sales had peaked at $156,050. The store had greater traffic this past season; however, they had no fresh product to sell, and sales tumbled to $53,396.

Out of 36 original suppliers, only one would not care to work out some form of continuing relationship with this company under a new owner. The dissenter is apparently under financial pressure and feels it cannot afford the risk. The 10 major suppliers to this firm expressed sincere hopes of reestablishing business relationships with the company. According to the trustee, they would be content to settle old accounts at $.50 on the dollar and consented to establish open lines to a qualified buyer of this distressed company. The remainder offered various terms that could be worked out short term, since none represents major annual buys. My feeling is that if we could obtain better than $.50 on the dollar for the unsecured, we could negotiate quite acceptable terms from these minor suppliers as well.

Stripped to meet these lower sales forecasts, the business could be operated for a year or more from a two-car garage of someone's home. The two peak mailings each year might overflow work into the living room temporarily. An ideal buyer would be a husband-and-wife team with mass-marketing experience who would concentrate on the catalog end of the business. The retail store is open six months of the year and could be staffed with contract labor. Although the retail store is open, the new owners must contend with two minor-season mailings that might still afford sufficient time to oversee the retail operation. Such an arrangement would be intense while it lasted; however, it appears that $150,000 more sales could be realized. Staying lean and mean, they might be ready to add one or two employees to help at various times of the year. With the power of present-day personal computers, both the mailing list and business records could be maintained for the purchase of around $5,000 in hardware and software.

Although business records are in poor shape, a thorough examination of the past two years' purchase orders is convincing evidence that this business has not yet died. Given 12 months of no mailings, and it's gone. If it can be sold during the next six months, I believe it can be resurrected to prosper and grow. Bear in mind that the mail-order structure did not expose the customer to the shambles of the shop. The retail operations thrive on transient customers who change from year to year. It is on this basis that we enter the plea for a six-month holding status under Chapter 11.

1. We recommend trustee, rather than debtor, be in possession.

2. We recommend that the real property follow the traditional foreclosure route; however, we also suggest that it be listed by a local real estate company in attempting to secure outright sale prior to auction.

3. We recommend that in the event a real property buyer is closed prior to business assets sale, the second floor of attached structure be reserved for business asset storage for up to three months beyond real property purchase.

4. Inasmuch as the business assets are not pledged to the bank that holds the mortgage on real property, we recommend that we negotiate "hands-off" storage at the site until five days prior to auction, or in accordance with item #3 above.

5. We recommend that the present computer be released to the lessor under the condition that we be permitted to produce both hard copy and tape facsimiles of all records contained therein. Software should be retained. We should also delete any copies stored once facsimiles are made.

6. With the assistance of the trustee, the bank to which the business assets have been pledged in a working line of credit has given verbal consent to provide up to three months of marketing time prior to proceeding with foreclosure. Add the normal three-month procedural time and we would have approximately six months to sell the

business assets. This bank has agreed to give serious consideration to financing a qualified buyer.

7. Included is both the business interim operating and marketing plans.

8. The following summarizes our expectation through business asset sale. The targeted objective would translate into $.70 on the dollar for unsecured creditors.

Allocation of Selling Price

Tangible Assets	Estimated Value	Use
Mailing List	$ 43,500	$ 43,500
Inventory (rounded)	29,000	53,000
Fixture/Equipment	5,000	5,000
Total Tangible	$ 77,500	$101,500
Intangible Assets		
Goodwill/Trade Name	$ 45,000	$ 5,000
Copyright	—	16,000
Noncompete	5,000	5,000
Aggregate Selling Price	$127,500	$127,500

We have structured the allocation to provide the most favorable tax status to a buyer. The previous owner has agreed to enter into a noncompete agreement as well as to provide whatever information about past operations that a buyer might wish. Wife and husband now separated, their financial condition is such that they will be unable to do more than provide information by mail or telephone. One has moved to California, the other to Wisconsin, where they are now employed.

Can a Buyer Pay This Price

Hypothetical Buyout	
Purchase Price	$127,500
Minimum Cash Down	75,000
Bank Loan	$ 52,500*

*Most likely to involve pledging other personal assets up to $30,000.

Therefore:

Annual Principal/Interest Payments	
(15 years/10%, ballooning at the end of 5 years)	$ 6,770
5th-Year Balloon	$ 43,255

Using projected cash flow, the following would appear to be the start-up scenario:

Low Probability Unencumbered Cash	$ 30,414
Less: Debt Service	6,770
Free Cash Flow	$ 23,644
Median Probability Unencumbered Cash	$ 45,804
Less: Debt Service	6,770
Free Cash Flow	$ 39,034
High Probability Unencumbered Cash	$ 61,194
Less: Debt Service	6,770
Free Cash Flow	$ 54,424

This all suggests that an appropriate buyer would want to have 6 to 12 months' living expenses tucked away in addition to the $75,000 required as down payment. The bank has indicated its willingness to provide up to a $25,000 working capital loan for such a buyer. This bank has had five years of rewarding experience from working with the previous owner, and it feels the business has good potential. The bank is aware of the conditions leading to bankruptcy and had refused to lend additional money for expansion in the direction the owner took the business.

This case has been included in a book on valuation primarily to show the very wide ways in which business valuation might be put to use. Many see valuation as a static process offering no more than a periodic snapshot of business value. Others use elements of the process to assist in capital equipment expansion planning and to measure growth. With imagination, this case suggests to the reader other possible ways to mold findings into further use beyond the report. Gathered under the heading of a successful company, the low, median, and high technique could be used to show lenders the extent of exposure under varying possible outcomes. For example, this technique helps bankers evaluate risk and, quite importantly, shows the lender that the buyer or owner is also thinking about risk . . . and planning to avoid it. With the odds of business success stacked so high against small companies, it is also my hope that this chapter provides some help to those struggling to overcome hard times.

The business was ultimately sold . . . yielding $.70 on the dollar for unsecured creditors. Be aware, however, that many businesses entering Chapter 11 bankruptcy never recover. Some months ago, a major U.S. newspaper carried a story estimating that 9 out of 10 businesses failed to survive restructuring under "11." My own experience through consulting with the courts and trustees is considerably bleaker than that. We are a proud people in general, and most of us take pride in paying our bills.

When times get rough, we become embarrassed and go into hiding. The cover-up that ensues pulls us further and further into the hole. By the time we either can't take the stress any longer or are forced to close, our troubled businesses are in such shambles that there's little or nothing to salvage. Creditors may have reached such anxiety that no amount of negotiation can pacify them. By the time protection is sought and awarded by the courts, there quite regularly is no fuse left to burn between the dynamite and the explosion. Once in a great while, a situation like this case can be found. Mail-order businesses were prime candidates for ready, willing, and able buyers at the time it occurred. As we now know, the mail-order industry has been hard hit during recent years. However, I'm pleased to report that this small company survives nicely in the niche it ultimately created. Moving the operation to the Deep South several years ago, the company now markets its products exclusively through catalog sales. Annual sales have reached in excess of $2 million, and the owners thrive.

For reasons I can't go into at this time, I must admit that two other similar mail-order cases did not survive. In these two instances, I'm still convinced that opportunity was there but never seized upon by their buyers. Both valuation and purchase in the realm of bankruptcy proceeding are risky business to say the least.

> *"Bankruptcy changes a man's nature. I feel as though every person has lost confidence in me. . . ."*
> Henry John Heinz '57

> *"Time is a circus, always packing up and moving away."*
> Ben Hecht

15

Retail Home-Decorating Business Valuation

(With Production and Retail Sales)

Small retail operations can be any number of combinations that to the public look to be pure retail. They might include resale of merchandise only, or combine to include wholesale, manufacturing, and/or catalog sales. When these businesses include significant revenues apart from straight retail, each element must be examined for its contribution to profits or losses.

These businesses are more apt to take on the personalities of their owners because of direct customer contacts. Elements of business operation may change with each new owner's particular interests and skills. It is not uncommon for "parts" of these businesses to remain with sellers as they dispose of the mainstay of operations through sale. Thus one must examine product-line issues not just for profitability but also for what remains to be valued and/or sold.

Forecasting is complicated where such multiplicity of product lines exists. Seasonality, waxing and waning within lines, makes straightforward forecasting of sales and cost of goods sold inappropriate for major items of sale. Inventories are more apt to contain larger measures of unsalable or slow-moving merchandise than in most other types of businesses in general.

Sales promotion and product display devices add considerably to the costs of doing business in many retail stores. Samples and display apparatuses generally are not provided free to the retailer, and a mortality in such items can be quite significant on an annual basis. Thus, in larger stores there will tend to be inventory of retained sales promotion items as well as "expensed" items of a discontinued nature.

Repair and maintenance expenses, for lack of interest, may contain many costs that do no more than support the retail selling effort. Retail stores, since they are so bent upon *point-of-purchase merchandising,* make innumerable cosmetic improvements in facilities to encourage consumer preferences. Annual write-offs can grow quite large in bigger stores. Thus this category can seem unduly high to the nondiscerning eye.

BRIEF CASE BACKGROUND

This business was purchased in a condition near to bankruptcy by its present owner in 1986. Sales were substantially below subsistence levels, and service to customers was nonexistent. The entire operation had suffered years of neglect; however, its earlier history revealed successes and a gradual winding down. At the time of purchase, the business offered carpet, draperies, wallpaper, paint, kitchen cabinets, and light fixtures.

The new owner "leveraged" his purchase by pledging personal assets, reserving cash for facility and business rehabilitation. He remodeled the real estate and revamped product lines. The kitchen cabinet and light fixture lines were dropped, distributor carpet lines cut back from 17 to 8' and a direct-mill purchase added, wallpaper books carved from 500 to 200, drapery lines reduced from 21 to 10 and a "designer-exclusive" line added. Both paint lines were replaced with a major brand name. Extensive residential and commercial drapery hardware lines were added along with drapery material and supplies. Because of the new owner's background, three lines of tile and stone flooring were added, along with an art gallery line of prints that the owner produced and also sold wholesale to various gift shops locally and nationally.

Carpet installation and drapery fabrication stood in shambles due to poor workmanship and installation. Two full-time flooring and tile installers were hired, and two drapery seamstresses were employed for improved quality and overall control. Installers are paid a combination of base wage and piece rate. Seamstresses are paid by piece rate only. Two decorators were employed and paid in a combination of base salary plus commissions paid on product sales made external of store resources.

The operation was contained in 4,000 square feet of a 10,000-square-foot building, and 6,000 square feet was revamped for rent to other retail shops. In 1988 a two-story specialized ministorage building was added to the six acres of prime road-frontage land. Occupancy rose to 100% in late 1991 when all construction was completed.

The business implemented and maintains a separate direct-mill wholesale carpet line that is drop-shipped to various locations without overhead costs beyond the owner's personal time. However, the store benefits by a 3.1% discount on carpet at wholesale. Since this aspect of the business is contracted for sale to another wholesaler, carpet/tile (cost of goods sold) are adjusted in the reconstructed statements to reflect these more than likely higher costs to a new owner.

The purpose of valuation is to ascertain a listing price for sale of both the business and real estate. The owner's stated objective through sale was to clear $250,000 before personal taxes. He would carry debt beyond the cash and bank financing if needed.

As stated at the outset, various ways of reviewing statements would be presented throughout to control redundancy and increase general interest in reading each case example. Each type of business offers a new slant on the valuation problem; however, what works particularly well in one type can often be adapted in another. One should always review several years of income and balance sheet data for trends and/or unusual occurrences. Too much is left to the imagination when you don't, and imaginations have the real tendency to follow the positive, which may not be the best choice. My motto has always been: "Statements are guilty until proven innocent." Not because people intentionally misstate events, but because small-business financial statements are constructed to blindside the casual observer. First, many small companies simply cannot afford extensive accounting procedures. Second, small-business owners minimize tax obligations. Third, too many small-business owners don't know what they need in the way of reports. And fourth, many owners use statement preparation only for IRS reporting purposes . . . it's the crumpled notes in the owner's pocket that he or she uses daily to run his or her business. Subsequently, you may not be able to obtain some of the formats I've outlined in the various valuation chapters. However, if you want the best possible accuracy in estimating values, you're advised to dig deeply for all you can get and then try to reconstruct what you might suspect is happening to operations.

Following are balance sheets as booked and as reconstructed to contain items offered in prospective sale, a detail of product sales and costs, taxes, and rental income, and three years of reconstructed income statements. *There is no forecast year due to the owner's own estimate that 1993 will be no better than 1992.* The assignment took place within less than two weeks from the close of 1992. This owner felt that he had pretty well saturated the local market, and the remaining choices for growth seem mostly in adding product lines and/or cloning the operation elsewhere. These choices, although he considered them good ideas for this business's growth, were not of interest to him since he had an opportunity to purchase another business in distress. His self-professed talent is turnaround, and he claimed to get bored with aftermath operations.

Retail Home-Decorating Business
Balance Sheet Reconstructed for Valuation

	Recast 1992
Current Assets	
Accounts Rec.	$ 66,390
Inventory	220,660
Sales Promo.	92,155
Prepaid Exp.	7,005
Total Current Assets	$ 386,210
Property & Equipment	
Land (Fair Market Value)	$ 75,000
Buildings (FMV)	577,900
Furniture/Fixture (FMV)	42,100
Machinery/Equipment (FMV)	4,000
Vehicle(s) (FMV)	27,250
Net Property/Equipment	$ 726,250
TOTAL ASSETS	$1,112,460
Current Liabilities	
Accounts Payable	$ 48,540
Customer Advances	12,455
Total Current Liabilities	$ 60,995
TOTAL LIABILITIES	$ 60,995
Adjusted Stockholder Equity	$1,051,465
TOTAL LIABILITIES & EQUITY	$1,112,460

Retail Home-Decorating Business
Reconstructed Income Statements

	1990	1991	1992
Sales	$1,236,425	$1,204,880	$1,107,585
Cost of Sales	754,920	756,205	677,580
Gross Profit	$ 481,505	$ 448,675	$ 430,005
Expenses			
Wages	$ 69,620	$ 95,885	$ 92,725
Advertising	26,585	21,465	20,965
Vehicle Exp.	20,890	18,610	20,220
Bank Charges	475	1,270	1,280
Commissions	21,495	11,215	11,130

	1990	1991	1992
Dues/Subs./Cont.	1,530	2,485	1,840
Freight	29,675	20,985	14,765
Insurance	24,400	25,475	14,675
Prof. Fees	4,755	4,195	6,595
Miscellaneous Exp.		810	200
Office Exp.	3,515	7,380	5,410
Equip. Lease	360	225	—
Repair/Maint.	21,105	12,085	13,985
Rubbish/Snow Rem.	2,340	2,295	2,385
Sales Promotion	6,000	17,665	9,710
Shop Supplies	3,485	3,690	6,540
Taxes	31,340	32,525	32,560
Telephone	9,905	10,925	8,500
Travel/Meetings	445	8,895	3,500
Utilities	16,590	25,530	16,835
Total Expenses	$ 294,510	$ 323,610	$ 283,820
Rental Income	$ 54,875	$ 61,250	$ 75,750
Recast Income	$ 241,870	$ 186,315	$ 221,935
Income Without Rental	$ 186,995	$ 125,065	$ 146,185

Retail Home-Decorating Business
Balance Sheet

	1992
Current Assets	
Cash	$ 25,785
Accounts Rec.	66,390
Inventory	220,660
Sales Promo.	92,155
Prepaid Exp.	7,005
Total Current Assets	$411,995
Property & Equipment	
Land	$ 25,000
Buildings	547,080
Furniture/Fixture	59,615
Machinery/Equipment	6,885
Vehicle(s)	68,205
Less: Accum. Deprec.	− 170,980
Net Property/Equipment	$535,805

Other Assets

Organization Exp.	$ 190
Security Deposits	1,500
Const. in Process	18,850
Total Other Assets	$ 20,540
TOTAL ASSETS	$968,340

Current Liabilities

Current L-T Debt	$ 10,260
Accounts Payable	48,540
Accrued Expense	8,800
Customer Advances	12,455
Total Current Liabilities	$ 80,055

Long-Term Debt

Mortgage & Notes	$313,270
Total Long-Term Debt	$313,270
TOTAL LIABILITIES	$393,325

Stockholder Equity

Common Stock	$474,715
Retained Earnings	$100,300
Total Stockholder Equity	$575,015
TOTAL LIABILITIES & EQUITY	$968,340

Retail Home-Decorating Business
Detail Reconstructed Income Statements

	1990	1991	1992
Sales			
Paint	$ 122,985	$ 116,220	$ 159,900
Wallpaper	111,530	115,115	118,340
Custom Drapery	275,285	294,030	252,500
Carpet/Tile	529,520	468,430	394,375
Art Gallery	6,380	18,870	19,015
Labor	215,995	191,615	166,685
Accounts Receivable	− 21,675	—	—
Miscellaneous	3,625	3,760	210
Less Returns	− 7,220	− 3,160	− 3,440
Total Sales	$1,236,425	$1,204,880	$1,107,585

	1990	1991	1992
Cost of Sales			
Paint	$ 87,105	$ 81,175	$ 109,965
Wallpaper	63,840	72,560	71,120
Custom Drapes	142,575	153,670	126,000
Carpet/Tile	321,800	280,975	227,445
Art	4,650	12,910	10,125
Subcontracting	15,610	37,330	36,150
Labor	117,630	112,930	79,230
Miscellaneous	2,415	—	—
Inventory Variance	− 705	4,655	17,545
Total Cost of Sales	$ 754,920	$ 756,205	$ 677,580
Taxes			
FICA	$ 12,830	$ 12,870	$ 11,870
Fed. Unemployment	1,450	1,300	945
State Unemployment	5,585	6,905	6,755
Excise/Registration	620	765	675
Real Estate	10,855	10,685	12,315
Total Taxes	$ 31,340	$ 32,525	$ 32,560
Rental Income			
Plaza Shops	$ 12,000	$ 12,000	$ 12,000
Mini-Storage Units	42,875	49,250	63,750
Total Rental Income	$ 54,875	$ 61,250	$ 75,750

Note: This table adds minimally to the analysis section here; however, it is included primarily to show that sales and expenses comprise many items, some of which can seasonally offset the seasonability of other items. In this respect, it will help point out that items as they may appear in "total" on many income statements can lead to inaccurate conclusions in forecasting, until one assesses the contribution each item makes.

FINANCIAL ANALYSIS

This business presents a number of issues that should be of concern to the value processor. Sales appear to have reached a plateau and, in fact, are waning. Gross profits, however, seem tightly woven to sales in each of the three years. Recast income reveals that the business took quite a hit in 1991, sinking from $241,870 to $186,315, while sales remained essentially the same. Without rentals, cash flow is quite subdued. Forty-seven percent of the $55,555 hit came in the way of increased wages and 37% through increased sales promotion expenses and utilities. Sales promotion was a onetime write-off of derelict items, and utilities contained $9,000 of onetime construction expenses. Labor, however, was considered necessary to sustain sales and was considered partially justified by an offset of lower commissions. The owner expressed satisfaction in the level of 1992 expenses in relationship to either 1991 or 1992 sales. At this point, we could either reconstruct 1991 expenses to reflect the reduction of extraordinary cost or simply accept the 1992 column as being indicative of an appropriate cash stream to value. In light of the owner's earlier remarks that his business had peaked out at this location, we might accept this premise and proceed with the analysis. Also, in making this assumption, we would not ordinarily calculate a weighted average cash stream.

Ratio Study

Financial experts will not always agree as to which ratios are particularly germane to the small and privately owned enterprise. I feel that it is essential to examine the following.

$$\textbf{Ratio for Gross Margin} \ = \ \frac{\text{Gross Profit}}{\text{Sales}} \ \text{ or}$$

1990	1991	1992	Industry Median
38.9	37.2	38.8	37.7

This ratio measures the percentage of sales dollars left after cost of goods sold (sometimes referred to as cost of sales) are deducted. The significant trend in our retail company is for acceptable efficiency of the selling process; however, in calculating this ratio we need to assure ourselves that we included "apples" in our cost of goods that are comparable to "apples" in the cost of goods in surveyed samples. Thus it is important to explore the survey's definition of items included in cost of goods and perhaps even restructure the target company's statements to reflect same-case scenarios.

It should be noted that ratios for net profit, before and after taxes, can be most useful ratios. But the fact that private owners frequently manage their businesses to "minimize" the bottom line will often produce little meaningful information from these ratios applied to smaller businesses. Therefore, these ratios are not included. Balance sheet data necessary for calculating certain ratios for 1990 and 1991 are not included in the text; however, I have presented the ratios in those categories affected to complete the range of values.

The current ratio provides a rough indication of a company's ability to

service its obligations due within one year. Progressively higher ratios signify increasing ability to service short-term obligations. Bear in mind that
liquidity in a specific business is an element of asset composition. Thus,
the "acid test" ratio that follows is perhaps a better indicator of liquidity
overall. In this particular business, we must note that $92,155 of current
assets are sales promotion devices that are unlikely to be turned back into
cash per se.

$$\textbf{Current Ratio} \;=\; \frac{\text{Total Current Assets}}{\text{Total Current Liabilities}} \quad \text{or}$$

			Industry
1990	1991	1992	Median
3.2	2.6	5.1	1.7

Note: Unreconstructed balance sheet used.

The quick, or acid test, ratio is a refinement of the current ratio and
more thoroughly measures liquid assets of cash and accounts receivable
in the sense of ability to pay off current obligations. Higher ratios indicate
greater liquidity as a general rule.

$$\textbf{Quick Ratio} \;=\; \frac{\text{Cash and Equivalents + Receivables}}{\text{Total Current Liabilities}} \quad \text{or}$$

			Industry
1990	1991	1992	Median
.8	.7	1.2	.7

Note: Cash and equivalents equal all-cash, marketable securities, and other near-cash items. It
excludes sinking funds.

Less than a ratio of 1.0 can suggest a struggle to stay current with
obligations. The median offers that the industry as a whole may wrestle
with liquidity problems by the nature of doing business; however, the top
25% of reported companies reflect a ratio of 1.6.

$$\textbf{Sales/Receivable Ratio} \;=\; \frac{\text{(Income Statement)}}{\underset{\text{(Balance Sheet)}}{\text{Receivables}}}^{\text{Sales}} \quad \text{or}$$

1990	1991	1992	Industry Median
17.1	11.3	16.7	13.9–22.4

This is an important ratio and measures the number of times that receivables turn over during the year. Our target company seems to turn these over in tune with the industry median.

$$\text{Day's Receivable Ratio} = \frac{365}{\text{Sale/Receivable Ratio}} \quad \text{or}$$

1990	1991	1992	Industry Median
21	32	19	26–16 days

This highlights the average time in terms of days that receivables are outstanding. Generally, the longer that receivables are outstanding, the greater the chance that they may not be collectible. Slow-turnover accounts merit individual examination for conditions of cause. In our case example, three years show inconsistency in collections although they do fall within the industry median range.

$$\text{Cost of Sales/Payables Ratio} = \frac{\text{Cost of Sales}}{\text{Payables}} \quad \text{or}$$

1990	1991	1992	Industry Median
16.4	16.5	14.0	14.3

Note: Cost of sales and cost of goods sold are interchangeable terms.

Generally, the higher their turnover rate, the shorter the time between purchase and payment. Lower turnover suggests that the company may frequently pay bills from daily in-store cash receipts due to slower receivable collections. This practice can be somewhat misguided in light of investment principles whereby one normally attempts to match collections relatively close to payments so that more business income can be directed into the pockets of owners. Some businesses may, however, have little choice.

$$\text{Sales/Working Capital Ratio} = \frac{\text{Sales}}{\text{Working Capital}} \quad \text{or}$$

1990	1991	1992	Industry Median
4.6	4.4	3.4	11.7

Note: Current assets less current liabilities equals working capital.

A low ratio may indicate an inefficient use of working capital, whereas a very high ratio often signals a vulnerable position for creditors. Our target company has been below the median and may increasingly be growing inefficient in the use of its working capital.

To analyze how well inventory is being managed, the cost of sales to inventory ratio can identify important potential shortsightedness.

$$\text{Cost of Sales/Inventory Ratio} \; = \; \frac{\text{Cost of Sales}}{\text{Inventory}} \; \text{or}$$

1990	1991	1992	Industry Median
3.5	3.2	3.1	7.2

A higher inventory turnover can signify a more liquid position and/or better skills at marketing, whereas a lower turnover of inventory may indicate shortages of merchandise for sale, overstocking, or obsolescence in inventory. Our case example falls into the lower quartile as regards inventory management. This should signal the need for a particular examination of inventory as to quality and size.

Conclusions

Financial analysis does not conclude with ratio study, but for our purpose it will suffice. Sales have been flat, the owner losing interest, and perhaps his territory "maxed" out. If his assessment for growth is accurate, the value of his business is to be found in the history up to 1992. Growth by way of new product development or new locations can be costly growth. Certainly the values in these ideas belong to the person who pays for and executes them, and maintaining present levels in sales may take more than just labors of love. This case exhibits conditions where the use of "discounted" processes may be *least likely* to produce satisfactory results.

THE VALUATION EXERCISE

Book Value Method

Total Assets at Year-End 1992	$968,340
Total Liabilities	393,325
Book Value at Year-End 1992	$575,015

Adjusted Book Value Method

Assets	Balance Sheet Cost	Fair Market Value
Cash	$ 25,785	$ 25,785
Acct./Rec.	66,390	66,390
Inventory	220,660	220,660
Sales Promo.	92,155	92,155[1]
Prepaid Exp.	7,005	7,005
Real Estate	572,080	652,900[2]
Equipment, Etc.	134,705	73,350[2]
Other	20,540	20,540
Accumulated Deprec.	− 170,980	—
Total Assets	$ 968,340	$1,158,785
Total Liabilities	$ 393,325	$ 393,325
Adjusted Book Value at 1992	$ 575,015	$ 765,460

[1]While sample material may have little resale value, promotional devices are necessary to generate sales. Subsequently, when the business is sold as a "going concern," these items can be included at book value. I caution, however; sales promotion items can experience very short life spans, particularly in a home decorating business where styles change rapidly.
[2]Stated at appraised and, thus, fair market value.

Hybrid Method

(This is a form of the capitalization method.)

1 = High amount of dollars in assets and low-risk business venture

2 = Medium amount of dollars in assets and medium-risk business venture

3 = Low amount of dollars in assets and high-risk business venture

	1	2	3
Yield on Risk-Free Investments Such as Government Bonds[a] (Often 6%–9%)	8.0%	8.0%	8.0%
Risk Premium on Nonmanagerial Investments[a] (corporate bonds, utility stocks)	4.5%	4.5%	4.5%
Risk Premium on Personal Management[a]	7.5%	14.5%	22.5%
Capitalization Rate	20.0%	27.0%	35.0%
Earnings Multipliers	5	3.7	2.9

[a]These rates are revised periodically to reflect changing economies. They can be composed through the assistance of expert investment advisers if need be.

This particular version of a hybrid method tends to place 40% of business value in book values.

Book Value at Year-End 1992	$575,015	
Add: Appreciation in Assets	190,445	
Book Value as Adjusted	$765,460	
Weight to Adjusted Book Value	40%	$ 306,184
1992 Net Income	$221,935	
Times Multiplier	×3.7	$ 821,160
Total Business Value		$1,127,344

Excess Earnings Method

(This method considers cash flow and values in hard assets, estimates intangible values, and superimposes tax considerations and financing structures to prove the most-likely equation.)

1992 Cash Flow	$ 221,935
Less: Comparable Salary	− 45,000
Less: Contingency Reserve	− 5,000
Net Cash Stream to Be Valued	$ 171,935
Cost of Money	
Market Value of Tangible Assets, Minus Liabilities[1]	
(see reconstructed balance sheet)	$1,051,465
Times: Applied Lending Rate	×10%
Annual Cost of Money	$ 105,147

Excess of Cost of Earnings

Return Net Cash Stream to Be Valued	$ 171,935
Less: Annual Cost of Money	− 105,147
Excess of Cost of Earnings	$ 66,788

Intangible Business Value

Excess of Cost of Earnings	$ 66,788
Times: Intangible Net Multiplier Assigned	×2.5*
Intangible Business Value	$ 166,970
Add: Tangible Asset Value	1,051,465
TOTAL BUSINESS VALUE (Prior to Proof)	$1,218,435
	(Say $1,220,000)

Financing Rationale

Total Investment	$1,220,000
Less: Down Payment	− 300,000
Balance to Be Financed	$ 920,000

[1]Minus liabilities whenever liabilities are sold with business.
*Refer to Figure 9.1 "Guide to Selecting Net Multipliers," in Chapter 9.

At this point, we must gauge the amount in prospective bank financing. It's important to use a good deal of logic at this stage of valuation or you will waste a lot of time coming up with reliable estimates. One can set up the financing scenario any way appropriate to the local conditions, but my guess is that the following would be pretty close.

Real Estate ($652,900) at 70%	$457,030*
Furniture/Fixture ($42,100) at 30%	12,630
Equipment ($4,000) at 0 Value	–0–
Vehicles ($27,250) at 25%	6,813
Inventory ($220,660) at 50% of Book Value	110,330
Receivables Minus Payables ($17,850 at 0 Value)	–0–
Estimated Bank Financing	$586,803
	(Say $590,000)

*Bankers often calculate a strange configuration when real estate that has separate cash flow is included in business financing. Noting the reconstructed income statements, rental income equals $75,750 in 1992. 70% of $75,750 equals $53,025 and annual payments of principal and interest on $460,000 of debt equals $53,269. Neat little "cushion," wouldn't you say?

I must interrupt the process flow for a moment to remind readers that real estate sold with a "going concern" should be treated just as all other assets for the purpose of business valuation. Unless, of course, *intangible* business value in the foregoing calculation is "0" or a negative number. In that case, there is **no** business value to report in excess of the values in hard assets, including real estate. Such being exhibited translates into assets-only for sale, and, subsequently, appraisal of assets versus business valuation would be the assignment undertaken. However, one should not neglect a possibility that real estate could be leased rather than sold. In our example, real estate enjoys strong cash flows and could remain an excellent investment for the previous business owner. In this event, business value would be examined without the real estate asset, expenses increased to include "rent" paid, and the rental income removed from reconstructed cash flows. So many years using the "excess" method have taught me the "gut-feel" as to which way to initially proceed. When in doubt, I start as I have here, because *a* facility is necessary to conduct business, and one way or the other, there will be a cost associated with housing. The formula walks me into examining the correct pew I must ultimately consider. In spite of what I've just said, real estate and other hard assets will always have "stand-alone values." These must be known to the best of your ability, regardless of the strengths or weaknesses of business cash flow. Business-value estimating that portends to depress fair market values of real estate and other hard assets is irresponsible reporting.

Bank (10% × 20 years)	
Amount	$590,000
Annual Principal/Interest Payment	68,324
Testing Estimated Business Value	
Return: Net Cash Stream to Be Valued	$171,935
Less: Annual Bank Debt Service (P&I)	− 68,324
Pretax Cash Flow	$103,611
Add: Principal Reduction	11,700*
Pretax Equity Income	$115,311
Less: Est. Dep. & Amortization (Let's Assume)	− 33,930
Less: Estimated Income Taxes (Let's Assume)	− 1,600
Net Operating Income (NOI)	$ 79,781

*Debt service includes an average $11,700 annual principal payment that is traditionally recorded on the balance sheet as a reduction in debt owed. This feature recognizes that the "owned equity" in the business increases by this average amount each year.

Return on Equity:

$$\frac{\text{Pretax Equity Income}}{\text{Down Payment}} = \frac{\$115,311}{\$300,000} = 38.4\%$$

Return on Total Investment:

$$\frac{\text{Net Operating Income}}{\text{Total Investment}} = \frac{\$ 79,781}{\$1,120,000} = 7.1\%$$

Although return on total investment is abysmally low in relationship to conventionally expected investment returns, the return on equity is attractively high and cash flow is strong.

Basic Salary	$ 45,000
Net Operating Income	79,781
Gain of Principal	11,700
Tax-Sheltered Income (Dep.)	33,930
Effective Income	$170,411*

*There is also the matter of $5,000 annually into the contingency and replacement reserve that would be at the discretion of the owner if not required for emergencies or asset replacements.

At this time we have taken our first shot at estimating business value, but we are still missing a vital element in the process. A $300,000 cash down payment plus $590,000 in bank financing, or $890,000, leaves us with a $330,000 shortfall of the all-cash target specified by the generic definition of fair market value. It also leaves us $330,000 short in closing a deal. If we leave the price at $1,220,000, either the buyer has to make up the difference outside this business, or the seller must become flexible toward providing $330,000 of seller financing, or find another buyer with more cash, or the estimated price must be "squeezed" to fit the conditions of the projected buyer. Stated at the outset, our seller agreed to provide some financing, as long as he could realize at least $250,000 prior to personal taxes. The $890,000 forecast through down payment and institutional financing more than meets the target, thus we can proceed to insert seller debt into the equation.

Financing Rationale	
Total Investment	$1,220,000
Less: Down Payment	− 300,000
Balance to Be Financed	$ 920,000
Bank (10% × 20 years)	
Amount	$ 590,000
Annual Principal/Interest Payment	68,324
Seller (8% × 10 years)	
Amount	$ 330,000
Annual Principal/Interest Payment	48,046
Total Annual Principal/Interest Payment	$ 116,370

Testing Estimated Business Value

Return: Net Cash Stream to Be Valued	$ 171,935
Less: Annual Bank Debt Service (P&I)	− 116,370
Pretax Cash Flow	$ 55,565
Add: Principal Reduction	26,334*
Pretax Equity Income	$ 81,899
Less: Est. Dep. & Amortization (Let's Assume)	− 33,930
Less: Estimated Income Taxes (Let's Assume)	–0–*
Net Operating Income (NOI)	$ 47,969

*Debt service includes an average $26,334 annual principal payment that is traditionally recorded on the balance sheet as a reduction in debt owned. This feature recognizes that the "owned equity" in the business increases by this average amount each year. Tax obligations are reduced since increased interest expense is deductible from business cash flow.

Return on Equity:

$$\frac{\text{Pretax Equity Income}}{\text{Down Payment}} = \frac{\$ 81,899}{\$300,000} = 27.3\%$$

Return on Total Investment:

$$\frac{\text{Net Operating Income}}{\text{Total Investment}} = \frac{\$ 47,969}{\$1,220,000} = 3.9\%$$

Note that returns change quite a bit under our new scenario, but the return on equity is still high in relationship to alternative investments for the $300,000 cash being used as down payment.

Buyer's Potential Cash Benefit

Forecast Annual Salary	$ 45,000
Pretax Cash Flow (contingency not considered)	55,565
Income Sheltered by Depreciation	33,930
Less: Provision for Taxes	–0–*
Discretionary Cash	$134,495
Add: Equity Buildup	26,334
Discretionary and Nondiscretionary Cash	$160,829

*Assumes that buyer would increase salary to avoid double taxation by paying taxes at the business level.

As a matter of practicality, I know that the owner of this business withdrew take-home pay slightly over $160,000 in pretax 1992 dollars. The actual earnings of a present owner has always been somewhat of a benchmark criterion that I shoot for in terms of evaluating a prospective buyer's potential earnings. Some people remark that this is giving away the "kitchen sink," but I don't think so, particularly when you consider that owners can stay in their businesses and continue to earn if they wish to do so. I have another philosophy to share: Buyers are not obligated to feather the nest of sellers . . . ever! There's a happy median for both, and that's usually the point at which sellers and buyers are *equally* stretched by the process of actual sale. To my way of thinking, that is where true business value lies. Prospective buyers should not, in the process of purchase, be able to immediately earn more than sellers have earned, but at the same time, sellers cannot expect to earn from their buyers what they could not earn from their business while they ran it. The debt leverage of cash streams can be tight as a drum in the purchase of fast-growing companies, but in cases like this retail operation, where sales, earnings, and growth are stagnant, the prospective buyer deserves *wiggle room* to expand the business in years to come. That means that more "jingle" must be dumped into the buyer's equation or the business simply won't sell. If the estimated value does not forecast a likely sale, then the estimate is wrong . . . period!

Seller's Potential Cash Benefit in Sale

Cash Down Payment	$300,000
Bank Financing Receipts	590,000
Gross Cash at Closing	$890,000*

*From which must be deducted capital gains and other taxes. Structured appropriately, the deal qualifies as an "installment" sale with the proceeds in seller financing put off regarding taxes until later periods.

Projected Cash to Seller by End of 10th Year

Cash at Closing	$ 890,000
Add: Projected 10-Year Principal and Interest Payments to Seller	480,457
Pretax 5-Year Proceeds	$1,370,457

This owner paid $600,000 for his business seven years ago. That's 128.4% return on his original purchase, or an average dollar return of $110,065 per each of the seven years between 1986 and now. This does not include what he earned in the way of salary for operating his business. $290,000 over his original purchase ($890,000 in cash minus $600,000) might be likely realized on a date of sale. Calculated any way one wishes, return to this owner is just and wouldn't be likely to be repeated in the stock market or in a job with corporate America. Want to know the end of the story? I'm happy—this was *my* business . . . I was the seller! I sold the business separate of real estate, ultimately sold the real estate later to an investment group, sold the wholesale carpet division separately, and I grew richer in the process. The years were 1969, 1970, and 1971—not

1990, 1991, and 1992 as herein stated to keep a secret up to this point. I returned to college during 1970 and spent less than two hours per business day in my operation. Thus labor costs fit the scenario for me. However, my time away did have an impact on business.

Today, I value other businesses as I did through the purchase and sale of five small companies—from the trenches, not from academia! Today I own two enterprises alone, and two others with partners. I didn't have two sticks to make fire when I started my small-business rampage nearly 30 years ago. Business valuation is estimating what real players will do, and real players add eons to the yardsticks of conventionally accepted measurement. Ignore how buyers think and act, and you're guaranteed to miss your target estimation. Comparable business sales are virtually useless because there are no comparable business operators. Individuals are unique and not very predictable . . . less so for buyers who read books.

Forget the Scientist, This Is What Counts Method

Offering Price	$1,220,000
Less: Down Payment	− 300,000
Less: Financing	− 920,000
"Uncovered" Debt	− 0–
Cash Flow (commonly used last completed year, assuming that conditions of the business warrant such)	$ 221,935
Less: Principal/Interest	− 116,370
Cash Flow Free of Debt	$ 105,565
At 7 times earnings value =	$ 738,955
At 9 times earnings value =	$ 950,085

Business Is Fairly Priced If:

1. Asking price is not greater than 150% of net worth (except where reconstructed profits are 40% of asking price).

   a. Net worth $1,051,465 times 150% equals $1,577,198.

   b. Reconstructed profits $221,935 divided by asking price $1,220,000 equals 18.2%.

2. At least 10% sales growth per year being realized.

   a. No growth.

3. Down payment is approximately the amount of one year's recon-structed profits.

   a. $300,000 minus $221,935 or $78,065 (35.2%) more.

4. Terms of payment of balance of purchase price (including interest) should not exceed 40% of annual reconstructed profit.

   a. Debt service $116,370 divided by $221,935 equals 52.4%.

What does all this mean for estimated value? It means that the price in the deal through the eyes of buyers, if they have read a multitude of publications whence this information was gleaned, could be viewed as a bit much to pay. Thus, we might conclude that $1,220,000 would be the maximum estimated value. Perhaps a most-likely selling price might be in the range of $900,000 to $950,000. Quite honestly, that is the reason that I split my sale of business and real property; because, as with many sellers, I too wanted my price. That's what is so good about small business—owners and purchasers can be flexible as to final deals.

RULE-OF-THUMB ESTIMATES

Well-established small retail companies with strong evidence of good operating performances have been known to change hands in the range of 4 to as high as 6 times reconstructed earnings. Thus for this case, estimated value ranges from a low of $887,740 to a high of $1,331,610 could be expected in any given market. The $1,220,000 price tag in our example translates into 5.5 times earnings. Another "rule" suggests .75 to 1.5 times net plus equipment and inventory. Bear in mind that the projected sale included receivables, payables, sales promotion samples, and customer advances that need to be reconciled and included when using this rule. If we were to average the low and high at 1.12, $640,127 would be forecast as value . . . not including real estate. When using rule-of-thumb estimating, these ratios rarely, if ever, take the value of real estate into consideration. Real estate cannot be arbitrarily added to the rule-of-thumb value, and purchase of facilities must meet the test of cash flow.

Results

Book Value Method	$ 575,015
Adjusted Book Value Method	765,460
Hybrid (capitalization) Method	1,127,344
Excess Earnings Method	1,220,000
Forget the Scientist Method	$738,955 to 950,085
Rule-of-Thumb Estimate	$887,740 to 1,331,610

As mentioned elsewhere, I traditionally calculate the book and adjusted book value scenarios, although I know that good operations will rarely change hands at these prices. Data from these, however, are an important consideration to the hybrid and excess earnings formulas; and because some businesses have not produced cash flows strong enough to support values beyond these hard-asset values. Thus overall business values may not be greater than the values they hold in these hard assets.

We guessed from initial review of the balance and income statements that this retail operation had an added overall intangible value that was greater than the value in its assets. What we didn't know at that time was how much more could be justified.

For added flavor, the new business owner leased the facilities for $14,400 per year. This plus the $75,750 rental income came to $90,150 triple net real estate income. The business was sold for $550,000 and real estate later at $700,000. Together, these sales derived $1,250,000. The wholesale portion was another source of profit. Needless to say, I'm pleased to report that seller financing kept my kids in shoes for quite a while.

The Japanese have a philosophy about life that we Americans might well be advised to adopt: kaizen *(continuous improvement). Business valuation processors cannot possibly know it all, but they can always benefit through continuous improvement. I, for one, have no other choice; I do it to survive.*

W.M.Y.

16

Retail Hardware Stores

Smaller retail hardware stores can be distinguished from other retail operations by the vast complexity of diversified lines of merchandise. For example, most serve virtually every trade contractor, such as plumbers, electricians, millers, roofers, painters, and builders, as well as do-it-yourselfers. Lines can include lawn and garden suppliers, power generators, garden tractors, tools, housewares, unpainted furniture, car supplies, Christmas items, sportswear, artist supplies, toys, interior decorating materials, greeting cards, glassware, farm equipment, and so on. Individual-store inventory tends to model the general needs within the community wherever the store is located.

Sales in hardware stores are less likely to be affected by seasonal ups and downs, since much of their merchandise can be "shifted" to meet seasonal characteristics. Fall and spring may provide a little more volume, and as with many other retail stores, the first two months of each new calendar year can be somewhat slack from overexpenditures leading up to Christmas.

Independent retail stores are faced with tough competition on many fronts these days. Chain and discount stores, lumber dealers with hardware (and few don't have it), and specialty dealers such as paint, electrical, and plumbing wholesalers affront daily the small independent from all angles. Because of quantity buying discounts enjoyed by the "bigs," independents have been forced to model their general inventories after lower-priced merchandise and/or be very selective over what, if any, high-quality products might be carried. However, many independents benefit and survive by joint buying cooperatives such as Ace, True Value, Coast-to-Coast, and others. The key to successful operation and survival can weigh heavily in effective management of contribution ratios per department or product line. Computerization plays a vital role, or should do so, in daily management.

Inventory control is essential if one is to be successful in the retail hardware game. Misguided purchasing decisions, particularly seasonal merchandise, can create costly storage and holding problems. Daily cash and charge sales, stock replenishment, pricing, and so on can quickly get out of control if not rigorously watched.

Brief Case History

This retail hardware business serves customers from three leased facilities located approximately 30 miles apart. The two larger units now suffer major competition caused by the opening of a Wal-Mart midyear 2000, which is situated equidistant from these stores. The units are absentee-owned by a wealthy medical professional who bought them originally as an investment.

I am including this case for several reasons: (a) to show you should never be impressed by the size of sales alone; (b) to point out pitfalls of absentee ownership, especially in this type of business; and (c) to show how value is affected by the distressed nature of a business.

When assignments involve multiple sites, financial analysis should always include the study of each store individually, as well as profit contributions for each product line by individual store. However, for the purpose of brevity in this chapter, we will use the following consolidated statements.

Retail Hardware Stores
(Three Locations Consolidated)
Balance Sheets (Not Reconstructed)

	1998	1999	2000	2001
Assets				
Current				
Cash	$ 142,676	$ 77,635	$ 189,505	$ 13,820
Acct./Rec.	125,296	125,266	178,552	99,090
Inventory	410,574	678,524	713,088	377,592
Total Current	$ 678,546	$ 881,425	$1,081,145	$ 490,502

	1998	1999	2000	2001
Prop. Equip.				
Lease Imp.	$ 10,559	$ 10,559	$ 22,529	$ 13,436
Vehicles	12,906	12,906	32,263	7,772
Furn./Fixture	54,724	59,208	61,268	48,414
Less: Deprec.	− 41,814	− 52,744	− 67,624	− 52,825
Total Prop. Equip.	$ 36,375	$ 29,929	$ 48,436	$ 16,797
Other				
Note/Rec.—Officer	$ 91,760	$ 106,986	$ 264,738	$ 41,114
Security Deposit	592	592	592	592
Total Other	$ 92,352	$ 107,578	$ 265,330	$ 41,706
TOTAL ASSETS	$ 807,273	$1,018,932	$1,394,911	$ 549,005
Liabilities				
Current Liab.				
L-T Debt (Current)	$ 15,117	$ 38,780	$ 48,316	$ 16,867
Acct./Pay.	142,891	247,514	254,202	255,280
Accrued Exp.	40,055	71,122	30,898	8,388
Taxes Payable	20,151	15,390	15,945	6,677
Total Current Liab.	$ 218,214	$ 372,806	$ 349,361	$ 287,212
Noncurrent				
Long-Term Debt	$ 374,585	$ 424,244	$ 812,703	$ 391,506
Total Noncurrent	$ 374,585	$ 424,244	$ 812,703	$ 391,506
TOTAL LIABILITIES	$ 592,799	$ 797,050	$1,162,064	$ 678,718
Shareholder Equity	$ 214,474	$ 221,882	$ 232,847	$ − 129,713
TOTAL LIABILITIES & SHAREHOLDER EQUITY	$ 807,273	$1,018,932	$1,394,911	$ 549,005

Retail Hardware Stores
(Three Locations Consolidated)
Reconstructed Balance Sheets for Valuation

	Recast 2001
Assets	
Current	
Cash	$ 13,820
Acct./Rec.	99,090
Inventory	377,592
Total Current	$490,502

	Recast 2001
Prop. Equip.	
Lease Imp.	$ 10,000
Vehicles	5,000
Furn./Fixture	26,550
Total Prop. Equip.	$ 41,550
Other	
Security Deposit	592
Total Other	$ 592
TOTAL ASSETS	$532,644
Liabilities	
Current Liab.	
Acct./Pay.	$255,280
Accrued Exp.	8,388
Taxes Payable	6,677
Total Current Liabilities	$270,345
TOTAL LIABILITIES	$270,345
Equity	$262,299
TOTAL LIABILITIES & SHAREHOLDER EQUITY	$532,644

Retail Hardware Stores
(Three Locations Consolidated)
Reconstructed Income Statements—Valuation for Sale Purposes

	1998	1999	2000	2001
Sales	$1,182,354	$1,977,453	$2,167,160	$2,404,836
Cost of Sales	777,807	1,290,564	1,486,823	1,679,628
Gross Profit	$ 404,547	$ 686,889	$ 680,337	$ 725,208
% Gross Profit	34.2%	34.7%	31.4%	30.2%
Expenses				
Wages	$ 118,479	$ 222,694	$ 237,380	$ 248,212
Insurance—Group	3,520	7,298	13,366	23,028
Insurance—Gen.	17,168	4,949	8,850	12,954
Advertising	40,140	98,107	99,730	118,806
Freight	4,596	15,677	22,676	19,814
Utilities	8,132	21,750	23,230	43,159
Telephone	6,152	13,181	16,834	17,441
Office Supplies	4,777	7,909	9,779	13,237
Contributions	775	—	1,324	—
Bad Debt	860	1,776	2,148	464
Prof. Fees	8,449	12,863	8,164	7,022

	1998	1999	2000	2001
Repair/Maint.	3,018	6,188	9,470	2,713
Miscellaneous	8,940	4,149	2,142	11,211
Travel/Ent.	2,586	4,129	4,955	10,188
Property Taxes	1,576	7,106	6,511	17,390
Package/Process	1,118	7,357	4,969	7,357
Rent	75,381	90,952	95,990	77,200
Store Supplies	4,701	13,397	18,977	15,165
Dues & Subs.	730	2,333	378	1,637
Bank Charges	193	1,347	3,676	8,528
Total Expenses	$ 311,291	$ 543,162	$ 590,549	$ 655,526
Recast Income	$ 93,256	$ 143,727	$ 89,788	$ 69,682
Recast Income as a Percent of Sales	7.9%	7.3%	4.1%	2.9%

FINANCIAL ANALYSIS

Three key points on this business's nonreconstructed balance sheet should trigger immediate alarm to the value processor. The amount of increased long-term debt in 2000, the staggering decrease in total assets for 2001, and the ensuing negative net worth of −$129,713 at the end of 2001. This balance sheet, because of so many irregularities year to year, provides an ideal example of where ratio study can prove especially useful to an overall analysis. Although it is clear that a financial problem more than likely predated 1998, it is also clear that the situation has grown progressively worse during the past four years. Ratio study will highlight where difficulties are most pronounced, but before calculating this information, we must discover what happened to cause a near doubling of long-term debt. On the strength of the balance sheet through 1999, it appears inconceivable that this business could have been able to refinance its debt at all.

That, in fact, was the case . . . the absentee owner pledged a mortgage on his personal home. In addition, he auctioned the assets at a "fourth" site during late 2000 and used the proceeds to reduce long-term debt. Unfortunately, auction returns were inadequate to both reduce debt and pay off that location's pro rata share of accounts payable. One could offer any number of criticisms with regard to the best use of proceeds; however, it became obvious that he was bothered considerably by leaving business debt tied for long to his personal home. Given these conditions, it makes sense to be concerned about the "reliability" of 2001 sales and expenses. For simplicity, 2001 reflects the necessary adjustments to operations that remained after closing the fourth store; extraordinary and/or onetime costs have been removed, and 2001 income data reflect the remaining three stores.

Ratio Study

$$\textbf{Ratio for Gross Margin} \quad = \quad \frac{\text{Gross Profit}}{\text{Sales}} \quad \text{or}$$

1998	1999	2000	2001	Industry Median
34.2	34.7	31.4	30.2	39.1

This ratio measures the percentage of sales dollars left after cost of goods sold is deducted. The significant trend in our hardware company is for decreasing efficiency of the selling process, ending with the latest year nearly 9% below industry median. The two stores near to Wal-Mart have been heavily discounting to remain competitive. This situation alone steals nearly $208,000 of gross profit away from operations.

It should be noted that ratios for net profit, before and after taxes, can be most useful ratios. But the fact that private owners frequently manage their businesses to "minimize" bottom lines will often produce little meaningful information from these ratios applied to smaller businesses. Therefore, these ratios are not included.

The current ratio provides a rough indication of a company's ability to service its obligations due within the time frame of one year. Progressively higher ratios signify increasing ability to service short-term obligations. Bear in mind that liquidity in a specific business is a critical element of asset composition. Thus, the acid test ratio that follows is perhaps a better indicator of liquidity overall.

$$\textbf{Current Ratio} \quad = \quad \frac{\text{Total Current Assets}}{\text{Total Current Liabilities}} \quad \text{or}$$

1998	1999	2000	2001	Industry Median
3.1	2.4	3.1	1.7	2.6

Note the significant drop in the ratio for 2001.

The quick, or acid test, ratio is a refinement of the current ratio and more thoroughly measures liquid assets of cash and accounts receivable in the sense of ability to pay off current obligations. Higher ratios indicate greater liquidity as a general rule.

$$\text{Quick Ratio} \quad = \quad \frac{\text{Cash and Equivalents + Receivables}}{\text{Total Current Liabilities}} \quad \text{or}$$

1998	1999	2000	2001	Industry Median
1.2	.5	1.1	.4	.4

A ratio lower than 1.0 can suggest a struggle to stay current with obligations. The median offers that the industry as a whole may wrestle with liquidity problems by the nature of doing business, and the top 25% of reported companies reflect a ratio of only .8.

$$\text{Sales/Receivable Ratio} \quad = \quad \frac{\text{(Income Statement)}\ \text{Sales}}{\text{Receivables}\ \text{(Balance Sheet)}} \quad \text{or}$$

1998	1999	2000	2001	Industry Median
9.4	15.8	12.1	24.3	31.8–57.9

This is an important ratio and measures the number of times that receivables turn over during the year. Our target company seems to turn these over quite below the industry median, which suggests that credit extension and collection processes may not be adequately managed.

$$\text{Days's Receivable Ratio} \quad = \quad \frac{365}{\text{Sales/Receivable Ratio}} \quad \text{or}$$

1998	1999	2000	2001	Industry Median
39	23	30	15	11–6 days

This highlights the average time in terms of days that receivables are outstanding. Generally, the longer that receivables are outstanding, the greater the chance that they may not be collectible. Slow-turnover accounts merit individual examination for conditions of cause. In our case example, four years show irregularity in collections, although 2001 has improved closer to the industry median range. Much of the problem rests in the notion of large-trade contractor accounts who have found their customers to be slow paying.

$$\text{Cost of Sales/Payables Ratio} \ = \ \frac{\text{Cost of Sales}}{\text{Payables}} \quad \text{or}$$

1998	1999	2000	2001	Industry Median
5.4	5.2	5.8	6.6	11.8

Generally, the higher the turnover rate, the shorter the time between purchase and payment. Lower turnover, which our target company experiences, indicates that the company may frequently pay bills from daily in-store cash receipts due to slower receivable collections. This practice may be somewhat misguided in light of investment principles whereby one normally attempts to match collections relatively close to payments so that more business income can be directed into the pockets of owners. Some businesses may, however, have little choice. Our target company has felt that a "competitive edge" over Wal-Mart has been the company's extension of terms to contractors who represent major sales to the stores. However, what good are sales if cash can't be collected?

$$\text{Sales/Working Capital Ratio} \ = \ \frac{\text{Sales}}{\text{Working Capital}} \quad \text{or}$$

1998	1999	2000	2001	Industry Median
2.6	3.9	3.0	11.8	4.6

Note: Current assets less current liabilities equals working capital.

A low ratio may indicate an inefficient use of working capital, whereas a very high ratio often signals a vulnerable position for creditors. Our target held its own until 2001 when the bottom fell out.

To analyze how well inventory is being managed, the cost of sales to inventory ratio can identify important potential shortsightedness.

$$\text{Cost of Sales/Inventory Ratio} \ = \ \frac{\text{Cost of Sales}}{\text{Inventory}} \quad \text{or}$$

1998	1999	2000	2001	Industry Median
1.9	1.9	2.1	4.4	2.1

A higher inventory turnover can signify a more liquid position and/or better skills at marketing, whereas a lower turnover of inventory may indicate shortages of merchandise for sale, overstocking, or obsolescence. Our case example in 2001 suggests the company may have eliminated slow-turning stock from the other three stores in the auction of the fourth . . . which it in fact did. Subsequently, this higher turnover for 2001 may or may not continue long term.

Conclusions

This case is further complicated by the fact that the owner added another store in 1999 (not the one auctioned), for a total of three stores retained. Subsequently, we really don't have three recent contiguous years to evaluate. I cannot overstate just how important it is to evaluate individual locations separately when the valuation assignment consists of more than one site. At the time of the actual assignment, we focused a great deal of attention on recasting the 2001 year. In conversations with the owner and his managers, we concluded that figures from this year would largely be representative for the next year or two, and/or until they could make changes to operations such that expenses could be reduced. Above all else, $69,682 as recast income on $2.4 million of sales is no simple valuation task, and the question remained: Is there a "business" per se to sell?

THE VALUATION EXERCISE

Book Value Method

Total Assets at Year-End 2001 (unreconstructed balance sheet)	$549,005
Total Liabilities	678,718
Book Value at Year-End 2001	− $129,713

Adjusted Book Value Method

Assets	Balance Sheet Cost	Fair Market Value
Cash	$ 13,820	$ 13,820
Acct./Rec.	99,090	99,090
Inventory	377,592	377,592
Lease Improv.	13,436	10,000*
Vehicles	7,772	5,000*
Furn./Fixture	48,414	26,550*
Other	41,706	592
Accumulated Deprec.	− 52,825	
Total Assets	$ 549,005	$ 532,644
Total Liabilities	$ 678,718	$ 678,718
Business Book Value	$ − 129,713	
Adjusted Book Value at 2001		$ − 146,074

*Stated at appraised and, thus, fair market value.

Hybrid Method

(This is a form of the capitalization method.)

The hybrid method is not useful in this case because of both negative net worth and negative cash flow conditions. In the language of mathematics, a positive multiplier times a negative flow translates into a negative product.

Excess Earnings Method

(This method considers cash flow and values in hard assets, estimates intangible values, and superimposes tax considerations and financing structures to prove the most-likely equation.)

2001 Recast Cash Flow	$ 69,682
Less: Comparable Salary	− 35,000
Less: Contingency Reserve	− 5,000
Net Cash Stream to Be Valued	$ 29,682

Cost of Money	
Tangible Assets Minus Liabilities	
(see reconstructed balance sheet)	$ 262,299
Times: Applied Lending Rate	×10%
Annual Cost of Money	$ 26,230
Excess of Cost of Earnings	
Net Cash Stream to Be Valued	$ 29,682
Less: Annual Cost of Money	− 26,230
Excess of Cost of Earnings	$ 3,452
Intangible Business Value	
Excess of Cost of Earnings	$ 3,452
Times: Intangible Net Multiplier Assigned	×2.0*
Intangible Business Value	$ 6,904
Add: Tangible Asset Value	262,299
TOTAL BUSINESS VALUE (Prior to Proof)	$ 269,203
	(Say $270,000)
Financing Rationale	
Total Investment	$ 270,000
Less: Down Payment	− 50,000
Balance to Be Financed	$ 220,000

*Refer to Figure 9.1, "Guide to Selecting Net Multipliers" in Chapter 9.

At this point, we must decide what to do about bank financing. Accounts payable are about 2.6 times greater than receivables, and this business has suffered a very poor performance history to boot. The reconstructed balance sheet indicates how the seller wished to market his business. Regardless of how the deal might be ultimately structured, it seems unlikely that this seller can recover entirely from long-term debt or the pressure from short-term payables. Looming were choices of filing bankruptcy, auctioning assets to pay debt or payables, or continuing to operate with hopes of bringing the business into line. Long-term debt in this case was entirely a condition of loans made by the owner. He was unwilling at this stage to encumber his medical practice in the throes of bankruptcy. What he elected to do was to provide an owner-financed sale to five key employees. Under this arrangement, since these employees had earnings built in, the additional recast income was made available for the payment of debt and accounts payable. About 60% of the company's suppliers agreed to longer payout, as long as these five employees did not increase their own salaries until these obligations were retired. The seller agreed to pay the remaining 40% from his down payment and personal cash. Not a happy scenario for the seller, but a choice he made. A far larger number of businesses, once getting into this condition, have virtually no choice. Perhaps some element of bank financing could have been structured, but by the looks of the balance and income sheets, there might also have been the devil to pay. Financing went as follows:

Financing Rationale	
Total Investment	$ 270,000
Less: Down Payment	− 50,000
Balance to Be Financed	$ 220,000
Seller (8% × 20 years)	
Amount	$ 220,000
Annual Principal/Interest Payment	− 22,082
Available to Creditors	
2001 Recast Cash Flow	$ 69,682
Less: Contingency Reserves	− 5,000
Less: Debt Service	− 22,082
Benchmark Funds to Creditors	$ 42,600

As one might surmise, little benefit is added by refining business value estimates when cash streams do no more than cover the cost of asset purchase. In these instances, however, business valuation can serve to bring reality "close in" and assist owners with decisions they must make. I've included this case not for its added benefit to issues in methodology but primarily because, so frequently, negative net worth conditions precipitate seller motivations to sell. These five new owners are not out of the woods as of this writing, but it has become clear that they are making good progress. Hardware stores can be particularly poor investments for absentee owners, and it's amazing how employees perform more astutely when they assume ownership roles.

17

Retail Garden Center

Garden centers may or may not also be "growers" for both retail and wholesale distribution. Some produce their own vegetable and flower seeds and seedlings and engage in mail-order distribution. Others provide landscape horticultural services and engage in landscape planning, architectural, and counseling services, as well as offer a variety of ornamental shrub and tree pathology services. Many offer garden tools and, depending on location, may also sell and provide repair services for larger gas- and electric-powered tractors and implements. However, smaller centers tend mostly to sell products purchased from others; some may also sell plants and shrubs that they grow themselves. Services specifically offered at individual garden centers depend largely on the size of operations and/or skills of owners.

If, for example, an owner is formally trained in landscaping and/or horticulture, significant parts of historical cash flows may be directly tied to these skills. Persons having acquired these types of skills can be somewhat akin to licensed professionals, whereby "followings" are developed over time. Subsequently, it is important for the value processor to recognize the roles played in garden centers by their owners. If some part of a cash stream is unique to a specific owner, then that part must be removed or "subdued" in the equation of fair market value. On the other hand, if a prospective buyer is "defined" or limited to persons with similar skills, then this portion may be included. Bear in mind, however, that when one substantially narrows the field to unique prospective buyers, then one also tends to compress price or value. It's all in the economics of supply and demand . . . and supply and demand are always major ingredients in estimating business value.

Brief Case History

Our retail garden center is situated on a major road between two similar-sized small communities. Although the center offers a wide range of ornamental shrubs, flowers, and seeds, it specializes in growing and culturing small bonsai trees. In addition, the company has specialty plantings that should reach harvest size in two years. Traditional nursery stock and supplies are offered from a 6,600-square-foot building situated on a three-acre site. An independent landscaper works from the premises. No rent or utilities are borne by the tenant insofar as all plants, shrubs, and supplies are purchased from the garden center. One section of the store contains arts and crafts supplies, as well as holiday decorating products. The center has been under the same husband/wife ownership for nine years. Due to the owners' age and physical health, the purpose for valuation is business sale.

Up to this point I have not covered my secondary reasons for including ratio analysis in business valuation assignments. You've heard me talk often about supply and demand issues. Short supply, when there is high demand, raises prices and vice versa. It has been long said that good small companies are hard to find and buy. Those in the market for small businesses can guess, if they don't already know, that there are far too many buyers chasing too few good deals. In my companion book on buying and selling small companies, I show estimates that only one out of five businesses on the market actually sell. Ratio analysis can tip us off to the *positioning* enjoyed by target assignments. If, for example, the target fits into the top 25% of comparable firms, then we might secure greater yield from actual sale. On the other hand, exacerbating conditions may compress the target's yield from sale. As value processors, we can never afford to lose sight of those conditions predicting marketability. Since cash rules quite often in business sales, high cash flows being thrown off can serve to offset some undesirable aspects of a business's marketability. Thus, strong ratio evidence can enhance the selling scene and value estimate. On the other hand, weak ratios can tip the value processor into a mood of cautious estimating.

Retail Garden Center
Balance Sheets

	1998	1999	2000	2001
Assets				
Current				
Cash	$ 11,198	$ 12,418	$ 13,288	$ 25,205
Accounts Rec.	3,510	4,323	4,868	11,468
Inventory	185,640	175,865	168,493	163,370
Total Current	$200,348	$192,606	$186,649	$200,043
Fixed				
Land	$ 65,525	$ 65,525	$ 65,525	$ 65,525
Buildings	174,195	174,195	174,195	174,195
Vehicles	13,498	34,748	50,080	50,080
Equip./Fixtures	22,083	22,083	24,293	31,270
Less: Depreciation	− 40,268	− 59,020	− 93,795	− 117,290
Total Fixed	$235,033	$237,531	$220,298	$203,780
Other				
Goodwill	$ 7,500	$ 7,500	$ 7,500	$ 7,500
Deposits	250	250	250	250
Total Other	$ 7,750	$ 7,750	$ 7,750	$ 7,750
TOTAL ASSETS	$443,131	$437,887	$414,697	$411,573
Liabilities				
Current Liab.				
Notes	$ 26,250	$ 9,740	$ 14,740	$ 9,400
Acc. Payable	17,473	12,088	18,120	19,370
Taxes Payable	4,395	3,668	1,380	1,023
Mortgages	11,520	12,780	13,525	14,695
Total Current Liab.	$ 59,638	$ 38,276	$ 47,765	$ 44,488
Long Term				
Notes	—	$ 11,510	$ 13,905	$ 693
Mortgages	207,215	194,358	181,678	165,135
Total Long Term	$207,215	$205,868	$195,583	$165,828
TOTAL LIABILITIES	266,853	244,144	243,348	210,316
Equity	$176,278	$193,743	$171,349	$201,257
TOTAL LIABILITIES & EQUITY	$443,131	$437,887	$414,697	$411,573

Retail Garden Center
Reconstructed Income Statements

	1998	1999	2000	2001
Sales	$424,933	$417,173	$465,070	$553,700
Cost of Sales	226,968	235,900	259,543	296,135
Gross Profit	$197,965	$181,273	$205,527	$257,565
% Gross Profit	46.6%	43.5%	44.2%	46.5%
Coop Royalties	1,250	2,750	3,375	3,700
Recast GP	$199,215	$184,023	$208,902	$261,265
Expenses				
Wages	$ 66,720	$ 52,378	$ 46,680	$ 60,855
Taxes—Emp.	7,898	6,593	5,933	8,553
Supplies	2,200	2,750	3,868	3,030
Office Exp.	1,440	713	7,428	1,890
Vehicle Exp.	5,730	5,503	1,278	5,453
Insurance	4,853	6,970	7,930	5,058
Dues & Subs.	1,090	988	868	938
Utilities	5,648	6,928	5,218	4,553
Telephone	3,255	3,240	4,225	4,823
Repair/Maint.	1,850	2,223	2,140	2,798
Prof. Fees	2,548	2,053	7,290	6,418
Advertising	9,793	4,733	6,345	4,018
Freight	4,060	2,000	2,105	1,473
Miscellaneous	1,370	590	328	73
Total Expenses	$118,455	$ 97,662	$101,636	$109,933
Recast Income	$ 80,760	$ 86,361	$107,266	$151,332
Recast Income as a Percent of Sales	19.0%	20.7%	23.1%	27.3%

Balance Sheet Reconstructed to Show Fair Market Value of Assets Being Offered for Sale

Assets	2001
Current	
Inventory	$163,370
Total Current	$163,370
Fixed	
Land	$ 75,000
Buildings	245,000
Vehicles	21,250
Equip./Fixtures	23,770
Total Fixed	$365,020
TOTAL ASSETS	$528,390

Financial Analysis

One key point on this business's *non*reconstructed balance sheet might bother the average value processor a bit: the disproportionate amount of payables to receivables. Classic accounting texts tell us that a ratio of one to one is reasonably healthy, and of course, higher receivables than payables suggest greater liquidity. Let's think about the nature of the garden center business for a moment. Retail purchasers, since these products are not "basic necessities," will tend to pay in cash or charge to a credit card what they buy. Bad debt tends to be low, because retail purchasers who may be at risk tend not to extend themselves buying these products. Receivables are most often limited to landscape contractors, and these contractors, more often than not, will seek wholesale distributors rather than retail garden centers as sources of supply. Subsequently, low receivables in relationship to payables are not uncommon for businesses such as this.

Growth of equity in our target business has been limited to principal paydown on mortgages and notes. These owners elected to "zero" their bottom lines each year through salaries paid to owners; thus, no retained earnings . . . and no increase of equity provided by business cash flows. While I personally prefer to allow small amounts of "trickle-down" earnings, if for no other reasons than for possible refinancing or for securing working capital loans, these owners felt no need to worry about bank expectations.

Ratio Study

$$\textbf{Ratio for Gross Margin} \quad = \quad \frac{\text{Gross Profit}}{\text{Sales}} \quad \text{or}$$

1998	1999	2000	2001	Industry Median
46.6	43.5	44.2	46.5	39.8

This ratio measures the percentage of sales dollars left after cost of goods sold is deducted. Higher than the industry median, this garden center enjoys a good yield due to the bonsai segment. The owners employ two "specialists" who grow and cultivate these small trees. These skills can be learned by a new owner, if so choosing, and local market conditions indicate reasonable ease of finding employee replacements if required.

Once again it should be noted that ratios for net profit, before and after taxes, can be most useful ratios. But the fact that private owners frequently manage their businesses to "minimize" bottom lines will often produce little meaningful information from these ratios applied to smaller businesses. Therefore, these ratios are not included.

The current ratio provides a rough indication of a company's ability to service its obligations due within the time frame of one year. Progressively higher ratios signify increasing ability to service short-term obligations. Bear in mind that liquidity in a specific business is critically an element of asset composition. Thus, the acid test ratio that follows is perhaps a better indicator of liquidity overall.

$$\text{Current Ratio} \ = \ \frac{\text{Total Current Assets}}{\text{Total Current Liabilities}} \quad \text{or}$$

1998	1999	2000	2001	Industry Median
3.4	5.0	3.9	4.5	1.3

The quick, or acid test, ratio is a refinement of the current ratio and more thoroughly measures liquid assets of cash and accounts receivable in the sense of ability to pay off current obligations. Higher ratios indicate greater liquidity as a general rule.

$$\text{Quick Ratio} \ = \ \frac{\text{Cash and Equivalents} \ + \ \text{Receivables}}{\text{Total Current Liabilities}} \quad \text{or}$$

1998	1999	2000	2001	Industry Median
.2	.4	.4	.8	.3

A ratio less than 1.0 can suggest a struggle to stay current with obligations. The median suggests that the industry as a whole may wrestle with liquidity problems, and the top 25% of reported companies reflect a ratio of only .9. Thus we might conclude that this garden center has moved close to the upper quartile from an industry perspective.

$$\text{Sales/Receivable Ratio} \ = \ \frac{\overset{\text{(Income Statement)}}{\text{Sales}}}{\underset{\text{(Balance Sheet)}}{\text{Receivables}}} \quad \text{or}$$

1998	1999	2000	2001	Industry Median
121.1	96.5	95.5	48.3	54.7–209.3

This is an important ratio and measures the number of times that receivables turn over during the year. It symbolically represents my preceding comments wherein garden centers tend largely to generate cash sales. Although our target company seems to have slipped a bit in 2001, this could be no more than a quirk, since other years have been relatively stable. However, it points to questioning why receivables more than doubled in 2001.

$$\text{Days Receivable Ratio} \ = \ \frac{365}{\text{Sales/Receivable Ratio}} \quad \text{or}$$

1998	1999	2000	2001	Industry Median
3.0	3.8	3.8	7.6	6.7–1.7 days

This highlights the average time in terms of days that receivables are outstanding. Generally, the longer that receivables are outstanding, the greater the chance that they may not be collectible. Slow-turnover accounts merit individual examination for conditions of cause. In our case example, four years show regularity in collections, and a sharp peak occurs in 2001. Much of the problem rests in two larger "jobs" where there was joint agreement for 90-day terms.

$$\text{Cost of Sales/Payable Ratio} \ = \ \frac{\text{Cost of Sales}}{\text{Payables}} \quad \text{or}$$

1998	1999	2000	2001	Industry Median
13.0	19.5	14.3	15.3	24.7

Generally, the higher the turnover rate, the shorter the time between purchase and payment. Lower turnover, which our target company experiences, indicates that it may frequently pay bills from daily in-store cash receipts due to slower receivable collections. This practice may be somewhat misguided in light of investment principles, whereby one normally attempts to match collections relatively close to payments so that more business income can be directed into the pockets of owners. Some businesses may, however, have little choice. Our company owner admits to being lax at pursuing collections but claims never to have suffered bad debt as a result.

$$\text{Sales/Working Capital Ratio} \ = \ \frac{\text{Sales}}{\text{Working Capital}} \ \text{or}$$

1998	1999	2000	2001	Industry Median
3.0	2.7	3.4	3.6	15.2

Note: Current assets minus liabilities equals working capital.

A low ratio may indicate an inefficient use of working capital, whereas a very high ratio often signals a vulnerable position for creditors.

To analyze how well inventory is being managed, the cost of sales to inventory ratio can identify important potential shortsightedness.

$$\text{Cost of Sales/Inventory Ratio} \ = \ \frac{\text{Cost of Sales}}{\text{Inventory}} \ \text{or}$$

1998	1999	2000	2001	Industry Median
1.2	1.3	1.5	1.8	4.9

A higher inventory turnover can signify a more liquid position and/or better skills at marketing, whereas a lower turnover of inventory may indicate shortages of merchandise for sale, overstocking, or obsolescence. Our case example, while improving, falls into the lower quadrant and suggests inventory may be quite heavily overstocked or contain large amounts of distressed or unsalable merchandise.

Conclusions

This case presents a fairly stable operation with one possible exception caused by what appears to be excessive inventory. Close examination of inventory revealed two important facts. Six years ago, two acres were planted with seedling ornamental shrubs of their highest turnover category. These are harvestable in two years, and a rotational grow/sell plan has been developed. The present owner believes that this move curtails increasing problems with supply and will increase gross profits if the practice is continued. Inventory, therefore, has been accepted at current levels for the purpose of business valuation.

THE VALUATION EXERCISE

Book Value Method

Total Assets at Year-End 2001	$411,573
Total Liabilities	210,316
Book Value at Year-End 2001	$201,257

Adjusted Book Value Method

Assets	Balance Sheet Cost	Fair Market Value
Cash	$ 25,205	$ 25,205
Acct./Rec.	11,468	11,468
Inventory	163,370	163,370
Land	65,525	75,000*
Buildings	174,195	245,000*
Vehicles	50,080	21,250*
Equip./Fixtures	31,270	23,770*
Other	7,750	7,750
Accumulated Deprec.	− 117,290	
Total Assets	$ 411,573	$ 572,813
Total Liabilities	$ 210,316	$ 210,316
Business Book Value	$ 201,257	
Adjusted Book Value at 2001		$ 362,497

*See reconstructed balance sheet.

Hybrid Method

(This is a form of the capitalization method.)

    1 = High amount of dollars in assets and low-risk business venture

    2 = Medium amount of dollars in assets and medium-risk business venture

    3 = Low amount of dollars in assets and high-risk business venture

	1	2	3
Yield on Risk-Free Investments Such as Government Bonds[a] (Often 6%–9%)	8.0%	8.0%	8.0%
Risk Premium on Nonmanagerial Investments[a] (corporate bonds, utility stocks)	4.5%	4.5%	4.5%
Risk Premium on Personal Management[a]	7.5%	14.5%	22.5%
Capitalization Rate	*20.0%*	*27.0%*	*35.0%*
Earnings Multipliers	5	3.7	2.9

[a]These rates are revised periodically to reflect changing economies. They can be composed through the assistance of expert investment advisers if need be.

This particular version of a hybrid method tends to place 40% of business value in book values.

Weighted Cash Streams

Prior to completing this and the excess earnings method, we must reconcile how we are going to treat earnings so that we have a "single" stream of cash to use for reconstructed net income. I prefer the following technique:

	(a)	Assigned Weight	Weighted Product
1998	$ 80,760	(1)	$ 80,760
1999	86,361	(2)	172,722
2000	107,266	(3)	321,798
2001	151,332	(4)	605,328
Totals		(10)	$1,180,608
		Divided by:	10
Weighted Average Income Reconstructed			$ 118,061

This presents a classic example of where weighting schemes may miss their target. This garden center's free cash flow has progressed nicely, with sales jumping up by 19.1% in 2001. The free cash stream grew by 41.1% that year. Mathematicians may not agree with my following simple logic, but it works for me every time. If nothing more, it gives tangible recognition for unusually good performance, all of which is verified in previous years. However, valuators should always assure themselves that there is reasonable likelihood for future repeat performances and that an exceptional year is not a quirk occurrence.

2001 Sales	$553,700	(1)	$ 553,700
2001 Income	$151,332	(2)	302,664
Totals		(3)	$ 856,364
		Divided by:	3
Weighted Sales/Income Factor			$ 285,455

What we now need to decide is the "power" of the sales/income factor in the weighted cash stream. Again, not from the books of mathematicians, but working well: Sales grew by 19.1%, and income by 41.1%, thus, divide 41.1% by 19.1% and we get 2.2%—rounded, a factor of (2). We can now complete our weighting process.

	(a)	Assigned Weight	Weighted Product
1998	$ 80,760	(1)	$ 80,760
1999	86,361	(2)	172,722
2000	107,266	(3)	321,798
2001	151,332	(4)	605,328
Factor	$285,455	(2)	570,910
Totals		(12)	$1,751,518
		Divided by:	12

Weighted Average Income Reconstructed		$ 145,960
Book Value Year-End 2001	$201,257	
Add: Appreciation in Assets	161,240	
Book Value as Adjusted	$362,497	
Weight to Adjusted Book Value	40%	$144,999
Weighted Average Income	$145,960	
Times Multiplier	×3.7	$540,052
Total Business Value		$685,051

Excess Earnings Method

(This method considers cash flow and values in hard assets, estimates intangible values, and superimposes tax considerations and financing structures to prove the most-likely equation.)

Reconstructed Cash Flow	$145,960
Less: Comparable Salary	− 45,000
Less: Contingency Reserve	− 7,000
Net Cash Stream to Be Valued	$ 93,960
Cost of Money	
Market Value of Tangible Assets	
(what's being offered for sale)	$528,390
Times: Applied Lending Rate	×10%
Annual Cost of Money	$ 52,839
Excess of Cost of Earnings	
Return Net Cash Stream to Be Valued	$ 93,960
Less: Annual Cost of Money	− 52,839
Excess of Cost of Earnings	$ 41,121
Intangible Business Value	
Excess of Cost of Earnings	$ 41,121
Times: Intangible Net Multiplier Assigned	×5.0*
Intangible Business Value	$205,605
Add: Tangible Asset Value	528,390
TOTAL BUSINESS VALUE (Prior to Proof)	$733,995
	(Say $735,000)
Financing Rationale	
Total Investment	$735,000
Less: Down Payment (approximately 25%)	− 185,000
Balance to Be Financed	$550,000

*See Figure 9.1 in Chapter 9 for net muliplier.

Once again we must draw assumptions (best to specifically check out with local bankers) prior to completing our assessments. The following represents preliminary quotes from a commercial bank in the locale of our target company.

Land & Building ($320,000) at 70% of Appraised Value	$224,000
Equipment ($23,770) at 70% of Appraised Value	$ 16,639
Inventory ($163,370) at 50% of Book Value	81,685
Estimated Bank Financing	$322,324*
	(Say $325,000)

*Inventory contains approximately $40,000 of shrubs and plants in the "growing" stage that are possibly not harvestable for about two years. This business is located in a northern zone where seasonally unsold plants and shrubs must be planted or maintained through winter months. Subsequently, winter kill could be high as viewed by the bank.

Bank (10% × 15 years)
Amount	$325,000
Annual Principal/Interest Payment	37,636

Testing Estimated Business Value
Return: Net Cash Stream to Be Valued	$ 93,960
Less: Annual Bank Debt Service (P&I)	− 37,636
Pretax Cash Flow	$ 56,324
Add: Principal Reduction	6,100*
Pretax Equity Income	$ 62,424
Less: Est. Dep. & Amortization (Let's Assume)	− 18,313
Less: Estimated Income Taxes (Let's Assume)	− 10,137
Net Operating Income (NOI)	$ 33,974

*Debt service includes an average $6,100 annual principal payment that is traditionally recorded on the balance sheet as a reduction in debt owed. This feature recognizes that the "owned equity" in the business increases by this average amount each year.

Return on Equity (ROE):

$$\frac{\text{Pretax Equity Income}}{\text{Down Payment}} = \frac{\$ 62,425}{\$185,000} = 33.7\%$$

Return on Total Investment (ROI):

$$\frac{\text{Net Operating Income}}{\text{Total Investment}} = \frac{\$ 33,974}{\$735,000} = 4.6\%$$

Although return on total investment is abysmally low in relationship to conventionally expected investment returns, the return on equity is attractively high and cash flow is strong. As mentioned so often along the way, I do not believe that small-company buyers pay all that much heed to ROI . . . it's King Cash that leads the way.

Buyer's Potential Cash Flow Benefit
Basic Salary	$ 45,000
Net Operating Income	33,975
Gain of Principal	6,100
Tax Sheltered Income (Dep.)	18,313
Effective Income	$103,388*

*There is also the matter of $7,000 annually into the contingency and replacement reserve that would be at the discretion of the owner if not required for emergencies or asset replacements.

On the one hand, we have estimated business value; on the other hand, we may not have hit our target estimation. A $185,000 cash down payment plus $325,000 bank financing, or $510,000, leaves us with a $225,000 shortfall yet to be financed. If we leave the price at $735,000, either the buyer has to make up the difference outside this business or the seller must become flexible toward providing $225,000 of seller financing, or find another buyer with more cash, or the estimated price must be "squeezed" to fit the conditions of this buyer. How then might we resolve the discrepancy?

1. We know that we are $225,000 short of financing.
2. We know that we have an income stream of $97,288 ($103,388 minus noncash equity buildup $6,100). A decent stream in light of cash outlay at purchase.
3. We know that most sellers are anxious to receive cash as quickly as possible.
4. Assuming that a salary of $45,000 is typical to equivalent work being done by other managers in this field, then we can also assume that we have wiggle room to retrofit additional financing into the equation (but we must still leave room for down payment investment returns of some sort).

In attempting to solve for this question, we return to the point in the equation for Financing Rationale.

Financing Rationale	
Total Investment	$ 735,000
Less: Down Payment (25%)	− 185,000
Balance to Be Financed	$ 550,000
Bank (10% × 15 years)	
Amount	$ 325,000
Annual Principal/Interest Payment	37,636
Seller (8% × 5 years)	
Amount	$225,000
Annual Principal/Interest Payment	54,746
Total Annual Principal/Interest Payment	$ 92,382
Testing Estimated Business Value	
Return: Net Cash Stream to Be Valued	$ 93,960
Less: Annual Bank Debt Service (P&I)	− 92,382
Pretax Cash Flow	$ 1,578
Add: Principal Reduction	$ 10,031
Pretax Equity Income	$ 11,609
Less: Est. Dep. & Amortization (Let's Assume)	− 18,313
Less: Estimated Income Taxes (Let's Assume)	−0−
Net Operating Income/Loss (NOI)	*$ −6,704*

A bit "tight" you say? You're right . . . it is too tight to sell to a buyer of this garden center. Bear in mind that we did just this in a previous example, but that case had much higher cash flow and personal earnings to a potential buyer. I use a rule-of-thumb earnings (as full cash proceeds) to a buyer predicting a return of down payment in about three years. Thus, in this example, $185,000 divided by three equals approximately $62,000 between estimated salary and business returns. This will not always be the case, of course, but it is a reasonable expectation. So, let's try the "financing" and "testing" portions again.

Financing Rationale	
Total Investment	$ 735,000
Less: Down Payment (25%)	− 185,000
Balance to Be Financed	$ 550,000
Bank (10% × 15 years)	
Amount	$ 325,000
Annual Principal/Interest Payment	37,636
Seller (8% × 10 years)	
Amount	$ 225,000
Annual Principal/Interest Payment	32,758
Total Annual Principal/Interest Payment	$ 70,394
Testing Estimated Business Value	
Return: Net Cash Stream to Be Valued	$ 93,960
Less: Annual Bank Debt Service (P&I)	− 70,394
Pretax Cash Flow	$ 23,566
Add: Principal Reduction	21,063*
Pretax Equity Income	$ 44,629
Less: Est. Dep. & Amortization (Let's Assume)	− 18,313
Less: Estimated Income Taxes (Let's Assume)	− 1,875*
Net Operating Income (NOI)	$ 24,441

*Debt service includes an average $21,063 annual principal payment (increases from $10,031 with addition of seller financing) that is traditionally recorded on the balance sheet as a reduction in debt owed. This feature recognizes that the "owned equity" in the business increases by this average amount each year. Tax obligations are reduced since interest expense is deductible from business cash flow.

Return on Equity:

$$\frac{\text{Pretax Equity Income}}{\text{Down Payment}} = \frac{\$\,44,630}{\$185,000} = 24.1\%$$

Return on Total Investment:

$$\frac{\text{Net Operating Income}}{\text{Total Investment}} = \frac{\$\,24,441}{\$735,000} = 3.3\%$$

Note that return on equity drops considerably under our new scenario but is still in the range of good return on the $185,000 down payment. Let's now look at how the buyer might view this posture.

Buyer's Potential Cash Benefit

Forecast Annual Salary	$ 45,000
Pretax Cash Flow (contingency not considered)	23,567
Income Sheltered by Depreciation	18,313
Less: Provision for Taxes	−1,875
Discretionary Cash	$ 85,005
Add: Equity Buildup	21,063
Discretionary and Nondiscretionary Cash	$106,068

Although the business's cash flow would be quite leveraged ($70,394 P & I) during the first 10 years, the buyer would have earned slightly less than the seller was earning at the time of his exit. Some folks disagree with this belief, but in my opinion, another "test" of estimating value is a *finished equation* that predicts cash outflows roughly equal to what a seller had been capable of earning in the year of transition.

Seller's Potential Cash Benefit

Cash Down Payment	$185,000
Bank Financing Receipts	325,000
Gross Cash at Closing	$510,000*

*From which must be deducted capital gains and other taxes. Structured appropriately, the deal qualifies as an "installment" sale with the proceeds in seller financing put off regarding taxes until later periods.

Projected Cash to Seller By End of Tenth Year

Gross Cash at Closing	$510,000
Add: Projected Annual Principal/Interest Payments	327,580
Pretax Ten-Year Proceeds	$837,580

If our garden center owner wishes to obtain maximum yield on price, then the seller financing must be considered. Chapter 10, "Practicing with an Excess Earnings Method," demonstrates how one can experiment with alternative modules that provide wiggle room for seller negotiations with buyers. Decreasing bank and seller debt in our example leaves room for the possibility of refinancing both notes at about year seven-and-one-half. But a five-year balloon payment on seller debt would be impractical, since restructure in five years would be unlikely to cover all debt. An all-cash at closing scenario would forecast price compression near to the value of hard assets.

Forget the Scientist, This Is What Counts Method

Offering Price	$ 735,000
Less: Down Payment	– 185,000
Less: Bank Financing	– 550,000
"Uncovered" Debt	–0–
Cash Flow (commonly used last completed year, assuming that conditions of the business warrant such)	$ 151,332
Less: Principal/Interest	– 70,394
Cash Flow Free of Debt	$ 80,938

Return on Equity: $80,938 minus salary $45,000 equals $35,938, divided by $185,000 equals 19.4%.

Business Is Fairly Priced If:

1. Asking price is not greater than 150% of net worth (except where reconstructed profits are 40% of asking price).
   a. Net worth $528,390 times 150% equals $792,585.
   b. Reconstructed profits $151,332 divided by asking price $735,000 equals 20.6%.
2. At least 10% sales growth per year being realized.
   a. Three growth periods in the four years equal 30% or about 10% per year average.
3. Down payment is approximately the amount of one year's reconstructed profits.
   a. $185,000 minus $151,332 or $33,668 (22.2%) more.
4. Terms of payment of balance of purchase price (including interest) should not exceed 40% of annual reconstructed profit.
   a. Debt service $70,394 divided by $151,332 equals 46.5%.

What does all this mean for estimated value? It means that the price of the deal in the eyes of buyers, if they have read from a multitude of publications whence this information was gleaned, could be viewed as just about right. Subsequently, we might estimate *most-likely* value to be

$735,000. Considering that garden centers or nurseries sit on the higher end of the desirability scale for all buyers in general, we might also recommend that a seller offer the business in the market at $750,000 to start.

Results

Book Value Method	$ 201,257
Adjusted Book Value Method	362,497
Hybrid (capitalization) Method	685,055
Excess Earnings Method	735,000
Forget the Scientist Method	735,000

As you might note, this is the first time in our examples that the forget the scientist and excess earnings methods show the same results. Assuming that forget the scientist models general buyer practice, then this fact might suggest an early sale of this garden center. To some it might also suggest that we have underpriced the business . . . but that's not really true. As a general rule, any time that down payment requirements exceed $100,000 there is a great tendency in buyers to seek cash flows of substance and, usually, above average personal earnings capacities. As we approach the $200,000 down payment mark, we begin to tap buyers of a more sophisticated category. Garden centers and nurseries, while they do enjoy good buyer appeal, largely fit into the category of "lifestyle" enterprises. Thus, growth of revenues can be quite slow under even the best of circumstances. Buyers of these and similar businesses are inclined to negotiate much harder to achieve "day-one" cash flows because they recognize that the growth of personal earnings is likely to be slow in coming.

For many reasons, the issue of forecasting practical levels for growth must be fully understood by value processors. Sellers quite normally get caught up in "dream" rates of growth (and they shouldn't unless previous actions show that they have done it themselves), and buyers quite normally are doubt-ridden about seller's predictions; therefore, value estimating that tips too far one way or the other tends to unleash "no-interest/no-sale" results. Pricing for lifestyle businesses will tend to fall into the "where is, as is" model.

18

Grocery Store

Once in a great while, value processors will run up against sellers who refuse to provide balance sheet information. Perhaps their malingering fear is rooted in historical purchase prices they paid and, subsequently, they worry that prospective buyers will use these data to their disadvantage at the time of negotiations. I have a bone to pick with this reluctance or refusal on the part of sellers. Yes, what one originally paid for something being sold today has no bearing on its present value. However, history tells the best story about present values. Outstanding performances recorded from the past can become a major selling point to the benefit of sellers. Inabilities to complete a range of ratio studies in support of hard-asset values serve only to weaken the sellers' overall case. At some point in the negotiation process, it is likely they are going to be required to disclose this information to buyers or their accountants . . . so why not up front? Withholding, in my opinion, smacks of impropriety and leaves me suspicious as heck. What do you think it does for buyers?

BRIEF CASE HISTORY

The owner purchased this business approximately 25 years ago. Sales were less than $100,000 and the store occupied about one-third the present-day selling space of 3,700 square feet. The U.S. Postal Service leases an attached storefront with 10 years remaining on the lease. The building was completely renovated in 2000 and has been appraised at $270,000. Fixtures and equipment have been appraised at $54,000, and inventory taken three weeks prior to valuation was set at $58,500. Wages include $18,500 for a shift supervisor that might be filled by a purchaser's grown son or daughter if desired. The position is necessary due to 18-hour operating days, and therefore, not removed from expenses.

The store is located in a mixed residential/light industrial area. Five small manufacturing plants are within reasonable walking distance and afford the owner a 60% windfall gross profit on approximately $158,000 of sales from the store's no-table-service luncheonette. The closest "superstore" grocer lies 22 miles away, and the semirural setting makes it unlikely that a larger competitor will locate closer to his facility. Retirement and sale of the store are the owner's stated purpose for valuation.

What's Being Sold in the Way of Hard Assets

Assets	Fair Market Value
Inventory	$ 58,500
Land	67,500
Buildings	202,500
Equip./Fixtures	54,000
Total	$382,500

Grocery Store
Reconstructed Income Statements for Valuation

	1998	1999	2000	Estimate 2001
Sales	$1,078,854	$1,075,653	$1,088,408	$1,077,524
Cost of Sales	790,578	756,609	728,785	711,166
Gross Profit	$ 288,276	$ 319,044	$ 359,623	$ 366,358
% Gross Profit	26.7%	29.7%	33.0%	34.0%
Expenses				
Wages & Tax	$ 101,993	$ 113,540	$ 123,972	$ 130,022
Advertising	3,111	4,003	1,126	1,142
Vehicle Exp.	2,505	2,016	1,512	1,512
Insurance—Gen.	14,294	8,114	8,824	8,640
Insurance—Emp.		5,807	2,337	2,340
Prof. Fees	2,606	1,883	2,526	2,520
Office Exp.	50	68	413	414
Repairs/Maint.	8,609	11,880	11,364	8,820
Supplies	10,006	11,470	7,837	7,920
Taxes	3,600	3,655	3,579	3,600
Utilities	21,691	21,196	23,668	22,500

	1998	1999	2000	Estimate 2001
Rubbish/Snow	2,187	1,580	1,380	1,350
Cleaning	5,895	6,449	8,336	7,830
Bookkeeping	323	430	1,202	1,260
Miscellaneous	1,661	1,791	1,526	1,593
Total Expenses	$ 178,531	$ 193,882	$ 199,602	$ 201,463
Recast Income	$ 109,745	$ 125,162	$ 160,021	$ 164,895
% Recast Income	10.2%	11.6%	14.7%	15.3%
Other				
Rental Income	$ 5,580	$ 2,610	$ 3,735	$ 5,400
Pur./Div. Income	5,225	5,363	5,313	5,310
Total Other	$ 10,805	$ 7,973	$ 9,048	$ 10,710
Free Cash Flow	$ 120,550	$ 133,135	$ 169,069	$ 175,605

FINANCIAL ANALYSIS

Without exception, expenses appear well under control. Sales, however, are flat nearly to the penny during the past three years. One can immediately note the beneficial effect of the luncheonette on cost of goods sold and gross profit. Overall, however, the picture is that store sales have peaked . . . supported entirely by the owner's *own* estimate for the balance of 2001.

Ratio Study

Since the seller's balance sheet was withheld, we are unable to complete balance sheet comparative ratios. However, we can still do a couple.

$$\textbf{Ratio for Gross Margin} \quad = \quad \frac{\text{Gross Profit}}{\text{Sales}} \quad \text{or}$$

1998	1999	2000	Industry Median
26.7	29.7	33.0	28.7

This ratio measures the percentage of sales dollars left after cost of goods sold are deducted. Slightly higher than the industry median, this small grocery store shows the results of opportunity management.

Ratios for net profit, before and after taxes, can be the most useful ratios; however, private owners frequently manage their businesses to "minimize" bottom lines and this often produces little meaningful information from these ratios applied to smaller businesses. Therefore, these ratios are not included.

To analyze how well inventory is being managed, the cost of sales to inventory ratio can identify important potential shortsightedness at this time.

$$\text{Cost of Sales/Inventory Ratio} = \frac{\text{Cost of Sales}}{\text{Inventory}} \text{ or}$$

Per Current Inventory and 2001 Cost of Sales	Industry Median
12.5	11.9

A higher inventory turnover can signify a more liquid position and/or better skills at marketing, whereas a lower turnover of inventory may indicate shortages of merchandise for sale, overstocking, or obsolescence. In our case, the higher turnover is a positive note.

Unfortunately, due to the lack of balance sheets, further ratio study on historical performance is limited. But we can use ratios to examine the purchasing structure of a new buyer. These will be included near the end of our valuation exercise.

Overview

This case presents a fairly stable operation, but one that seems to have reached its pinnacle in sales. Past operations appear to be efficient, but there could be a future concern to buyers—"how much more can be squeezed out of operations?" From the looks of the data, this business may not be able to meet even cost-of-living growth. A trap could be waiting for unwary buyers who only casually observe the surface of these income statements. Recast income has grown nicely during the three years, but can it continue? Subsequently, from a buyer's perspective, one should be asking if the business is worth today's cash flow value. Thus, this business might be a candidate for discounted cash flow methods, *calculated in reverse!*

THE VALUATION EXERCISE

Hybrid Method

(This is a form of the capitalization method.)

1 = High amount of dollars in assets and low-risk business venture

2 = Medium amount of dollars in assets and medium-risk business venture

3 = Low amount of dollars in assets and high-risk business venture

	1	2	3
Yield on Risk-Free Investments Such as Government Bonds[a] (Often 6%–9%)	8.0%	8.0%	8.0%
Risk Premium on Nonmanagerial Investments[a] (corporate bonds, utility stocks)	4.5%	4.5%	4.5%
Risk Premium on Personal Management[a]	7.5%	14.5%	22.5%
Capitalization Rate	*20.0%*	*27.0%*	*35.0%*
Earnings Multipliers	**5**	**3.7**	**2.9**

[a]These rates are revised periodically to reflect changing economies. They can be composed through the assistance of expert investment advisers if need be.

This particular version of a hybrid method tends to place 40% of business value in book values.

Weighted Cash Streams

Prior to completing this and the excess earnings method, we must reconcile how we are going to treat earnings to ensure we have a "single" stream of cash to use for reconstructed net income. I prefer the weighted average technique as follows:

	(a)	Assigned Weight	Weighted Product
1998	$120,550	(1)	$ 120,550
1999	133,135	(2)	266,270
2000	169,069	(3)	507,207
Totals		(6)	$ 894,027
Divided by:			6
Weighted Average Income Reconstructed			$ 149,004

Why haven't I included the estimated 2001 year, you ask? That's a fair question, since we've done that in past chapters. However, flat sales and diminishing prospects for greater returns demonstrate that we should be cautious in estimating value. Future value of today's returns may in fact grow less and less. There's no assurance that 2000 can be repeated, and with sales being forecast at about $11,000 less for 2001, there is no proof that 2001 will yield at the forecast. Look hard at sales, cost of sales, and bottom lines year by year. As a value observer, I find concerns that operations have been "squeezed" to the limits either for the purpose of planned future sale, or through management efficiency that is "causing" the sale at this time. In either event, there seems to be no wiggle room for growth, and there is supporting evidence forecasting diminishing returns; thus, to select some cash-flow number between 1999 and 2000 seems quite appropriate.

Book Value as Adjusted	$382,500	
Weight to Adjusted Book Value	40%	$ 153,000
Weighted Average Income	$149,004	
Times Multiplier	×3.7	$ 551,315
Total Business Value		$ 704,315

Excess Earnings Method

(This method considers cash flow and values in hard assets, estimates intangible values, and superimposes tax considerations and financing structures to prove the most-likely equation.)

Reconstructed Cash Flow	$ 149,004
Less: Comparable Salary	− 45,000
Less: Contingency Reserve	− 10,000
Net Cash Stream to Be Valued	$ 94,004
Cost of Money	
Market Value of Tangible Assets	
(what's being offered for sale)	$ 382,500
Times: Applied Lending Rate	×10%
Annual Cost of Money	$ 38,250
Excess of Cost of Earnings	
Return Net Cash Stream to Be Valued	$ 94,004
Less: Annual Cost of Money	− 38,250
Excess of Cost of Earnings	$ 55,754

Intangible Business Value	
Excess of Cost of Earnings	$ 55,754
Times: Intangible Net Multiplier Assigned	×4.5*
Intangible Business Value	$ 250,893
Add: Tangible Asset Value	382,500
TOTAL BUSINESS VALUE (Prior to Proof)	$ 633,393
	(Say $635,000)
Financing Rationale	
Total Investment	$ 635,000
Less: Down Payment (Approximately 25%)	− 150,000
Balance to Be Financed	$ 485,000

*See Figure 9.1 in Chapter 9 for net multipliers.

Once again we must draw assumptions (best to specifically check out with local bankers) prior to completing our assessments. The following represents preliminary quotes from a commercial bank in the locale of our target company.

Land and Building ($270,000) at 70% of Appraised Value	$189,000
Equipment ($54,000) at 70% of Appraised Value	$ 37,800
Inventory ($58,500) at 50% of Book Value	29,250
Estimated Bank Financing	$256,050*
	(Say $256,000)

*Inventory contains largely perishable products. Spoilage and/or wastage can run quite high in retail grocery stores. While asset-based lending may be available to wholesale distributors who often enjoy "guaranteed" return policies from their suppliers, retail merchants, with a few exceptions, are stuck with inventory purchased in marketable condition. Some banks in the northeast will not go as high as lending 50%.

Bank (10% x 20 years)	
Amount	$256,000
Annual Principal/Interest Payment	− 29,645
Testing Estimated Business Value	
Return: Net Cash Stream to Be Valued	$ 94,004
Less: Annual Bank Debt Service (P&I)	− 29,645
Pretax Cash Flow	$ 64,359
Add: Principal Reduction	4,950*
Pretax Equity Income	$ 69,309
Less: Est. Dep. & Amortization (Let's Assume)	− 14,464
Less: Estimated Income Taxes (Let's Assume)	− 9,246
Net Operating Income (NOI)	$ 45,599

*Debt service includes an average $4,950 annual principal payment that is traditionally recorded on the balance sheet as a reduction in debt owed. This feature recognizes that the "owned equity" in the business increases by this average amount each year.

Return on Equity (ROE):

$$\frac{\text{Pretax Equity Income}}{\text{Down Payment}} = \frac{\$\ 69{,}309}{\$150{,}000} = 46.2\%$$

Return on Total Investment (ROI):

$$\frac{\text{Net Operating Income}}{\text{Total Investment}} = \frac{\$\ 45{,}599}{\$635{,}000} = 7.2\%$$

At this point, we must categorically recognize that grocery stores are labor intensive and can therefore be unattractive to most white-collar buyers. However, in these times of corporate downsizing, both white- and blue-collar candidates could be prospective buyers, since purchasing a "job" might be the only alternative their outplacement now offers. Returns on equity and total investment may not be at issue, since finding replacement work is more of a concern. The purchase of a grocery store, however, will not usually be the white-collar's early or first choice, and when they do move in this direction, return on down payment (equity) will be the "hook" that causes them to do so; return on equity will normally need to be strong.

Basic Salary	$ 45,000
Net Operating Income	45,599
Gain of Principal	4,950
Tax-Sheltered Income (Dep.)	14,464
Effective Income	$110,013*

*There is also the matter of $10,000 annually into the contingency and replacement reserve that would be at the discretion of the owner if not required for emergencies or asset replacements.

You will notice that in all of my examples we seem to be "short" on the financing end in each case. I'm not coming up with this arbitrarily. Only rare cases in the 1,000-plus closely held valuation assignments I've completed met conditions that eliminated a need for some form of seller participation in debt financing. Public companies have stock infrastructures to help make up the differences, but the smaller company usually has only the seller to close the "loop," or the seller must find another buyer with more cash, or they must squeeze the estimated price to fit the conditions of buyers. As mentioned often in my companion buying and selling book, 70% or more of small business deals go down with sellers carrying paper. Those where they don't are generally so small that we're only talking peanuts as the difference, and something flighty is usually worked out on the side. In our case grocery store, we are short $229,000 ($635,000 − $256,000 − $150,000).

In attempting to solve for this shortage, we return to the point in the equation for Financing Rationale.

Financing Rationale

Total Investment	$ 635,000
Less: Down Payment (approximately 25%)	− 150,000
Balance to Be Financed	$ 485,000
Bank (10% × 20 years)	
Amount	$ 256,000
Annual Principal/Interest Payment	29,645
Seller (8% × 10 years)	
Amount	$ 229,000
Annual Principal/Interest Payment	33,341
Total Annual Principal/Interest Payment	$ 62,986
Testing Estimated Business Value	
Return: Net Cash Stream to Be Valued	$ 94,004
Less: Annual Bank Debt Service (P&I)	− 62,986
Pretax Cash Flow	$ 31,018
Add: Principal Reduction	22,217
Pretax Equity Income	$ 53,235
Less: Est. Dep. & Amortization (Let's Assume)	− 14,464
Less: Estimated Income Taxes (Let's Assume)	− 2,484
Net Operating Income (NOI)	$ 36,287

Why 8% spread over 10 years? This business is a "labor-intensive" grocery store and as such, cash flow after debt service will normally be required to attract buyers from all walks of life. Labor-intense businesses are not attractive to the more affluent buyer (and one with $150,000 for down payment certainly fits into this mold) unless a *strong* return on that down payment (equity) is provided to overcome what might be loss of a lifestyle previously accorded. Therefore, we can't expect to stretch the financing "rubber band" anywhere near as tight as, say, for a manufacturing or wholesale distribution firm. Let's now see how the new scenario translates in light of a potential buyer.

Return on Equity:

$$\frac{\text{Pretax Equity Income}}{\text{Down Payment}} = \frac{\$ 53,235}{\$150,000} = 35.5\%$$

Return on Total Investment:

$$\frac{\text{Net Operating Income}}{\text{Total Investment}} = \frac{\$ 36,287}{\$635,000} = 5.7\%$$

Buyer's Potential Cash Benefit	
Forecast Annual Salary	$ 45,000
Pretax Cash Flow (contingency not considered)	31,018
Income Sheltered by Depreciation	14,464
Less: Provision for Taxes	− 2,484
Discretionary Cash	$ 87,998
Add: Equity Buildup	22,217
Discretionary and Nondiscretionary Cash	$110,215

Although the business's cash flow would be increasingly leveraged ($62,986 P & I), in the minds of most folks who might consider a grocery store as a business purchase, the available discretionary cash flow and business's stability seem to offset what anxiety could exist.

Seller's Potential Cash Benefit	
Cash Down Payment	$150,000
Bank Financing Receipts	256,000
Gross Cash at Closing	$406,000*

*From which must be deducted capital gains and other taxes. Structured appropriately, the deal qualifies as an "installment" sale, with the proceeds in seller financing put off regarding taxes until later periods.

Projected Cash to Seller by End of 10th Year	
Gross Cash at Closing	$406,000
Projected Annual Principal and Interest	
Payment After 10 Years	333,408
Pretax 10-Year Proceeds	$739,408

Forget the Scientist, This Is What Counts Method

Offering Price	$ 635,000
Less: Down Payment	− 150,000
Less: Financing	− 485,000
"Uncovered" Debt	−0−
Cash Flow (commonly used last completed year, assuming that conditions of the business warrant such)	$ 169,069
Less: Principal/Interest	− 62,986
Cash Flow Free of Debt	$ 106,083

Return on Equity: $106,083 minus salary $45,000 equals $61,083, divided by $150,000 equals 40.7%.

Business Is Fairly Priced If:

1. Asking price is not greater than 150% of net worth (except where reconstructed profits are 40% of asking price).

   a. Net worth $382,500 times 150% equals $573,750.

   b. Reconstructed profits $169,069 divided by asking price $635,000 equals 26.6%.

2. At least 10% sales growth per year being realized.

   a. Flat sales exacerbated by flat forecast.

3. Down payment is approximately the amount of one year's reconstructed profits.

   a. $150,000 minus $169,069 or −$19,069 (11.3%) less. This is an attractive feature in the sale of this type of business.

4. Terms of payment of balance of purchase price (including interest) should not exceed 40% of annual reconstructed profit.

   a. Debt service $62,986 divided by $169,069 equals 37.3%. This is a noticeable requirement by buyers, and of course, quite often a requirement when banks participate in the financing.

All considered, $635,000 appears to be a quite good value when viewed through the eyes of potential buyers. In fact, assuming that the down payment does not exceed $150,000, a prospective buyer might be encouraged to pay as high as $670,000 for this business . . . assuming that forget the scientist approaches were used.

Results

Hybrid (capitalization) Method	$ 704,315
Excess Earnings Method	$ 635,000
Forget the Scientist Method	$635,000–670,000

In the early part of this book, I said that business valuation is not a precise science . . . and it's not. It is a useful benchmark by which owners can gauge their own thoughts with regard to the values contained by their businesses. Our case owner chose to list the business at $675,000 and sold it for $650,000. He had no debt on any element of his property, the buyer made a down payment of $100,000, and the seller elected to finance the remainder over 20 years, with a 10-year balloon. Those of you with pocket calculators can figure out that principal and interest payments on

$550,000 of debt at 8% interest comes to $55,205 per year . . . or $7,781 less debt-service outflow per year than the $62,986 "blend" shown above.

I suggested earlier that we could apply a few more ratios to a buyer scenario, in light of industry medians. We will use the pro forma balance sheet that the buyer offered in his business plan and the estimated income column for 2001.

Balance Sheet

ASSETS
Current
Cash	$ 15,000
Accounts Receivable	–0–
Inventory	58,500
Total Current	$ 73,500

Fixed
Land	$ 67,500
Buildings	202,500
Equipment/Fixtures	54,000
Total Fixed	$324,000

Other
Noncompete Agreement	$ 50,000
Goodwill	$217,500
Total Other	$267,500

TOTAL ASSETS	$665,000

LIABILITIES
Current
Current Portion Debt	$ 11,625
Accounts Payable	–0–
Total Current	$ 11,625

Long Term
Mortgages Payable	$538,375
Equity	$115,000
TOTAL LIABILITIES AND EQUITY	$665,000

The following is an abbreviation of the previous estimated 2001 income statement. I have amended it so that we may compare owner compensation and profit ratios.

Sales	$1,077,524
Cost of Sales	711,166
Gross Profit	366,358

Reconstructed Expenses	$ 201,463
Add: Other Income	10,710
Recast Income with Other	$ 175,605
Less: Owner Salary	− 45,000
Less: Depreciation	− 14,464
Less: Interest Expense	− 43,580
Net Income Before Taxes	$ 72,561

Ratio Study

The current ratio provides a rough indication of a company's ability to service its obligations due within the time frame of one year. Progressively higher ratios signify increasing ability to service short-term obligations. Bear in mind that liquidity in a specific business is critically an element of asset composition. Thus the acid test ratio that follows is perhaps a better indicator of liquidity overall.

$$\textbf{Current Ratio} \; = \; \frac{\text{Total Current Assets}}{\text{Total Current Liabilities}} \quad \text{or}$$

	Industry
2001	Median
6.3	2.4–5.5

The quick, or acid test, ratio is a refinement of the current ratio and more thoroughly measures liquid assets of cash and accounts receivable in the sense of ability to pay off current obligations. Higher ratios indicate greater liquidity as a general rule.

$$\textbf{Quick Ratio} \; = \; \frac{\text{Cash and Equivalents} + \text{Receivables}}{\text{Total Current Liabilities}} \quad \text{or}$$

	Industry
2001	Median
1.3	.8–1.5

Less than a ratio of 1.0 can suggest a struggle to stay current with obligations. The median offers that the industry as a whole may wrestle somewhat with liquidity problems by the nature of doing business; however, the top 25% of reported companies reflect a ratio of 1.5. Thus we might conclude that this grocery store starts out close to the upper quartile from an industry perspective.

$$\text{Sales/Working Capital Ratio} \ = \ \frac{\text{Sales}}{\text{Total Working Capital}^1} \quad \text{or}$$

2001	Industry Median
17.4	16.3–9.5

[1]Current assets minus current liabilities equals working capital.

A low ratio may indicate an inefficient use of working capital, whereas a very high ratio often signals a vulnerable position for creditors. Our case starts out slightly above the industry median.

At this point, we can add three more for comparison.

$$\text{EBIT/Interest Ratio} \ = \ \frac{\text{Earnings Before Int./Taxes}}{\text{Annual Interest Expense}} \quad \text{or}$$

2001	Industry Median
2.7	3.4–6.1

This ratio measures a business's ability to meet interest payments. A low ratio indicates that a borrower may have difficulty in meeting interest obligations.

$$\text{Debt to Worth Ratio} \ = \ \frac{\text{Total Liabilities}}{\text{Tangible Net Worth (Equity)}} \quad \text{or}$$

2001	Industry Median
4.8	1.4–.5

High ratios indicate high risk being assumed by creditors (in this case, the seller). A low ratio suggests that a business has more flexibility in future borrowing.

Now for the fun of it, let's try a discounted method to see what we come up with. Bear in mind that there is no evidence for growth. In fact, there should even be a question about using the 3.5% cost of living adjustment that we will use.

Discounted Cash Flow of Future Earnings (The theory is that the value of a business depends on the future benefits [earnings] it will provide to owners. Traditionally, earnings are forecast from a historical performance base into some number of future years [usually 5 to 10 years] and then discounted back to the present using present value tables.)

In our grocery business both sales and earnings may well have peaked. This leaves us with the prospect that "present" dollars will lose ground as we move into future years. Let's use just four years. For the sake of argument, we'll use the completed 2001 year as suggested in the buyer's ratio study above and use increases at no more than cost of living differentials of 3.5%.

Base	Forecast Earnings			
Year	1	2	3	4
$72,561	$75,101	$77,730	$80,451	$83,267

Establishing Expected Rate of Return (The rate expected as a return on invested capital) For the loss of liquidity and venture rate of returns in the range up to 25%, let's assume 20% as a level of return on risk associated with small-business ownership. We'll also assume the earnings plateau in the fifth year at $85,000.

Value of Grocery Business

$$\text{Forecast Year 1} \quad \frac{\$75,101}{(1 + .20)} \quad = \quad \$\ 62,584*$$

$$\text{Forecast Year 2} \quad \frac{\$77,730}{(1 + .20)^2} \quad = \quad \$\ 53,979*$$

$$\text{Forecast Year 3} \quad \frac{\$80,451}{(1 + .20)^3} \quad = \quad \$\ 46,557*$$

$$\text{Forecast Year 4} \quad \frac{\$83,267}{(1 + .20)^4} \quad = \quad \$\ 40,156*$$

$$\textbf{Plus} \quad \frac{(\$85,000 \text{ divided by } .20)}{(1 + .20)^4} \quad = \quad \$204,958*$$

Total Business Value $408,234*

*Future earnings discounted to present value.

On the basis of the discounting method, we might choose to negotiate the purchase of our grocery store business for a price of $408,234 or less.

SUMMARY

In this chapter I have attempted to provide a range of formulas applied to a business that enjoys quite a residual value but may not portend any substantial future growth. There are many small businesses in America such as this one. They may not provide investments for the adventuresome, but they do afford "catch basins" to many caught up in the downsizing likely to continue. This grocery business appears relatively safe from invasion by the "bigs" due to its particular location. However, growth, if any comes, will be through the innovation *and expense* of its new owner. I've included the discounted method not for any real practical use but mostly to show what can happen to investments made now without any real assurances for future growth. We all have been experiencing an erosion of our dollars in recent years. Although this business provides a good job for someone without great alternatives, the price paid for that job in terms of today's dollars could become quite high longer term. Casual observance of the bottom lines of the income statements by the unwary leads one to garner a sense of growth. However, the flatness of sales for three years, plus slim forecasts, should dispel any such sense and might well be painting the picture of a typical business that one should not overpay for in terms of price and terms at purchase. With dust settling on the information provided in this chapter, one can wonder if retirement was the sole reason this owner wished to sell.

> *"The art of life is to know how to enjoy a little and to endure much."*
>
> William Hazlitt

19

Manufacturer with Mail-Order Sales

This case adds a "twist" of mail-order distribution to the various complexities outlined in our earlier manufacturing valuation example. Methods of product distribution must be thoroughly understood before one undertakes financial statement reconstruction and enters the valuation task. More traditional forms of a manufacturer's primary distribution tend to be either the employment of direct sales forces or the use of independent manufacturing representatives, or a combination of both. In the first situation, "compensation" shows up on income statements as either direct salary or through blends of both salary and commissions. The second condition reflects commission only as a general rule.

On the other hand, mail-order distribution presents unique expense characteristics that make forecasting inordinately difficult. To understand why, we must specifically address features of this form of selling. Perhaps we pay little attention to this process when we, and we all do, receive catalogs from a wide variety of mail-order houses. Do you have any idea what these catalog production and mailing expenses might be per distribution? The expense for full-color catalogs from L. L. Bean and Sharper Image, for example, would make you shudder and question how these sorts of companies can make any money at all. Granted, when catalogs are produced in very large quantities, the price per issue is held down. But what about the cost of small-run production for the "little" guy? Most of us are aware of the "price-break points" we obtain when we need simpler printing jobs done. In the production of catalogs we must add the expense of folding and binding that might also enjoy quantity discounts.

Through another dimension, we must deal with shipping and postage expense. Both of these costs can be enhanced or exacerbated by factors of "weight." Thus, the cost of design, layout, and printing must be considered fully in light of "delivery" expense, and these costs balanced in relationship to projected consumer purchases.

That's not all, folks, because there is the very real (but quite hidden) cost when a catalog mailed does not produce greater than breakeven sales. According to national direct-mail marketing statistics, mail-order houses can count on little more than 2% to 5% returns from the total mailing list used. Some, such as the example in Chapter 14, "Seventy Cents on the Dollar," do a little better. To increase the odds of greater returns, these houses "clean" their customer lists frequently and spend considerable sums focused on catalog design and content. Many have policies of dropping potential customers when a "name" does not buy at least once or twice per year. It is costly to manage these customer lists. Smaller houses may engage "list-management" businesses to perform these cleaning tasks. Expense for list management is quite regularly subsidized through "renting" the lists to other mail-order businesses, *regularly including the names of customers who have not made purchases.* At the consumer end, this translates into a mounting plethora of unsolicited junk mail. Sometimes list rentals will entirely subsidize management fees, and sometimes not. The value of any list to its owner depends on the "quality" or number of frequent buyers. The value to a renter depends a great deal on the degree of "comparable" buyers in a list. Since each list owner attempts to whittle and model (make unique) a mailing list to his or her specific products and/or services, the process of others gleaning productive names for themselves from this list can be hit or miss. It is also costly in terms of the "experimentation" necessary to reduce the purchased list to the few more names added to the renter's base.

The variableness in catalog production and customer delivery makes sales and expense forecasting for mail-order businesses quite difficult, to say the least. One other irregularity must be highlighted as well. Shipping of actual products to the consumer can add to operating expense. Although most catalog distributors pass this freight expense along to the consumer on the basis of "average" weight/cost, without conducting frequent audit, these costs can get out of hand as well.

Forecasting in mail-order businesses, and subsequent management, presents a need to fully understand all of its stratified complexities of marketing. As was noted in Chapter 14, the mailing list itself requires substantial attention to hold down the cost of producing sales and to "massage" a company into greater revenues. As noted in our manufacturing example, the manufacturing process alone requires special treatments to stay in control of the game. When manufacturing and mail-order distribution are combined, we find the essence of very complex businesses.

I'm not saying that they can't be profitable, because many succeed; however, they tend to be inordinately labor-intense due to their many facets in production and marketing. In this age of technology, I can't think of a better example where computer numerical controllers (CNCs) and computer-assisted management can be more directly and cost effectively applied in a small business.

BRIEF CASE HISTORY

Our assignment is to provide an estimate of value for the business's "predictable" sale. The owner describes his business and personal financial conditions as not as good as he would like.

The company is housed in a large factory building containing first-floor production space and a sail-making loft. In addition to high-quality mainsails, headsails, and spinnakers, the company manufactures six items of boat hardware and two lines of winches. The business has been in operation for nearly 60 years and has had three owners in the past 8. Products are offered to the public through direct mail; however, the company dedicates a small front section to a retail factory outlet that is opened for two months in the spring of each year. The company enjoys an excellent after-market reputation for its products.

This company is, once again, my client; thus, for a number of reasons, I have elected to restate financial information, using a computer routine that downsizes its much larger operation. Data, however, are presented in the actual relationship as they appear in the company's statements. Subsequently, conclusions also reflect these smaller proportions and model results found in the larger company.

Boat Products Mail-Order Manufacturer
Balance Sheets

	1990	1991	1992
Assets			
Current Assets			
Cash	$ 6,647	$ 3,350	$– 7,708
Acct./Receivable	82,366	87,552	33,237
Inventory	546,675	591,651	508,528
Prepaid Exp.	17,077	11,886	11,397
Total Current Assets	$652,765	$694,439	$545,454

	1990	1991	1992
Property and Equip.			
Equipment	$170,092	$170,092	$170,092
Vehicles	28,202	28,202	28,202
Boats	168,236	155,941	138,279
Less: Accum Dep.	− 214,697	− 224,689	− 234,681
Total Property and Equip.	$151,833	$129,546	$101,892
Other			
Deposits	$ 2,659	$ 1,813	$ 2,303
Trademarks	2,940	2,940	2,940
Total Other	5,599	4,753	5,243
TOTAL ASSETS	$810,197	$828,738	$652,589
Liabilities & Equity			
Current			
Acct./Payable	$ 89,567	$109,711	$ 75,691
Notes, Current Port.	4,467	4,004	5,076
Mortgage, Current	12,511	13,481	12,698
Customer Deposits	40,901	37,322	43,718
Accrued Exp.	32,393	25,393	26,895
Total Current	$179,839	$189,911	$164,078
Long-Term Debt			
Notes	$ 43,498	$ 39,031	$ 49,482
Mortgages	461,863	449,353	384,642
Total Long-Term Debt	$505,361	$488,384	$434,124
Total Liabilities	$685,200	$678,295	$598,202
Total Stockholder Equity	$124,997	$150,443	$ 54,387
TOTAL LIABILITIES & EQUITY	$810,197	$828,738	$652,589

Boat Products Mail-Order Manufacturer
Reconstructed Income Statements for Valuation

	1990	1991	1992
Sales	$1,008,007	$1,304,903	$1,162,376
Cost of Sales	508,060	672,075	492,996
Gross Profit	$ 499,947	$ 632,828	$ 669,380
% Gross Profit	49.6%	48.5%	57.6%
Expenses			
Wages	$ 103,615	$ 174,162	$ 135,940
Payroll Tax	27,695	37,382	36,456
Adv. Catalog	48,387	69,433	76,720
Bank Charges	10,223	15,146	16,150

(continued)

	1990	1991	1992
Dues & Subs.	1,054	1,394	—
Freight-Out	17,959	23,666	22,759
Insurance	33,701	41,193	39,488
Prof. Fees	3,821	6,610	6,256
Office Exp.	7,839	5,565	7,089
Miscellaneous	10,333	2,645	13,618
Postage	3,341	4,950	5,854
Rent	47,926	22,246	39,396
Repair/Maint.	16,509	22,144	17,624
Sales Exp./Post.	19,118	25,655	26,914
Telephone	27,821	40,417	32,601
Travel/Show Exp.	36,359	26,045	36,035
Utilities	9,775	6,714	7,424
Total Expenses	$ 425,476	$ 525,367	$ 520,324
Recast Income	$ 74,471	$ 107,461	$ 149,056
Recast Income as a Percent of Sales	7.4%	8.2%	12.8%

Financial Analysis

This company offers a plethora of interesting dilemmas to resolve. I draw your attention to the income statements first. Recast income has grown from $74,471 to $149,056 in our "target" year of prospective sale. But I also caution you to observe accompanying balance sheet "confusion." Stockholder equity has decreased during this same period from $124,997 to $54,387. I don't know about you, but I suspect a "fly in the ointment" someplace. It's called pressure on the owner's pocketbook! 1992 cash is *negative,* receivables have decreased in one year by $54,315, and payables by $34,020 for that period. Although cash flow seems nicely increased, I'm quite naturally suspicious about whether "customer deposits" of $43,718 are reserved in liquid form at this point. I am also cognizant that "notes" under liabilities have increased by $11,523 between 1991 and 1992. An earlier concern that 1992 income and expenses might have been stretched or shrunk in preparation for business sale was alleviated through examination of the checkbook and other business records. I'm confident that the financially astute will find other concerning issues in these statements. However, for the purposes of our mission—the process of valuation—this allusion to financial analysis will suffice.

Ratio Study

I do not believe that this small company is uniquely alone in its classification, but I am unable to find an "industry resource" for comparison to both boat product manufacturer and mail-order selling. Another issue that complicates analysis further, and as happens in many small businesses, is that this company commingled its operations and financial record keeping such that it is impossible to sort various criteria into "pots" for appropriate comparison. This does not, however, mean that ratio study will not help better understand year-to-year performances.

$$\text{Ratio for Gross Margin} = \frac{\text{Gross Profit}}{\text{Sales}} \quad \text{or}$$

1990	1991	1992
49.6	48.5	57.6

This ratio measures the percentage of sales dollars left after the cost of manufactured goods is deducted. Significant swings in the cost of goods sold are unusual without significant events. The upward yield for 1992 was the result of a switch during the later part of 1991, to two new sources of supply for material and findings in sail manufacture. Though it is still too early to tell, no apparent sacrifice in quality is evidenced at the consumer level thus far.

$$\text{Sales/Receivable Ratio} = \frac{\text{(Income Statement)} \; \text{Sales}}{\text{Receivables (Balance Sheet)}} \quad \text{or}$$

1990	1991	1992
12.2	14.9	35.0

This is an important ratio and measures the number of times that receivables turn over during the year. Our target company significantly turned these over in 1992, suggesting they might be pressing hard for customers to pay bills. Combined with negative cash at the end of 1992, one becomes even more suspicious of what appears to be increasing financial struggle.

$$\text{Day's Receivable Ratio} = \frac{365}{\text{Sales/Receivable Ratio}} \quad \text{or}$$

1990	1991	1992
30	24	10

This highlights the average time in days that receivables are outstanding. Generally, the longer that receivables are outstanding, the greater the chance that they may not be collectible. Taken alone, this dramatic reduction in collection time seems positive, but it's the dramatic reduction over a relatively short period that should cause some alarm. Few consumers take kindly to being "muscled" and in an era of 30-day credit terms, the shrinking to 10 days might suggest undue pressure—and, ultimately, the potential for reduced sales.

$$\text{Cost of Sales/Payables Ratio} = \frac{\text{Cost of Sales}}{\text{Payables}} \quad \text{or}$$

1990	1991	1992
5.7	6.1	6.5

Generally, the higher their turnover rate, the shorter the time between purchase and payment. Increasingly higher turnover supports the likelihood that increasing pressure is being exerted on suppliers due to the company's cash shortages, but it also suggests that the owner is paying attention to debt owed with the cash generated.

$$\text{Sales/Working Capital Ratio} = \frac{\text{Sales}}{\text{Working Capital}} \quad \text{or}$$

1990	1991	1992
2.1	2.6	3.0

Note: Current assets less current liabilities equals working capital.

A low ratio may indicate an inefficient use of working capital, whereas a very high ratio often signals a vulnerable position for creditors. Our target company has been improving in this department, which might be a surprise to some readers. Although only a subtle indicator, this might be a signal that while the owner is struggling, he appears to be doing some of the right management things with the cash obtained.

To analyze how well inventory is being managed, the cost of sales to inventory ratio can identify important potential shortsightedness.

$$\text{Cost of Sales/Inventory Ratio} = \frac{\text{Cost of Sales}}{\text{Inventory}} \quad \text{or}$$

1990	1991	1992
.9	1.1	1.0

A higher inventory turnover can signify a more liquid position and/or better skills at marketing, whereas a lower turnover of inventory may indicate shortages of merchandise for sale, overstocking, or obsolescence. This company maintains what seems to be near-oppressive levels of inventory. As noted in the following, inventory builds up to a high level and then is largely depleted during a two- to four-month spring and summer period. While this may be a necessary characteristic for boating products in the northeast, it seems that there may be a management opportunity here for improvement.

Conclusions

To fully understand the benefit of examining ratios without industry comparisons, one must call on accumulated practical experience. Therefore, competent financial professionals should be consulted for that advice. However, in the front of the *Annual Statements Studies* conducted by Robert Morris Associates, one can find a brief but easy to understand meaning of the various ratios and their interpretations. One does not need to be a financial genius to recognize some of the problems being experienced by this company. Cash is obviously short and there may be undue pressure being exerted upon customers to pay their bills (obviously, too much might hurt future sales), but there is some indication that present management is directing available resources in an appropriate manner. The balance sheet seems inordinately burdened in light of present-day sales. The income statements, particularly 1992, seem inconsistent with the struggle indicated on the balance sheets. As a professional observer, my first inclination was to be quite suspicious that this owner had "tampered," by overstating sales, or understating expenses, in his IRS Form 1120 return. No formal audits had been conducted. Closer examination of business records indicated several peculiarities to this specific business. Huge lags are experienced between manufacturing and mail-order consumer delivery, thus inventories are being maintained at unusually high levels. Since most sales (boating products) are realized in the northern climate, revenues surge in the spring of the year. Those of us living in these areas can be most appreciative of consumer patterns in the north. We tend not to think about summer activities until the spring thaw . . . and then we expect "instant gratifications" to fill our soon-to-come activity needs. This company can predict permanent cancellations on any order that they cannot immediately fill. Subsequently, manufacturing of products (and inventory) builds up to a crescendo of sales in the spring of the year. Attempts at winter sale through catalog mailings have been costly and have generally failed to produce breakeven results. The balance sheet item for "Boats" includes the complete show regalia for a moment's notice exhibition (the owner admits that he does not plan well in advance for these shows). Show expenses contain losses in each of the three years on the sales (rather than pay transportation back to home base) of a 14- and 16-foot sailing dinghy used for these exhibitions. By the end of 1991, this company had implemented a piecework pay system on all production lines but winches. While all "bugs" are not ironed out, the owner feels that the 25% to 28% reduction in wages has not deterred quality in products. Sail makers seem content with the new pay system; however, the owner is concerned about increasing entry-level employee turnover in other lines. The system designer has returned to examine what might be done to reduce this problem. Apparently it takes about three months to reach earnings-level proficiency from the day of employment. A combination base-pay/piecework-rate arrangement is currently being discussed to accommodate new entrants.

The owner summarizes the major problem in his company as the operations being too seasonal. He has not explored the prospects for partial plant shutdowns or staggered production schedulings; nor has he calculated the alternatives in other forms of marketing. He admits that something must be done differently to survive long term, but he feels that too much of his time is taken up in brushfire management as opposed to examining various alternatives that might increase profits. A whole drawer in a file cabinet in his office is dedicated to the plethora of complimentary letters from satisfied customers. Several long-term employees have expressed interest in owning part of the company, but this owner is concerned that this may not be the answer. He claims his own strengths are highest in managing production, which is also the strength of these potential partners. His assessment suggests that needs lie in the areas of general and marketing management, thus he would entertain selling part of the company to someone possessing these attributes . . . or sell out completely. In the event that such a partner could be located, he feels that a significant cash infusion will be necessary to fund expected changes to operations. He is not opposed to some owner financing under this condition. As a backup scenario, he would consider selling to employees—but only for all cash at closing.

Before proceeding with the valuation task, however, we must ascertain what assets and liabilities will be offered for sale with the business. Including or excluding assets and liabilities should not be arbitrary and should minimally include what is necessary to reproduce past year's sales. What is excluded by sellers can become "added" start-up expense for buyers.

Balance Sheet Reconstructed for Sale Purposes

Assets	1992	Fair Market Value
Current		
Accounts Receivable	$ 33,237	$ 33,237
Inventory	508,528	493,272
Total Current	$541,765	$526,509
Property and Equipment		
Equipment	$170,092	$132,672
Vehicles	28,202	18,050
Boats	138,279	138,279
Less: Depreciation	− 234,681	0
Total Property and Equipment	$101,892	$289,001
TOTAL ASSETS	$643,657	$815,510
Liabilities		
Current		
Accounts Payable	$ 75,691	$ 75,691
Customer Deposits	43,718	43,718
Total Current	$119,409	$119,409
ASSET-BASED EQUITY VALUE	$524,248	$696,101

In taking this step of reconstructing balance sheets to reflect what owners wish to sell, it is important to recognize that "book value" and "adjusted book value" do not represent those sellers' true financial conditions. Instead, we are applying formulas, and extracting results, that can be misleading in terms of the "real" business value and, more important, misleading in how the reconstructed balance sheet might affect *re-creating* the historical picture of sales and expenses concurrently being presented to potential buyers. For example, the act of removing "cash" through reconstruction translates into the need for added working capital by a buyer. In our case, accounts payable exceed accounts receivable by $42,454 and predict an additional depletion of working capital resources as the business continues to function. Though overall asset values might increase in worth through reconstruction, "liquidity" can become severely strained in a process that fails to include working capital requirements. It is not uncommon for sellers of small companies to retain cash and other more liquid business assets at closing. And it is a common failure of buyers to put the required due diligence into assessing their needs for working capital after the closing.

I feel that this minor derailment from our task of valuation was necessary at this particular point. Many formulas tend to ignore this missing and vital link between needed working capital and a business's value.

The Valuation Exercise

Book Value Method (items for sale only)

Total Assets at Year-End December 1992	$643,657
Total Liabilities	119,409
Book Value at Year-End December 1992	$524,248

Adjusted Book Value Method (items for sale only)

Assets	Balance Sheet Cost	Fair Market Value
Acct. Rec.	$ 33,237	$ 33,237
Inventory	508,528	493,272
Equipment	170,092	132,672
Vehicles	28,202	18,050
Boats	138,279	138,279
Less: Depreciation	–234,681	0
Total Assets	$643,657	$815,510
Total Liabilities	$119,409	$119,409
Adjusted Book Value at 12/92 (relative to equity value)	$524,248	$696,101

Hybrid Method

(This is a form of the capitalization method.)

1 = High amount of dollars in assets and low-risk business venture

2 = Medium amount of dollars in assets and medium-risk business venture

3 = Low amount of dollars in assets and high-risk business venture

	1	2	3
Yield on Risk-Free Investments Such as Government Bonds[a] (often 6%–9%)	8.0%	8.0%	8.0%
Risk Premium on Nonmanagerial Investments[a] (corporate bonds, utility stocks)	4.5%	4.5%	4.5%

	1	2	3
Risk Premium on Personal Management[a]	7.5%	14.5%	22.5%
Capitalization Rate	*20.0%*	*27.0%*	*35.0%*
Earnings Multipliers	5	3.7	2.9

[a]These rates are revised periodically to reflect changing economies. They can be composed through the assistance of expert investment advisers if need be. Capitalization rates translate into earnings multipliers by dividing the capitalization rate into 100%.

This particular version of a hybrid method tends to place 40% of business value in book values. Experience in working with this instrument teaches one *not* to be too bold in assigning multipliers. For the convenience of readers, I have a saying in my firm that goes: "Only God gets a multiplier of much in excess of 5—and I've never been asked by him or her." The key to reducing labor hours in the assignment is to be conservative in determining multipliers.

Weighted Cash Streams

Prior to completing this and the excess earnings method, we must reconcile how we are going to treat earnings so that we have a "single" stream of cash to use for reconstructed net income. I prefer the weighted average technique as follows:

	(a)	Assigned Weight	Weighted Product
1990	$ 74,471	(1)	$ 74,471
1991	107,461	(2)	214,922
1992	149,056	(3)	447,168
Totals		(6)	$ 736,561
Divided by:			6
Weighted Average Income Reconstructed			$ 122,760

Eyeballing column (a), one might conclude that the weighted average reconstructed income seems reasonably low, on the surface at least. However, let's bear in mind what our discussion thus far has provided. Nothing in this epilogue suggests anything but conservatism . . . conservatism . . . conservatism. *And at this stage we need to be extra conservative because of the all-cash or high-cash infusion expected by the owner.*

Book Value at 12/92	$524,248
Add: Appreciation in Assets	171,853
Book Value as Adjusted	$696,101

Weight to Adjusted Book Value	40%	$ 278,440
Reconstructed Net Income	$122,760	
Times Multiplier	×3.0	$ 368,280
Total Business Value		$ 646,720

With any truth in this formula, we can immediately notice an impending problem—we are estimating a business value that is $49,381 *under* adjusted book value of hard assets ($696,101 − $646,720 = $49,381 shortfall). In other words, through this estimation we are saying to the owner that his business has *no* intangible value (at least in the view of the Internal Revenue Service's definition, which says that goodwill, or intangible value, is that amount paid in excess of the value of hard assets). But let's go on with our process before drawing any hard-line conclusions.

Excess Earnings Method

(This method considers cash flow and values in hard assets, estimates intangible values, and superimposes tax considerations and financing structures to prove the most-likely equation.)

Reconstructed Cash Flow	$ 122,760
Less: Comparable Salary	− 50,000
Less: Contingency Reserve	− 15,000
Net Cash Stream to Be Valued	$ 57,760
Cost of Money	
Market Value of Tangible Assets	$ 782,273*
Times: Applied Lending Rate	×10%
Annual Cost of Money	$ 78,227

*Equipment, vehicles, boats, and inventory.

Excess of Cost of Earnings	
Return Net Cash Stream to Be Valued	$ 57,760
Less: Annual Cost of Money	− 78,227
Excess of Cost of Earnings	$ − 20,467
Intangible Business Value	
Excess of Cost of Earnings	$ − 20,467
Times: Intangible Net Multiplier Assigned	×3.5
Intangible Business Value	$ − 71,635
Add: Tangible Asset Value	696,101*
TOTAL BUSINESS VALUE (Prior to Proof)	$ 624,466
	(Say $625,000)

*Equipment, vehicles, boats, and inventory plus accounts receivable, minus total current liabilities.

Financing Rationale

Total Investment	$ 625,000
Less: Down Payment (approximately 25%)	− 160,000
Balance to Be Financed	$ 465,000

At this point, because estimated value appears *less* than the fair market value in hard assets, we might be able to finance the balance through a "collateralized" position with traditional financing institutions. My guess is that the following would be a pretty close estimate as to what could be expected to occur at most banks.

Equipment ($132,672) at 70% of Appraised Value	$ 92,870
Vehicles ($18,050) at 30% of Value	5,415
Boats ($138,279) at 70% of Value	96,795
Inventory ($493,272) at 65% of Book Value	320,627
Estimated Bank Financing	$515,707*
	(Say $516,000)

*In effect, the difference of $51,000 might represent security for a working line of credit, which seems quite necessary as changes are made to the operation of this business.

Bank (10% × 15 years)	
Amount	$ 465,000
Annual Principal/Interest Payment	59,963

Line of Credit (10% × 11 months)	
Amount	$ 51,000
Interest Payments Only	4,675
Principal Payment Due Within 11 Months	51,000

Testing Estimated Business Value	
Return: Net Cash Stream to Be Valued	$ 57,760
Less: Annual Bank Debt Service (P&I)	− 59,963
Less: Line Interest	− 4,675
Less: Line Principal	− 51,000
Pretax Cash Flow (Year one only)	$− 57,878
Add: Principal Reduction (First year only)	14,097
Pretax Equity Income/Loss	$− 43,781
Less: Est. Dep. & Amortization (Let's Assume)	− 31,569
Less: Estimated Income Taxes (Let's Assume)	0
Net Operating Income/Loss (NOI)	$ − 75,350

At this stage, calculating rates of returns serves no useful benefit, since our formula is suggesting that only negative returns exist. The preceding discussion provides hints for buying this company, but let's take a look at a prospective purchaser's financial scenario . . . is there financial merit in the short term?

1992 Reconstructed Income	$149,056
Basic Salary	− 50,000
Gain of Principal	14,097
Less: Long-Term Debt Service	− 59,963
Less: Line Interest	− 4,675
Less: Line Princ./Repayment	− 51,000
Effective Income/Loss (Year 1)	$− 2,485*

*There is also the matter of $15,000 annually into the contingency and replacement reserve that would be available at the discretion of the owner if not required for emergencies or asset replacements.

Let's also look at this under an assumption that a purchaser did not need to use the line of credit.

1992 Reconstructed Income	$149,056
Basic Salary	− 50,000
Gain of Principal	14,097
Less: Long-Term Debt Service	− 59,963
Effective Income (Year 1)	$ 53,190

Subsequently, a prospective buyer might have between − $2,485 and + $53,190 in *discretionary cash* depending on use of a line of credit between $0 and $51,000. Assuming the "repeat" of at least 1992 reconstructed income, the worst case use of the line would decrease a purchaser's salary to $47,515 ($50,000 − $2,485). Without further ado, this says that we have reached the pinnacle in our estimation of value. A buyer would be unlikely to pay more than $625,000 for this business. Why would a seller consider the loss on hard assets? Mostly because of psychological pressure to sell (assuming such is the case), but also because of the hard reality that assets put under the "hammer" of auction rarely bring as much as those same assets sold in some form of "going-concern" status.

RULE-OF-THUMB ESTIMATES

Attempting to value and purchase any business experiencing similar conditions as this under the guise of rule-of-thumb methods is an invitation to gross personal disaster. Under no circumstances should one trust final purchase decisions to anything but thorough cash flow analysis. However, rule-of-thumb estimates can form benchmarks for additional study and can be useful supporting data when applying for loans. While I do not believe that such "rules" exist for this type of business, I elected to place this statement here as a reminder to the unwary that rule-of-thumb methods tend to reflect only the "tip of the iceberg." The "treasure," if one is to be found, is below the surface. For example, the income statements in this case could well lead one to accept that this is a "growing" business, while the balance sheets and assets tell quite another story. The existence of treasure in any business is generally hidden from plain sight . . . so are the problems.

Results

Book Value Method	$ 524,248
Adjusted Book Value Method	696,101
Hybrid (capitalization) Method	646,720
Excess Earnings Method	625,000

I mentioned earlier that this company had returned to me as a client in 1995. The owner of record at the time of valuation located a partner during 1993 who provided the strengths he sought. This partner's buy-in represented essentially one-half of an overall price of $625,000. At this time they are increasing use of independent manufacturing representatives to distribute products directly to retail or wholesale outlets throughout the United States. Dependency on retail catalog sales is being examined in relationship to wholesale distribution and changes in profit. Sales are approaching $2 million and did break above this level in 1996. They are not without continuing operational problems, but the scene improves with the few changes they have implemented. Both are enthused with their future, and the partnership appears to fit them both well.

20

Wholesale Distributor

Wholesale distribution businesses represent perhaps the second highest level (next to manufacturing) of broad general purchase-interest to prospective buyers. Operating in self-contained "cocoons" lodged between producers and secondary consumers, these businesses seem to many to afford the best of two worlds. Neither requiring the skills of production nor requiring direct confrontations with consumers, theirs is truly a service challenge based solely in marketing know-how and product transportation ... the people in the middle who move much of America's goods.

For many would-be buyers, these wholesale businesses are particularly attractive because their owners deal mostly with other businesspeople—a pass-on consumer not usually so fastidious as the general public. On the other hand, they are of considerable resource to producers in terms of communicating end user preferences, expediting product movements, and in parlaying the "positioning" of products in marketplaces.

Volume, status, and trend of the wholesaling trade have long been regarded as significant barometers of general business conditions. Yet considerable confusion exists as to the meaning of wholesaling and the distinction between wholesaling and retailing. One clear distinction is commonly found in the wholesaler's usual ability to bypass payment of sales taxes in states where such taxes apply.

Wholesaling is not limited solely to product distribution. A broad conception might well include the marketing of business services to other organizations, who in turn "resell" these services to consumers. Perhaps the word *middleman,* suggesting that "some functional element" exists between producer/provider and the organization through which a consumer "takes title" to goods and services, is best used to describe wholesaling for our purposes.

While this rather academic lead-in can seem unnecessary to some, the less astute might be warned by its inclusion that wholesaling businesses present formative problems that should not be overlooked. For example, a manufacturer produces a product for, let's say, $10.00. The wholesaler "adds" $3.00 for his or her services when sold to the retailer, who in turn adds $13.00 and sells to the final consumer for $26.00. Let's now examine the same pricing structure—but eliminate the middleman. The manufacturer sells *directly* to the retailer for $10.00, whereupon the retailer similarly doubles his or her price and sells the product to the consumer for $20.00—a $6.00 savings at street level for the same product. The *value added* by the wholesaler's service must be justified or the consumer will attempt to "go around" these middlemen. I call this "consumer substitution" or the revenge of the furious consumer who sees no value added by the services of middlemen.

Using this quite simple example, one can easily see the need to research compelling reasons for the "existence" of each wholesale business in the valuation assignment. Bear also in mind that producers and destination resale centers both will be striving to obtain their own maximum profits. Consumers will only pay so much, and it's the wholesaler who traditionally gets worked over in the squeeze play. In this process, it's hard for the wholesaler not only to hold on to stable pricing and profits but also to increase business yields. Downswinging economies tend to make doing business as a wholesaler that much harder. Margins are customarily quite narrow and there's just not a whole lot of wiggle room for error, or the viselike pressures brought on by producers, end sellers, and ultimate users.

The valuation of wholesale businesses must be tightly woven through tailored research, and the value processor must be discouraged from the assertive expectation that "growth" is easily derived.

BRIEF CASE HISTORY

This small 40-year-old wholesaler distributes mostly nonconsumable products. About 20% of business is generated from perishable/consumable lines. Their primary market is retail, industrial, and a number of public facilities. The company is the second largest of its kind, and a full-line supplier within the territory where it currently operates. The company operates a small but growing retail outlet—sales now amount to about 3.9% of total sales. Two new products were added to the general lines during the past three years and are demonstrating higher levels of profit than the other lines. This business has been under the current ownership for 15 years. The operations are housed in leased facilities with 8 years remaining on the base lease. Two 5-year options are provided, at what appear to be attractive future rates. Most products are stored on pallets, and, subsequently, costly storage fixturing is unnecessary.

A creative financing element is found in the company through the "liquidation" feature of its inventory. With the exception of damaged goods, about 95% of inventory *can* be returned for *full credit* to the wholesaler's suppliers. This presents an opportunity for the use of asset-based lending. Explained in general terms, banks with *asset-based lending* departments will be more apt to advance substantial funds against inventory values whenever they can be provided assurances that items in inventory have increased security, such as this ability to be returned to suppliers for full credit. However, not all commercial banks provide asset-based programs, because this form of lending has its own set of risks, not the least of which is the liquidity of the asset itself. In one sense, this could be called "labor-intensive" lending because the asset owner could promptly liquidate as easily as the bank. Thus, asset-based lenders are as much inventory specialists as are the bankers. If inventory is not frequently monitored in the context of loans outstanding, collateral securing the loan could slip away. This assignment involved working for the prospective *purchaser*, rather than the seller. Therefore, an expected outlook on value might be that of the most reasonable (or likely) purchase price for the buyer.

Company growth and development have been determined by the buyer to exist in five major areas: (a) new products, (b) new territories within the state's borders, (c) new territories outside the state, (d) increase profit margins from a 4.6% base, and (e) expansion of retail outlets in key locations where the company does not compete with its retail customers.

The buyer has stated that he feels $845,000 would be a fair price to pay and believes that the seller would accept that amount. A thorough analysis extracted the following information with regard to operations:

	1998	1999	2000	Forecast 2001
Sales	$2,799,926	$3,132,171	$3,501,953	$3,740,000
Cost	2,551,343	2,820,525	3,160,275	3,373,700
Gross Profit	$ 248,583	$ 311,646	$ 341,678	$ 366,300
% G.P.	8.9%	9.9%	9.8%	9.8%
Expenses	$ 133,558	$ 167,208	$ 181,866	$ 194,700
Recast Income	$ 115,025	$ 144,438	$ 159,812	$ 171,600
% R.I.	4.1%	4.6%	4.6%	4.6%

What's Being Offered For Sale

(The levels are determined by audit at time of negotiations or by fair market appraisal in the case of vehicles and furniture and fixtures.)

Accounts Receivable	$288,750
Inventory	330,000
Vehicles	57,500
Furniture/Fixtures	62,500
Total Value of Assets	$738,750

Levels in *Accounts Receivable* vary throughout the year, depending on the seasons. With more than 220 seasonal accounts, the seasonally high figure can often be $300,000 or more. "Aging" has been determined to be within acceptable payment practice. Receivables average about $187,000.

Inventory and Purchasing: Inventory levels also vary according to seasons. Since replenishment stock is mostly acquired with the aid of high-interest lines of credit, it has been this company's practice to purchase "lean" wherever possible. Items necessitating longer lead times for delivery are purchased through the use of operating cash, taking advantage of suppliers' normal terms for payment. Inventory fluctuates between a low of $180,000 to a high of $330,000. The seasonal high runs approximately three to four months' duration but peaks to about $260,000 at two other times of the year. A triple-pallet rotation system is employed to ensure first-in, first-out of goods being delivered to customers. An examination of aged A/R receipts and inventory replenishment, and cash inflows, suggest an approximate $25,000 required for start-up cash. Average inventory runs about $225,000.

For purposes of forecasting, this company has had nearly 10 years of consecutive growth in both sales and earnings. Although undramatic, growth has been steady and is predictable into the future without adding changes anticipated by the buyer. Thus, an "extended" forecast might be fairly included during the process of valuation.

Forecast	2001	2002	2003	2004
Sales	$3,740,000	$4,188,800	$4,730,000	$5,665,000
Cost	3,373,700	3,778,500	4,257,000	5,086,400
Gross Profit	$ 366,300	$ 410,300	$ 473,000	$ 578,600
% G.P.	9.8%	9.8%	10.0%	10.2%
Expenses	$ 194,700	$ 217,800	$ 233,200	$ 282,700

Forecast	2001	2002	2003	2004
Recast Income	$ 171,600	$ 192,500	$ 239,800	$ 295,900
% R.I.	4.6%	4.6%	5.1%	5.2%

I have included more forecast years than my experience using the excess earnings process recommends; however, this case *would appear to* lend itself to a more practical application of the discounted method provided later.

The Valuation Exercise

Hybrid Method

(This is a form of the capitalization method.)

1 = High amount of dollars in assets and low-risk business venture

2 = Medium amount of dollars in assets and medium-risk business venture

3 = Low amount of dollars in assets and high-risk business venture

	1	2	3
Yield on Risk-Free Investments Such as Government Bonds[a] (Often 6%–9%)	8.0%	8.0%	8.0%
Risk Premium on Nonmanagerial Investments[a] (corporate bonds, utility stocks)	4.5%	4.5%	4.5%
Risk Premium on Personal Management[a]	7.5%	14.5%	22.5%
Capitalization Rate	*20.0%*	*27.0%*	*35.0%*
Earnings Multipliers	**5**	**3.7**	**2.9**

[a]These rates are revised periodically to reflect changing economies. They can be composed through the assistance of expert investment advisers if need be.

This particular version of a hybrid method tends to place 40% of business value in book values.

Weighted Cash Streams

Prior to completing this and the excess earnings method, we must reconcile how we are going to treat earnings so that we have a "single" stream of cash to use for reconstructed net income. I prefer the weighted average technique as follows:

	(a)	Assigned Weight	Weighted Product
1998	$115,025	(1)	$ 115,025
1999	144,438	(2)	288,876
2000	159,812	(3)	479,436
2001	171,600	(4)	686,400
2002	192,500	(5)	962,500
Totals		(15)	$2,532,237
Divided by:			15
Weighted Average Income Reconstructed			$ 168,816

Why include forecast 2001 and 2002, you ask? Upon examination of several past years' "budgets," we find that the owner has customarily estimated earnings to within 10% to 12% accuracy. The 2001 forecast reflects this owner's budget for six months remaining in the present year. Working collectively with the buyer, 2002 through 2003 reflect a similar mode of estimating. 2004 earnings are heightened by the purchaser's anticipated improvements to operations.

Value of Assets Being Sold	$738,750	
Weight to Adjusted Book Value	40%	$ 295,500
Weighted Average Income	$168,816	
Times Multiplier	×3.7	$ 624,619
Total Business Value		$ 920,119

Excess Earnings Method

(This method considers cash flow and values in hard assets, estimates intangible values, and superimposes tax considerations and financing structures to prove the most-likely equation.)

Reconstructed Cash Flow	$ 168,816
Less: Comparable Salary	− 50,000
Less: Contingency Reserve	− 25,000*
Net Cash Stream to Be Valued	$ 93,816

*Largely cash for inventory purchase.

At this stage, for purposes of the next calculation, we must separate *average* accounts receivable and inventory from assets. Inventory turns at a rate of 9.6 times per year, and receivables have an average history of payment within 37.2 days. In this regard, they are quite liquid forms of working capital and therefore should be considered "resources" rather than fixed assets. (Total assets = $738,750 − [avg. a/r] $187,000 − [avg. inv.] $225,000 = $326,750). Of course, one could argue that all receivables and inventory are "liquid" and should be removed if we are to follow this logic. This is a reasonable position, but then we would be ignoring the "carrying costs" for average levels that must be maintained at all times. You won't find this approach in standard textbooks ... it's my process and it works for me.

Cost of Money

Market Value of *Less-Liquid* Tangible Assets	
(what's being offered for sale)	$ 326,750
Times: Applied Lending Rate	×10%
Annual Cost of Money	$ 32,675

Excess of Cost of Earnings	
Return Net Cash Stream to Be Valued	$ 93,816
Less: Annual Cost of Money	− 32,675
Excess of Cost of Earnings	$ 61,141

Intangible Business Value	
Excess of Cost of Earnings	$ 61,141
Times: Intangible Net Multiplier Assigned	×2.5*
Intangible Business Value	$ 152,853
Add: Tangible Asset Value	
(including A/R & Inventory)	738,750
TOTAL BUSINESS VALUE (Prior to Proof)	$ 891,603
	(Say $892,000)

*See Figure 9.1 in Chapter 9 for net multipliers.

Financing Rationale

Total Investment	$ 892,000
Less: Down Payment (Approximately 25%)	− 225,000
Balance to Be Financed	$ 667,000

Once again we must draw assumptions (best to specifically check out with local bankers) prior to completing our assessments. The following represents preliminary quotes from a commercial bank in the locale of our target company.

Furn./Fixtures ($62,500) at 50% of Appraised Value	$ 31,250
Vehicles ($57,500) at 30% of Blue Book Value	17,250
Inventory at Average Levels ($225,000)	
Asset-Based Lending (90%)	202,500
Accounts Receivable	–0–*
Estimated Bank Financing	$251,000

*While accounts receivable could provide a large addition to cash by "factoring" and/or used as collateral to secure bank financing, we must bear in mind that this business traditionally has enjoyed no more than 10% gross profits. The cost of debt, with bank rates running near 10%, and/or factoring could wipe out profits from these assets. On the other hand, provided through initial sale, they represent the past owner's profit, rather than future profits of the buyer. However viewed, it seems more practical in the long run that they be used to secure working lines of credit for replenishment of inventories and other short-term capital needs. In this manner, cost of capital can be managed more accurately to minimize dilution of already skinny gross profits.

What made this purchase particularly attractive to the buyer was the seller's objective that most proceeds should provide long-term retirement income. Sales at the time of the seller's purchase 15 years ago were below $600,000, and debt had long since been retired. Thus we have both a vehicle and the motivation to end other than line-of-credit discussions with a bank. The seller would fix his interest rate at 8% for 5 of the 20 years.

Seller (8% × 20 years)	
Amount	$667,000
Annual Principal/Interest Payment	– 66,949
Testing Estimated Business Value	
Return: Net Cash Stream to Be Valued	$ 93,816
Less: Annual Bank Debt Service (P&I)	– 66,949
Pretax Cash Flow	$ 26,867
Add: Principal Reduction	16,305*
Pretax Equity Income	$ 43,172
Less: Est. Dep. & Amortization (Let's Assume)	– 20,430
Less: Estimated Income Taxes (Let's Assume)	– 9,107
Net Operating Income (NOI)	$ 13,635

*Debt service includes an average $16,305 annual principal payment that is traditionally recorded on the balance sheet as a reduction in debt owed. This feature recognizes that the "owned equity" in the business increases by this average amount each year.

Return on Equity (ROE):

$$\frac{\text{Pretax Equity Income}}{\text{Down Payment}} = \frac{\$ 43,172}{\$225,000} = 19.2\%$$

Return on Total Investment (ROI):

$$\frac{\text{Net Operating Income}}{\text{Total Investment}} \quad = \quad \frac{\$ 13,635}{\$892,000} \quad = \quad 1.5\%$$

Although these calculations do reflect much lower returns than conventional wisdom recommends, bear in mind that "distribution" businesses, like manufacturing firms, claim a high percentage of buyer-at-large interests. And on the supply side of the equation, distribution firms are not that plentiful. Taken together, purchase prices being paid for wholesale distribution companies tend to be higher overall. Forgetting returns for a moment (and I'm certain that a large number of small-company buyers do not use "returns" as their final yardsticks of purchase), what might be the picture of cash flow to this buyer?

Basic Salary	$ 50,000
Net Operating Income	13,635
Gain of Principal	16,305
Tax-Sheltered Income (Dep.)	20,430
Effective Income	$100,370*

*There is also the matter of $25,000 annually into the contingency and replacement reserve that would be at the discretion of the owner if not required for emergencies or asset replacements.

One could argue price indefinitely, as some buyers and sellers seem to do. Explained more fully in my book *Self-Defense Finance for Small Businesses,* price/value is as much an issue of *gaining* personal objectives to buyers and sellers as it might otherwise involve financial logic. These more personal features cannot be measured through the use of formulas. Value processors who do not interact with both players miss the boat in terms of assisting them to do deals. Business valuations that check the "temperature" of deals, such as this assignment, should not deny access by the parties to their own negotiations, so long as these discussions lead up to fair agreements. In our case example, the buyer indicated that he could purchase this business for $845,000. This excess earnings method is forecasting up to a price of $892,000. The 5.6% variance is insignificant, and more or less confirmed this buyer's evaluation of what he wished to do.

Buyer's Potential Cash Benefit	
Forecast Annual Salary	$ 50,000
Pretax Cash Flow (contingency not considered)	26,867
Income Sheltered by Depreciation	20,430
Less: Provision for Taxes	− 9,107
Discretionary Cash	$ 88,190

Add: Equity Buildup	16,305
Discretionary and Nondiscretionary Income	$104,495

Seller's Potential Cash Benefit	
Cash Down Payment	$225,000
Gross Cash at Closing	$225,000*

*From which must be deducted capital gains and other taxes. Structured appropriately, the deal qualifies as an "installment" sale with the proceeds in seller financing taxed at lower rates in later periods.

Projected Cash to Seller by End of 20th Year	
Gross Cash at Closing	$ 225,000
Add: Principal and Interest Payments	1,338,974
Pretax 20-Year Proceeds	$1,563,974

ALL WELL AND GOOD

You bet! We're missing something here! Business valuation, as we have learned, is no more than an act of "estimating" fair market values. Considered in this light, the effects of conventional bank lending should always be included in any equation of value, regardless of prospects for seller, and perhaps, lower rates that might substitute institutional funding. In some regards, this could be termed "alternative planning," but specifically it establishes fair market value in terms of significantly more readily available funding—and those *conditions* of funding *always* affect price. It is rare indeed for buyers to locate small businesses and sellers who can, or will, provide the entire "banking" infrastructure. When sellers provide greater flexibility in the nature of lower rates and longer terms, prices being paid for these businesses by buyers can often be higher than when banks provide the funding. Thus, benchmark values that include institutional financing must be recognized, regardless of the parameters offered by specific deals. Once again, we return to the Financing Rationale section of the formula:

Financing Rationale	
Total Investment	$ 892,000
Less: Down Payment (25%)	− 225,000
Balance to Be Financed	$ 667,000
Bank (10% × 15 years minus [hard assets])	
Amount (furn./fixture/vehicle)	$ 48,500
Annual Principal/Interest Payment	7,691
Bank (10% × 5 years [asset-based on inventory])	
Amount	$202,000
Annual Principal/Interest Payment	51,630

Seller (8% × 20 years)

Amount	$416,000
Annual Principal/Interest Payment	41,755
Annual Combined Bank/Seller P&I	*101,076*

Testing Estimated Business Value

Return: Net Cash Stream to Be Valued	$ 93,816
Less: Annual Bank Debt Service (P&I)	− 101,076
Pretax Cash Flow	$ − 7,260
Add: Principal Reduction	54,016*
Pretax Equity Income	$ 46,756
Less: Est. Dep. & Amortization (Let's Assume)	− 20,430
Less: Estimated Income Taxes (Let's Assume)	-0-
Net Operating Income (NOI)	$ 26,326

*Debt service includes an average $54,016 annual principal payment that is traditionally recorded on the balance sheet as a reduction in debt owed. This feature recognizes that the "owned equity" in the business increases by this average amount each year.

Return on Equity (ROE):

$$\frac{\text{Pretax Equity Income}}{\text{Down Payment}} = \frac{\$ 46,756}{\$225,000} = 20.8\%$$

Return on Total Investment (ROI):

$$\frac{\text{Net Operating Income}}{\text{Total Investment}} = \frac{\$ 26,326}{\$892,000} = 3.0\%$$

Hmm ... ROE and ROI are better ... but there's a fly in the ointment, folks!

Basic Salary	$ 50,000
Net Operating Income	26,326
Gain of Principal	54,016
Tax-Sheltered Income (Dep.)	20,430
Effective Income	$150,772

Sound great? The $54,016 principal gain can't be spent paying bills!

Buyer's Potential Cash Benefit

Forecast Annual Salary	$ 50,000
Pretax Cash Flow (Contingency Not Considered)	− 7,260
Income Sheltered By Depreciation	20,430
Less: Provision for Taxes	–0–
Discretionary Cash	$ 63,170

Discretionary cash flow, by this insertion of bank debt, has been disadvantaged by nearly 40% (from the seller-financed structure). It doesn't take a mathematician to guess that the $892,000 value estimate might thus be less also. In Chapter 10, "Practicing with an Excess Earnings Method," we learned of a simple method to "back into" price/value discounting. Here's another twist to using this approach:

P&I Payments Under Bank/Seller Blended Financing	$101,076
P&I Payments Solely Under Seller Structure	66,949
Difference	$ 34,127
Per Month	2,844

View the difference as being made up of $251,000 in bank debt, of which 80.7% is just five years in term.

$$(80.7\%)\,(\$2,844) = \$2,295 \text{ per month at 5 years}$$

$$(19.3\%)\,(\$2,844) = \$549 \text{ per month at 10 years}$$

Using an "Equal Monthly Loan Amortization Payment" table, locate the page containing 10%, and 5 years, and then 10 years. We find that it takes $2.13 per month to amortize $100 dollars over 5 years, and $1.33 to amortize this amount over 10 years.

$2,295 divided by $2.13 (times 100) equals	$107,746
$ 549 divided by $1.33 (times 100) equals	41,278
Disadvantage Value	$149,024

Subsequently, we can generally draw an assumption that the former value estimate needs to be disadvantaged (reduced) by $149,024 (say $150,000), to accommodate purchase value under the combined bank/seller financing package: $892,000 − $150,000 = $742,000, under this scenario. To test this fundamental assumption, we return once again to the Financing Rationale:

Financing Rationale	
Total Anticipated Purchase Price	$ 892,000
Less: Down Payment (Approximately 25%)	− 225,000
Remainder	$ 667,000
Less: Anticipated Price Reduction	− 150,000
Balance to Be Financed	$ 517,000
Combined Annual Bank P&I Payments on $251,000 of Debt	$ 59,321

Buyer's New Annual P&I Payments to Seller
on $266,000, Versus Previous $416,000 Debt $ 26,699
                    ($517,000 − $251,000 = $266,000)

   Total P&I Payments $ 86,020

The scenario that led us to estimate value at $892,000 contained total P&I payments of $66,949. Under the new presumption, combined P&I is $86,020 (versus the previous $101,076). I would normally carry this out through the whole process, but for our purposes, let's go straight to the heart of the matter ... the buyer's discretionary cash flow.

Testing Estimated Business Value	
Return: Net Cash Stream to Be Valued	$ 93,816
Less: Annual Bank Debt Service (P&I)	− 86,020
Pretax Cash Flow	$ 7,796
Add: Principal Reduction	50,094*
Pretax Equity Income	$ 57,890
Less: Est. Dep. & Amortization (Let's Assume)	− 20,430
Less: Estimated Income Taxes (Let's Assume)	− 2,306*
Net Operating Income (NOI)	$ 35,154

*Debt service includes an average $50,094 annual principal payment that is traditionally recorded on the balance sheet as a reduction in debt owed. This feature recognizes that the "owned equity" in the business increases by this average amount each year. Estimated income taxes might increase slightly because of lower interest write-off.

Return on Equity (ROI):

$$\frac{\text{Pretax Equity Income}}{\text{Down Payment}} = \frac{\$ 57,890}{\$225,000} = 25.7\%$$

Return on Total Investment (ROI):

$$\frac{\text{Net Operating Income}}{\text{Total Investment}} = \frac{\$ 35,154}{\$742,000} = 4.7\%$$

Buyer's Potential Cash Benefit	
Forecast Annual Salary	$ 50,000
Pretax Cash Flow (contingency not considered)	7,796
Income Sheltered by Depreciation	$ 20,430
Less: Provision for Taxes	− 2,306
Discretionary Cash	$ 75,920

This, of course, does not set the equation equal to where the seller was solely providing financing infrastructure ... but, then, bank debt rarely models what sellers might provide to get their deals closed. What it does offer, however, is an estimate in terms of "fair purchase value." In this instance, if this seller required bank participation in his deal, the buyer's $845,000 negotiated price should be reduced to an offering price not exceeding $742,000.

I do not believe that valuation formulas should be used as static instruments. For nearly 30 years I have looked for ways to amend, modify, and/or restructure these processes to fit other needs of buyers and sellers. To the best of my knowledge, the amalgamation used herein for "backing into" another estimate of value will not be found in any other text. It took several years to develop a mathematical model that resembles what buyers and sellers actually do in the marketplace. Some may disagree with my approach, but I can assure you that this neat little trick, if you will, has proven quite reliable, time after time, for many years. "What to offer?" is a question most asked by buyers. Try the excess earnings method, and play around with the "back-into" routine outlined here. If you know what you need to earn personally after the purchase, this *whole* process can lead to answers for your question, "What do I offer?"

Discounted Cash Flow of Future Earnings (The theory is that the value of a business depends on the future benefits [earnings] it will provide to owners. Traditionally, earnings are forecast from a historical performance base into some number of future years [usually 5 to 10 years] and then discounted back to present using present value tables.)

In our wholesale case-business, sales and earnings plod ahead slowly but predictably. History reveals that the seller has been accurate in forecasting each year's working budget. Future estimates were completed by purchaser and buyer together, and thus, offer the prospect for levels of reliability in the use of discounted methods.

Base Year	Forecast Earnings			
	1	2	3	4
$159,812	$171,600	$192,500	$239,800	$295,900

Establishing Expected Rate of Return (The rate expected as a return on invested capital) For the loss of liquidity and venture rate of returns in the range up to 25%, let's assume 20% as a level of return on risk associated with small business ownership. We'll also assume the earnings plateau in the fifth year at $312,000.

Value of Wholesale Business

$$\text{Forecast Year 1} \quad \frac{\$171,600}{(1 + .20)} \quad = \quad \$143,000*$$

$$\text{Forecast Year 2} \quad \frac{\$192,500}{(1 + .20)^2} \quad = \quad \$133,681*$$

$$\text{Forecast Year 3} \quad \frac{\$239,800}{(1 + .20)^3} \quad = \quad \$138,773*$$

$$\text{Forecast Year 4} \quad \frac{\$295,900}{(1 + .20)^4} \quad = \quad \$142,699*$$

$$\text{Plus} \quad \frac{(\$312,000 \text{ divided by } .20)}{(1 + .20)^4} \quad = \quad \underline{\$752,315*}$$

Total Business Value $1,310,468*

*Earnings discounted to present value.

I hope you can now see why I am greatly concerned with the use of this so-called model formula in the valuation of small businesses. Unless arbitrarily "fudging" numbers along the way, this method tends nearly always to overvalue the smaller business. Granted, the formula varies from user to user, but this specific case was presented at three graduate business schools where results calculated by students and professors alike turned out similar high results. I know that I'm beating a dead horse once again, but discount methods of valuation are inappropriate in use with the smaller business. Rates of return used would have to be reduced from 20% to about 12% to 13% to simulate the results from other formulas. Lacking experienced judgments, most lay users of discounting methods will commonly overprice businesses.

Results

Hybrid (capitalization) Method	$ 920,119
Excess Earnings Method	
Exclusive Financing by Seller	892,000
Combination Bank/Seller Financing	742,000
Method (?) of the Buyer	845,000
Discounted Method	$1,310,468

The buyer did in fact purchase this business for $845,000, and this presents ample opportunity to show a buyer's beginning balance sheet. The cash down payment was $178,000.

ASSETS	
Current	
Cash	$ 25,000
Accounts Receivable	288,750
Inventory	330,000
Total Current	$643,750
Fixed	
Vehicles	$ 57,500
Furniture/Fixtures	62,500
Total Fixed	$120,000
Other	
Noncompete Agreement	$ 25,000
Transitional Employment	20,000
Trade Name	20,000
Customer List	41,250
Total Other	$106,250
TOTAL ASSETS	$870,000
LIABILITIES	
Current	
Current Portion Debt	$ 14,098
Accounts Payable	–0–
Total Current	$ 14,098
Long Term	
Mortgages Payable	$652,902
Equity	$203,000
TOTAL LIABILITIES & EQUITY	$870,000

I suspect that some are wondering why the "tally" balances to $870,000 and how "equity" stands at $203,000 rather than $178,000. The buyer infused an additional $25,000 into opening balances ($845,000 + $25,000 = $870,000, and $178,000 + $25,000 = $203,000).

This case brings us to the end of my case examples. In the next chapter I provide a working case for your own experimentation. My estimates of the value in this practice session will be found at the end of the book in Appendix A.

21

A Practice Session

A Marina Valuation

One of the most attractive and yet debilitating features for many marinas is their location. Often situated at or in close proximity to recreational bodies of water, the value of real estate most frequently presents a nemesis to what otherwise may be adequate cash flows (bear also in mind that costly real estate commonly translates into costly leases when such exist in lieu of land ownership). Subsequently, a great many sell at or near appraised values of real estate and other hard assets. This often presents a very real problem for sellers who have owned their marinas for shorter spans of time. As we all know, mortgages amortize "principal" debt very slowly in the early years. Thus, equities in properties held change so little in under 10 years.

Another shortcoming is the rather too frequent replacement costs necessary to maintain, especially, in-water assets, such as docks, moorings, and flotation devices. Storms and Mother Nature can and do raise havoc with the life spans of these vital assets. Exacerbating their replacements or expansions are a plethora of environmental regulations that rarely gestate favorable terms for marinas and their owners.

Marinas suffer high product-carrying costs similar to automobile dealerships and retail appliance businesses. Floor-plan financing for in-stock boats and other high-ticket items can run 2% to 4% per month. Most marinas in the United States are seasonal businesses—even in the Sunbelt states. Whereas most recreational products are subjected to the far end of the economic whip, marinas also suffer more during downturns that seem, with increasing frequency, to affect family units to a greater degree. Poor buying decisions leading to excess inventory at the end of seasons serve to dilute profits to what, for many, is already burdening operating costs.

Marinas can be quite profitable in season, but the onus of expensive real estate, asset replacements, and floor-plan carrying costs can frequently drain even a robust seasonal "windfall."

There is something, however, that is uniquely magnetic about marina ownership. The water, boating sports, fishing, the aroma, the outdoor environment itself . . . almost a call of the wild. Few persons, especially men, can pass through a marina without at least garnering thoughts, envisioning themselves as owners of this type of small business. During my years as a business broker, I have sold a half dozen marinas between Maine and Florida. None "went down" easy. Ads placed in the *Wall Street Journal,* to some extent, prove the charisma of these small businesses. After the second or third ad, one of my associates proclaimed, "We will have another week of telephone cauliflower ear." During my years of business brokerage, I never once handled any other small business that generated more ad-calls than marinas.

On the supply side of the equation, marinas "for sale" are quite plentiful throughout the United States. The largest single reason they seem to be for sale is echoed in this sentiment: I can't make a living here! However, many marinas, because of their valuable real estate resources, have been transformed into condominium associations; or their real estate now partially accommodates condominium-living complexes; and/or they have been replaced entirely by different ventures.

Many still do remain solely as marinas. Opportunity found, they are one of the great challenges for prospective buyers. Successful long-term operations frequently languish beyond the nature of the present marina itself. Thus, prospective buyers who are shy in net worth, and/or timid in creativity and risk, might best be advised not to apply.

With supply and demand briefly outlined, marinas that cash-accommodate the values of hard assets and, at the same time, provide minimal wages for new owners tend to sell quickly. Often located on real estate valuable for many other purposes, banks tend willingly to finance considerable portions of their purchase prices.

BRIEF CASE HISTORY

This marina is situated at the outlet of a tributary leading into a 32,000-acre lake in the mid-Atlantic states. The docking and mooring facilities are well sheltered along the riverbank, and the river channel provides easy, navigable access to and from the lake. Nestled on six wooded acres, a 2,000-square-foot modern building houses a retail showroom, service and repair facilities, *living quarters,* and the owner's office. At the riverbank there is adequate land mass for maneuvering of vehicles and some storage. Fuel, oil, and rental equipment are provided at the dock, where the marina offers 68 berthing slips, accommodating boats up to 32 feet. Other assets include two metal-clad cold-storage buildings housing between 150 and 170 boats off season; two pickup trucks, a tractor, forklift, and lowbed tandem trailer; and various showroom display fixtures, furniture, tools, and testing equipment. Part of the unused land overlooking the river might be developed for use as a boat owner's motel or other such commercial development.

While two larger and five smaller marinas compete on this lake, the sheltered location of this facility makes it particularly desirable. Boat slips can normally reach 120% occupancy by double-renting less-used seasonal tenants' slips. The marina rents boats and safety regalia as package leases to five summer youth camps situated on the lake. The bulk of revenues comes from sales of boats, motors, and accessories. Fiberglass boat repair and boat upholstering, including boat tops, are also provided.

Peak seasons extend just slightly over two months, with gradual up- and downswings, measuring about four additional months pre- and postseason. Off-season is generally limited to boat storage and engine repairs. The marina enjoys a wonderful business reputation, and most customers return year after year.

With the exception of floor-planned inventory, real estate and other assets are owned by the business. The company has been under the present tenure for 11 years.

The valuation problem is in two parts: *(a) what value or price should this business be listed for? and (b) what is the most likely sale price? (The owner will NOT provide any seller financing.)*

Following are historical balance sheets and reconstructed income statements. Also listed are assets included in sale (assume these to be stated at fair market or appraised value). If you choose to complete the ratio analysis section, data for the purpose of these calculations should be taken from historical statements. *Industry medians* relate to the last "completed" year of business and are provided herein. My own responses to ratios and the two-part task noted will be found in Appendix A. This is not a test; therefore, feel free to "cheat" open book if you get stuck. Better, and easier, to gain experience with the instruments along the way than to become frustrated and give up. Don't be too hard on yourselves; after 30 years, I'm still learning about valuation. I don't believe that anyone has all the "right" answers, if the so-called right answers do in fact exist. The highlight of this case exercise is . . . *we had a sale,* and you'll find the "punch-line" *price* in Appendix A. You may want to purchase an amortization table or business calculator for use with this exercise. If you're seriously in the market to sell or buy a small business, you'll use these implements quite often as you search for your lasting transaction. Good luck!

Practice Session—Marina
Balance Sheets

	1999	2000	2001
Assets			
Current Assets			
Cash	$ 5,049	$ 2,256	$ 2,307
Acct./Rec.	17,691	12,684	16,026
Inventory	215,814	204,300	212,385
Prepaid Expenses	8,733	6,933	—
Total Current Assets	$247,287	$226,173	$230,718
Fixed			
Land	$ 30,000	$ 30,000	$ 30,000
Bldg./Docks	368,178	368,178	368,178
Improvements	42,537	46,785	46,785
Vehicles	30,435	30,435	30,435
Furn./Equip.	7,608	7,608	7,608
Tools	14,565	14,565	14,565
Signs	6,438	6,438	6,438
Less: Deprec.	− 125,328	− 142,398	− 148,242
Total Fixed	$374,433	$361,611	$355,767
Other			
Reorg. Exp.	$ 756	—	—
Goodwill	30,000	30,000	30,000
Total Other	$ 30,756	$ 30,000	$ 30,000
TOTAL ASSETS	$652,476	$617,784	$616,485
Liabilities			
Current			
Acct./Payable	$ 3,270	$ 1,647	$ 2,604
Deposits	4,293	828	1,074
Notes—Floor Plan	104,529	97,242	72,261
Mortgage	57,567	43,500	45,990
Total Current	$169,659	$143,217	$121,929
Long-Term Mortgage	$257,709	$246,381	$234,234
Total Long Term	$257,709	$246,381	$234,234
TOTAL LIABILITIES	$427,368	$389,598	$356,163
Equity	$225,108	$228,186	$260,322
TOTAL LIABILITIES & EQUITY	$652,476	$617,784	$616,485

Practice Session—Marina
Reconstructed Income Statements for Valuation

	1999	2000	2001
Sales	$550,521	$583,656	$538,776
Cost of Sales	357,387	345,201	314,811
Gross Profit	$193,134	$238,455	$223,965
% Gross Profit	35.1%	40.9%	41.6%
Expenses			
Advertising	$ 13,392	$ 7,893	$ 10,650
Vehicle Exp.	231	1,608	696
Prof. Fees	6,924	5,031	4,311
Insurance	22,743	19,023	29,979
Office Supplies	1,944	1,986	1,596
Repair/Maint.	3,450	3,252	7,707
Wages	17,832	23,331	17,895
Floor-Plan Int.	19,107	19,434	16,671
Shop Supplies	6,420	6,288	10,686
Taxes—Real Est.	3,351	6,660	6,660
Taxes—Payroll	5,517	6,999	3,669
Telephone	3,729	3,747	3,711
Travel	3,891	1,992	2,043
Uniforms	450	540	630
Utilities	4,578	4,350	3,138
Miscellaneous	6,435	10,938	4,938
Total Expenses	$119,994	$123,072	$124,980
Recast Income	$ 73,140	$115,383	$ 98,985
% Recast Income	13.3%	19.8%	18.4%

Appraised Value of Assets Held Out for Sale

Land/Buildings/Docks (Includes Improvements)	$358,178
Vehicles	21,000
Furniture/Equipment	6,000
Tools	9,000
Other/Signs	5,000
"Owned" Inventory	212,385*
Total	**$611,563**

*$72,261 of the products are in "floor plan" inventory at a 2% per month carrying cost. For a properly qualified buyer, these may be *assumed* and, thus, do not require additional financing. However, bear in mind that a lender would add these costs to other debt-service payments as they consider the extent of other capital they might loan.

Based on the footnote above, total assets held out for sale could, subsequently, be reduced to $539,302. Floor-plan interest is already included in operating expenses.

Ratio Study

Financial experts will not always agree as to which ratios are particularly germane to the small and privately owned enterprise. I feel that it is essential to examine the following:

$$\textbf{Ratio for Gross Margin} \ = \ \frac{\text{Gross Profit}}{\text{Sales}} \quad \text{or}$$

1999	2000	2001	Industry Median
			58.0

This ratio measures the percentage of sales dollars left after goods are sold.

It should be noted that ratios for net profit, before and after taxes, can be most useful ratios. But the fact that private owners frequently manage their businesses to "minimize" bottom lines will often produce little meaningful information from these ratios applied to smaller businesses. Therefore, these ratios are not included.

The current ratio provides a rough indication of a company's ability to service its obligations due within the time frame of one year. Progressively higher ratios signify increasing ability to service short-term obligations. Bear in mind that liquidity in a specific business is a critical element of asset composition. Thus the acid test ratio that follows is perhaps a better indicator of liquidity overall.

$$\textbf{Current Ratio} \ = \ \frac{\text{Total Current Assets}}{\text{Total Current Liabilities}} \quad \text{or}$$

1999	2000	2001	Industry Median
			.8

The quick, or acid test, ratio is a refinement of the current ratio and more thoroughly measures liquid assets of cash and accounts receivable in the sense of ability to pay off current obligations. Higher ratios indicate greater liquidity as a general rule.

$$\textbf{Quick Ratio} \ = \ \frac{\text{Cash and Equivalents} \ + \ \text{Receivables}}{\text{Total Current Liabilities}} \quad \text{or}$$

1999	2000	2001	Industry Median
			.2

A ratio less than 1.0 can suggest a struggle to stay current with obligations. The median indicates that the industry as a whole may wrestle with liquidity problems, and even the top 25% of reported companies reflect only a ratio of 0.5.

$$\textbf{Sales/Receivable Ratio} \ = \ \frac{\text{(Income Statement)}}{\text{Receivables (Balance Sheet)}} \quad \text{or}$$

1999	2000	2001	Industry Median
			34.3–186.1

This is an important ratio and measures the number of times that receivables turn over during the year.

$$\textbf{Day's Receivable Ratio} \ = \ \frac{365}{\text{Sales/Receivable Ratio}} \quad \text{or}$$

1999	2000	2001	Industry Median
			11–2 days

This highlights the average time in terms of days that receivables are outstanding. Generally, the longer that receivables are outstanding, the greater the chance that they may not be collectible. Slow-turnover accounts merit individual examination for conditions of cause.

$$\textbf{Cost of Sales/Payables Ratio} \ = \ \frac{\text{Cost of Sales}}{\text{Payables}} \quad \text{or}$$

1999	2000	2001	Industry Median
			27.3

Generally, the higher their turnover rate, the shorter the time between purchase and payment. Lower turnover suggests that companies may frequently pay bills from daily in-house cash receipts due to slower receivable collections. This practice may be somewhat misguided in light of investment principles whereby one normally attempts to match collections relatively close to payments so that more business income can be directed into the pockets of owners. Some businesses may, however, have little choice.

$$\text{Sales/Working Capital Ratio} \ = \ \frac{\text{Sales}}{\text{Working Capital*}} \ \text{or}$$

1999	2000	2001	Industry Median
			− 21.9

*Current assets less liabilities equals working capital.

A low ratio may indicate an inefficient use of working capital, whereas a very high ratio often signals a vulnerable position for creditors. This *minus* industry median indicates that working capital is scarce or that inefficient uses of working capital prevail throughout this industry.

To analyze how well inventory is being managed, the cost of sales to inventory ratio can identify important potential shortsightedness.

$$\text{Cost of Sales/Inventory Ratio} \ = \ \frac{\text{Cost of Sales}}{\text{Inventory}} \ \text{or}$$

1999	2000	2001	Industry Median
			3.8

A higher inventory turnover can signify a more liquid position and/or better skills at marketing, whereas a lower turnover of inventory may indicate shortages of merchandise for sale, overstocking, or obsolescence.

The Valuation Exercise

Book Value Method

Total Assets at Year-End 2001	$ _____
Total Liabilities	
Book Value at Year-End 2001	$ _____

Adjusted Book Value Method

Assets	Balance Sheet Cost	Fair Market Value
Cash	$ _____	$ _____
Acct./Rec.	_____	_____
Inventory	_____	_____
Prepaid Exp.	_____	_____
Land	_____	_____
Real Estate/Docks	_____	_____
Improvements	_____	_____
Vehicles	_____	_____
Furniture/Equip.	_____	_____
Tools	_____	_____
Signs	_____	_____
Other	_____	_____
Accumulated Deprec.		
Total Assets	$ _____	$ _____
Total Liabilities	$ _____	$ _____
Business Book Value	$ _____	$ _____
Adjusted Book Value at 2001		$ _____

Weighted Average Cash Flow

1999	$ _____	(1)	=	$ _____	
2000	_____	(2)	=	_____	
2001	_____	(3)	=	_____	
Totals		(6)	=	$ _____	
Divided by					6
Weighted Reconstructed Income				$ _____	

The flip-side nature of three years of sales and income suggests the possibility that revenues might have peaked and that income is now largely dependent upon each year's economy. However, to assure oneself of such assumptions, several other years' performance should be examined. You can take this assumption for granted in our case.

Hybrid Method

(This is a form of the capitalization method.)

  1 = High amount of dollars in assets and low-risk business venture
  2 = Medium amount of dollars in assets and medium-risk business venture
  3 = Low amount of dollars in assets and high-risk business venture

	1	2	3
Yield on Risk-Free Investments Such as Government Bonds[a] (often 6%–9%)	8.0%	8.0%	8.0%
Risk Premium on Nonmanagerial Investments[a] (corporate bonds, utility stocks)	4.5%	4.5%	4.5%
Risk Premium on Personal Management[a]	7.5%	14.5%	22.5%
Capitalization Rate	*20.0%*	*27.0%*	*35.0%*
Earnings Multipliers	**5**	**3.7**	**2.9**

[a]These rates are revised periodically to reflect changing economies. They can be composed through the assistance of expert investment advisers if need be.

This particular version of a hybrid method tends to place 40% of business value in book values.

Book Value at Year-End 2001	$_____	
Add: Appreciation in Assets		
Book Value as Adjusted	$_____	
Weight to Adjusted Book Value	40%	$_____
Weighted Reconstructed Income	$_____	
Times Multiplier	×	$_____
Total Business Value		$_____

Excess Earnings Method

(This method considers cash flow and values in hard assets, estimates intangible values, and superimposes tax considerations and financing structures to prove the most-likely equation.)

Reconstructed Cash Flow	$ _____
Less: Comparable Salary (provided)	− 27,000
Less: Contingency Reserve	−
Net Cash Stream to Be Valued	$ _____
Cost of Money	
Market Value of Tangible Assets	
(see reconstructed balance sheet)	$ _____
Times: Applied Lending Rate	×10%
Annual Cost of Money	$ _____
Excess of Cost of Earnings	
Return Net Cash Stream to Be Valued	$ _____
Less: Annual Cost of Money	−
Excess of Cost of Earnings	$ _____
Intangible Business Value	
Excess of Cost of Earnings	$ _____
Times: Intangible Net Multiplier Assigned*	$ _____
Intangible Business Value	$ _____
Add: Tangible Asset Value	_____
TOTAL BUSINESS VALUE (Prior to Proof)	$ _____
(Say $)	_____

*Refer to Figure 9.1 in Chapter 9.

Financing Rationale	
Total Investment	$ _____
Less: Down Payment	−
Balance to Be Financed	$ _____

At this point, we must gauge the amount in prospective bank financing. It's important to use a good deal of logic at this stage of valuation or you will waste a lot of time calculating estimates. One can set up the financing scenario in any way appropriate to local conditions.

Real Estate ($ _____) at ___ % of FMV	$ _____
Furniture/Equip. ($ _____) at ___ % of FMV	_____
Tools ($ _____) at ___ % of FMV	_____
Vehicles ($ _____) at ___ % of FMV	_____
Inventory ($ _____) at ___ % of Book Value	_____
Estimated Bank Financing	$ _____
(Say $ _____)	

Bank (____ % × ____ years)

Amount	$ _____
Annual Principal/Interest Payment	− _____

Testing Estimated Business Value

Return: Net Cash Stream to Be Valued	$ _____
Less: Annual Bank Debt Service (P&I)	− _____
Pretax Cash Flow	$ _____
Add: Principal Reduction*	_____
Pretax Equity Income	$ _____
Less: Est. Dep. & Amortization	− _____
Less: Estimated Income Taxes	− _____
Net Operating Income (NOI)	$ _____

*Debt service includes annual principal payments that are traditionally recorded on the balance sheet as a reduction in debt owed. (I use an average of the first five or six years.) Unless you have use of a business calculator or an amortization table, you may have to obtain this answer from your accountant or banker.

Return on Equity:

$$\frac{\text{Pretax Equity Income}}{\text{Down Payment}} = \frac{\$\,\_\_\_\_}{\$\,\_\_\_\_} = \_\_\_\_ \%$$

Return on Total Investment:

$$\frac{\text{Net Operating Income}}{\text{Total Investment}} = \frac{\$\,\_\_\_\_}{\$\,\_\_\_\_} = \_\_\_\_ \%$$

A Bit of Proof

Basic Salary	$ _____
Net Operating Income	_____
Gain of Principal	_____
Tax-Sheltered Income (Dep.)	_____
Effective Income*	$ _____

*This number should not include dollars set aside in the contingency and replacement reserves.

At this time we have taken our first shot at estimating business value. The following is provided for the benefit of those who wish to experiment further with their own estimates of value. Although I conditioned this case in the beginning that the seller would not provide owner financing (all sellers say that), this does not mean such should not be figured. A tip: Few businesses in America sell without it.

Financing Rationale

Total Investment	$ _____
Less: Down Payment	− _____
Balance to Be Financed	$ _____

Bank (% ×   years)
  Amount $ _____
  Annual Principal/Interest Payment   − _____

Seller (% ×   years)
  Amount $ _____
  Annual Principal/Interest Payment   − _____

Testing Estimated Business Value
Return: Net Cash Stream to Be Valued $ _____
Less: Annual Bank Debt Service (P&I)   − _____
  Pretax Cash Flow $ _____
Add: Principal Reduction   _____
  Pretax Equity Income $ _____
Less: Est. Dep. & Amortization (Let's Assume)   − _____
Less: Estimated Income Taxes (Let's Assume)   − _____
  Net Operating Income (NOI) $ _____

Return on Equity:

$$\frac{\text{Pretax Equity Income}}{\text{Down Payment}} = \frac{\$ \rule{2cm}{0.4pt}}{\$ \rule{2cm}{0.4pt}} = \quad \%$$

Return on Total Investment:

$$\frac{\text{Net Operating Income}}{\text{Total Investment}} = \frac{\$ \rule{2cm}{0.4pt}}{\$ \rule{2cm}{0.4pt}} = \quad \%$$

Buyer's Potential Cash Benefit
Forecast Annual Salary $ _____
Pretax Cash Flow (contingency not considered)   _____
Income Sheltered by Depreciation   _____
  Less: Provision for Taxes   − _____
Discretionary Cash $ _____

  Add: Equity Buildup
Discretionary and Nondiscretionary Cash $ _____

Seller's Potential Cash Benefit in Sale
Cash Down Payment $ _____
Bank Financing Receipts   _____
  Gross Cash at Closing* $ _____

*From which must be deducted capital gains and other taxes. Structured appropriately, the deal qualifies as an "installment" sale with taxes on the proceeds in seller financing put off until later periods.

Projected Cash to Seller by End of 10th Year
Cash at Closing $ _____
Add: Principal and Interest Payments   _____
  Pretax 5-Year Proceeds $ _____

Considerations for Fairness in Pricing:

1. Asking price is not greater than 150% of net worth (except where reconstructed profits are 40% of asking price).
2. At least 10% sales growth per year being realized.
3. Down payment is approximately the amount of one year's reconstructed profits.
4. Terms of payment of balance of purchase price (including interest) should not exceed 40% of annual reconstructed profit.

Results

Book Value Method	$ _____
Adjusted Book Value Method	$ _____
Hybrid (capitalization) Method	$ _____
Excess Earnings Method	$ _____

Well, how did you do? They say that business valuators are the most independent, nonconforming individuals on earth. They never agree on anything. Frankly, they say that about writers, too. Personally, I believe both can find things to agree upon. If you haven't already, you can now turn to the Appendix A to see how you scored. Don't get upset with yourself if you "mushed" it a bit. It's like a lot of things in life . . . you often have to screw it up to learn. Quite honestly, I believe you did just fine.

Questions:

1. What should this business be listed for? _____
2. What is the *most-likely* sale price? _____
3. Would **you** pay this amount? _____

22

Concluding Thoughts about Value and Price

In this and my other books, I describe prices being paid for small businesses as fair or acceptable as long as those prices can be paid back to the purchaser from business earnings within a reasonable period of time. The essence or key to "acceptable price" within this thought rests in "paid back" and in "reasonable time." In early chapters I covered theory and personal perceptions associated with such academic definition. I'd now like to break this down into real terms.

DOWN PAYMENTS

Purchase prices paid for businesses generally include a combination of cash down payment and secured and/or unsecured debt instruments covering noncash balances for these prices being paid. Nothing startling about this. However, buyers far too frequently fail to consider the impacts on value that *down payments* create. Whatever prevailing rates of return one can normally expect to achieve from "safer" investments, such as stocks, bonds, CDs, or savings, must be considered, as a minimum, as one calculates estimated values. By my way of thinking, regardless of where my cash may be temporarily invested or stored, I prefer to use the market rate for bonds as the minimal standard since this choice is both stable and available to most people. At the time of this writing, for example, 8% could be a *generally expected* return from "savings" invested in bonds. Cash invested in these instruments provides (a) above-average safety of principal and (b) "no physical work" associated with earnings. In other words, risk is low and earnings are achieved without physical effort.

The question then becomes: What additional return on these funds might be fair and reasonable to put them at risk in small-business ownership? The basis for no risk/no work is 8% (or whatever prevails at the time) return. The problem gets a bit fuzzy at this stage because in buying a small company we expect to work and be paid for that work. Thus, the only real consideration for earnings beyond a basis-return has to do with *risk*. If I can get 8% without much risk to my capital, and don't have to work for a profit, then what amount "extra" will justify my putting this capital into greater risk? The answer to this, of course, is a very personal one, but I've found that prudent and ardent small-company buyers tend to place the *premium* expected at between 4% and 6%. Subsequently, if 8% is the "safe" rate, then to get prudent and ardent buyers to unleash cash for business purchase, we might generally expect that these individuals will not buy until the prices for purchase allow business cash flows to throw off *returns on equity* in the range of 12% to 14%.

We can build an economic model to help us work this through. Let's say that I want a down payment of $100,000 to return 12%:

$$\textbf{Return on Equity:}$$

$$\frac{\text{Pretax Equity Income}}{\text{Down Payment}} = \frac{?}{\$100,000} = 12\%$$

$$(\$100,000)\,(12\%) = \underline{\$12,000 \text{ per year equity income}}$$

Let's now assume that the business we are considering is throwing off a *reliable* $70,000 *reconstructed* (owner's "perks," depreciation, and interest removed) earnings per year. Using this as a starting point, we can begin our process of evaluating the "offering price" by saying that $12,000 of business cash flow is *not available* in our calculations. Before proceeding further, however, we must examine the element of "pay for expected work."

SALARY OR WAGE

Personal perception plagues what we "believe" we should be able to earn. Personal yardsticks often ensue from past experiences. We "were" earning X; therefore, to go into business for ourselves we want X plus Y. Subsequently, this too has two parts: (a) a fair amount that might be paid to "anybody" doing comparable work and (b) something "extra" for the skills we bring to the business that the present owner might not have had. Factor "a" can be ascertained through local employment agencies, personal knowledge, and/or government labor data. Pay rates for "similar" work must be the standard used at this stage in the calculation. For example, let us assume the "going rate" to be $35,000 to *manage* this type of business. By setting this standard, we are accepting that we *could hire* a qualified manager to run the business for this amount, and that $35,000 might have nothing to do with what we want or need to earn. Part "b" above cannot be answered at this point because we have yet to run the business and apply our skills to obtain this extra amount. *What we have historically earned, or believe we should earn, has nothing—nothing—to do with the value of a particular business.* To meet personal want/need earnings objectives we must "find" appropriate small businesses where down payments are within the reach of our pocketbooks . . . or *take chances* that we can perform feats within the allocated time frame established by our earning objectives. We have now added the second element leading to value or offering price.

Reconstructed Cash Flow	$ 70,000
Less: Return on Down Payment	− 12,000
Less: Comparable Management Wage	− 35,000
Cash Flow Available for Debt Servicing the Purchase Price	$ 23,000

THE REST OF THE STORY

We don't need to know what the seller is asking for his or her business to complete our assignment, because all we are interested in is what *we* would be willing to pay. The answer, once again, relies on two questions: (a) What principal amount can be amortized with $23,000 and (b) when added to a down payment of $100,000, what total amount is the projected offering price? Since we have used 10% as the commercial rate throughout this book, we will also use this in our example.

$23,000 divided by 12 equals approximately $1,917 per month. The "face amount" these payments will service over 10, 15, or 20 years can be estimated using amortization tables readily available through most bookstores, or by the use of business calculators. The following are examples for three different periods at 10%:

Using $1,917 per month available for debt service:

(10% over 20 years)	
Debt Principal	$198,648
Down Payment	100,000
Offering Price	$298,648

(10% over 15 years)

Debt Principal	$178,391
Down Payment	100,000
Offering Price	$278,391

(10% over 10 years)

Debt Principal	$145,062
Down Payment	100,000
Offering Price	$245,062

Noted throughout, the *terms of financing* bear heavily on the prices that can be paid by buyers for small companies. But under any of these financing terms, the buyer is provided (a) a return on equity of 12%, (b) a going-rate wage for comparable work, and (c) payment for debt . . . *all* out of the available cash flow of the business. The "over a reasonable period of time" factor is determined by a combination of *price paid* and the *terms of the loan*.

However, part b under the Salary or Wage section remains to be answered. This condition of "extra" is highly judgmental and the answer rests entirely in negotiations between buyer and seller. In one respect, dollars beyond comparable pay can be viewed as "extra" money for extra contributions. From that point of view, these earnings do not obligate sellers to feather the beds of buyers at the exact point of purchase. Rather, buyers need to perform exceptionally *after* the sale to glean these "extra" earnings. Few sellers price their businesses any other way. From the buyer's point of view, most will want some degree of a "fudge factor" protecting their initial investment. Not that sellers regularly lie or engage in deceptive practices, but buyers cannot know *all* about small businesses at the time of their purchases. It is not uncommon for machinery to fail shortly after purchase, or customers to leave, or employees to depart, or some other costly event to occur. Buyers are far from naive about the likelihood of these potential adverse happenings taking place. Subsequently, reasonable **contingency reserves** set aside can satisfy the seller's expectations to maximize personal returns and, at the same time, answer some part of a buyer's need to have safety cushions sheltering initial investments. Generally speaking, high motivations to sell might be the only conditions under which sellers permit more than contingencies into the formulas for price/value. In practical reality, few sellers will give away the ship unless they have no other choice. At the same time, few buyers will pay "tight-wire" prices for small companies unless surplus cash remains after payment for other conditions of purchase.

Contingency reserves should not be seen as monies that will be used to do something new by the buyer in the future. They are dollars set aside annually to maintain present assets in the similar condition that they were on the date of purchase. Since our example is purely hypothetical, we have no basis on which to develop a reserve. But we can pick a number to demonstrate the reserve's effect on the offering price. Let's use $3,000, and see what happens to our offering price with this additional deduction from reconstructed cash flow.

Reconstructed Cash Flow	$ 70,000
Less: Return on Down Payment	− 12,000
Less: Comparable Management Wage	− 35,000
Less: Contingency Reserve	− 3,000
Cash Flow Available for Debt Servicing the Purchase Price	$ 20,000

Using $20,000 divided by 12 equals $1,667 per month available for debt service:

(10% over 20 years)	
Debt Principal	$172,742
Down Payment	100,000
Offering Price	$272,742
(10% over 15 years)	
Debt Principal	$155,127
Down Payment	100,000
Offering Price	$255,127
(10% over 10 years)	
Debt Principal	$126,144
Down Payment	100,000
Offering Price	$226,144

In doing this, we set up several scenarios for the buyer: (a) If I manage the business to safeguard assets such that I do not have to spend the $3,000 for replacements, then I have "extra" for managing well; (b) if I need the $3,000 for replacements, then I have sheltered my initial capital investment and I'll have to do better next year; or (c) if this is not acceptable, I have the choice of seeking another business and another seller who might accommodate my wish. In the smaller of businesses, this is about all of the so-called extra that can be accomplished by buyers.

As businesses grow larger in market value, demands by buyers for risk/reward returns grow larger as well. Expected returns on equity can increase to upwards of 30%. There is no pat answer or formula to estimate rate of return expectations. As mentioned quite often in this book's companion edition, four out of five small businesses apparently do not sell at all. Thus we might conclude that a given marketplace will be the ultimate "manager" for both buyer's and seller's practice, assuming they want to do their deals at all. The simple formula above provides both a beginning and an end. It provides a beginning in that it offers a place to start negotiations on a reasonable plane. It provides an end in that it crystallizes a buyer's thoughts with regard to which boundaries the buyer will allow to be invaded emotionally and financially. Subsequently, it also crystallizes the choice to purchase or to pass. Businesses that cannot pass this minimal test of value should sound an alarm of impending personal disaster.

Buying and selling small companies are acts that are mixed thoroughly with emotional and financial concerns by both buyers and sellers. Both parties have rights to fairness and reasonable returns. True business "values" are found in the numbers game, but the *acts* of actual buying and selling often are hidden from the naked eye of mathematics. That is unfortunate for some because the grim reaper of bankruptcy looms for the unwary and the too emotional buyer or seller. The only small-company price or value that is "correct" is the one that can be paid for through business earnings during a reasonable period of time. Any greater price than that comes from the realm of emotion. As a gentle reminder to me personally, a sign on my wall reads: "People make money intellectually— and lose it emotionally."

In conclusion, I recommend that you reread Chapter 1 and the myths about business value. The contents of this book may not make you into a business valuation expert, but they will move you to the forefront and place you far ahead of buyers and sellers who take no time to study a subject that holds many of the characteristics forming survival after a deal is done. In writing this book I had the choice of being an educator by offering a plethora of valuation techniques or of being a practical provider of one or two formulas that could be mastered. Directed to an audience of real-time players, the latter purpose was my only choice. I would love to hear how you make out with your deals using these approaches.

Shalom, and may you live and prevail happily ever after . . . the deal.

"Symbolizing the thrust of Japanese approaches to life and to business is this alternative phrase. . . . Avoid: Muri, Muda, Mura. (Avoid: Excess, Waste, Unevenness)"

W.M.Y.

23

"Dot-Com"—Information Technology

"The best teacher in life is when we screw up as children."

OVERVIEW

We do well by continually reminding ourselves that true change is upon us. The Apache said, "Think what you want to think. You have to live with your thoughts." With change comes adjustment; with adjustment comes the leveling of playing fields. Not more than the blink of an eye ago, in entrepreneurial and investment communities alike, soap-box headlines proclaimed that the unlaunched information business might be worth as much as $1 to $2 million. Surprise! Surprise to all of us. But then, hindsight is quite the teacher, too.

We live in a culture of whining and complaining and excuses. People want the quick-fix answers to complex problems, but they're not so easily found. This dot-com revolution differs from any predecessor due to the wide-scale effect it has had on the worldwide communications scene. No previous period has globalized a world population so intensely and so quickly, or impacted how we do business in such a major way. It has brought invisibility to the forefront of the customer service equation. It has brought invisibility to customers themselves. It has kicked the funk out of how markets shop. It has mesmerized the brightest minds, seeking answers to the businessperson's ultimate nightmare—an impatient time where marketing madness rules. But behind the scenes lies a behemoth of old eras. The talent issue remains foremost as the Achilles' heel to the dot-com arena.

Plastering a landscape with buttons, bumper stickers, and one-liners promotes the concept that *starting* is 80 percent of the battle. Funny that we might *ever* choose to emphasize starting so heavily. It has always been the case that *finishing* is what society rewards. We seem endlessly to adore cutesy, clueless one-liners advocating the quick fix to whatever ails society. These one-liners, it seems, have come to symbolize the true grit of American dreaming. Our values as to where rewards should be given certainly went askew with regard to dot-com investors. Adult (meaning we should know best) urgencies for doing alchemy made more millionaires aged 15 to 30 than existed at any other time in our history. And, once again, the selective few walked away with the brass ring while most investors smarted from the mistaken emphasis on beginnings.

In life, we commonly get what we get used to. Place a frog in cold water, bring it slowly to a boil, and he stays there until he cooks. It used to be that we didn't need one, but for young people starting out today, the expectations of going through at least three orgasms of the mind during a lifetime is needed to survive. Career paths (and how we do business) have come to change that much. It's often said that an exciting life is a series of one-time experiences. With certainty, the youth of today believe this. Thus, the future holds far more of these one-time experiences than it holds duplication. The youth of our country—thus, the future of our country—is brought up knowing nothing other than one-time experiences. Think about this! Because people my age (around 60 or older) are going to miss out on the point of a new era if we don't finally grasp this self-perpetuating bent for life-renewing change.

Never in the history of humankind have generational differences been so distinct. Nor has a time brought such acute conflict on the subject of "how to do what about anything." Generational debate symbolizes one of the great differences between this dot-com era and transitions of the past. We should take a few moments to really look back on things we learned especially well—I mean *really* learned to the extent these made us experts at one thing or another later in life. That deep learning brought about through common-sense learning—failing at what we were attempting to do—was more valuable than formal educations. The dot-com era is a sibling just learning to walk—so, too, are its leaders. It will eventually gait forward in pride and there will be greater successes than we've ever before witnessed.

A few, no doubt, will criticize my use of the word "orgasm" in business writing. But I can't think of a more descriptive term—not one more widely or more fully understood—not one single word that better describes the incredible crescendo given up to everything happening around us. An orgasm of the mind is like a great steak to steak-lovers. Very satisfying. Dot-com founders (even those who failed) are very satisfied doing what they do or did.

Young generations do not have the patience to baby-step the success process. They rationalize, it seems, that if you include too many steps, when something goes wrong—then you're screwed. But the reality from human frailty—too few steps and you shoot yourself in the foot. Anything hurried too drastically is usually of poor quality. The new era founders avoided the acquisition of related experience before launching ideas; thus, the success equation got broken.

Somewhere out there, a dot-com has been or will be started that will bring this movement/revolution into its maturity and set the standards to come. How precisely to economically valuate for "the dream whose time has yet to come" may also change with time. But for the present, valuation tools of our recent past still work. With one exception, perhaps: The purely mechanical aspect used historically is not nearly enough now because the most invisible point in a dot-commer's business is its customers. Thus, the most viable question to field in the valuation exercise is, do they exist? Customers buying in large quantity have always been the strongest link in the chain of doing successful business. We who attempt dot-com valuation should not forget the adage, "The strongest link is also the weakest, because it can break all the rest." I therefore shift the emphasis for this chapter to the higher need to check marketing facts, in lieu of advancing anything more germane to valuation mechanics.

For the first time in history, a whole industry derives its present value from its yet-to-come business. That takes a remarkable amount of educated guesswork for even the most sophisticated mind. Spend just a week or two glued to NASDAQ reports and you'll prove for yourself the salient point I reference. The link that could break the chain demands that we vacate the closeted world of accounting tactics long enough to visit much more thoroughly the roots on which business forecasts are based, to assure that data presented are real-world. Financial forecasts hinged to marketing rubbish fooled us once. The job of valuation specialist changed too with this era. He or she must now be market researcher as well as financial technician. Working exclusively from the accounting closet will no longer get the job of valuation done.

I've relished the Chinese philosophy of sticking to the here and now since I was a young boy. But it took nearly a lifetime to understand fully in my heart and mind just how critical to life-doings this

*concept is to us. We can do nothing about changing the past. We can
do nothing, or very little, to make the future what we would have it
be. We have only the present moment. Our mission in life, therefore,
is to take the very moment we are in and move it forward—one step
at a time, one day to the next. Great happenings, or great disasters,
may befall the dot-com arena tomorrow. But we don't know that
now. What we know now about this industry is all I can address. An
hour from now—a month from now—things may be very different.
There is no gospel to things unknown.*

W.M.Y.

Why Is It So Difficult to Pick Winners— to Value Businesses Whose Time Hasn't Yet Come?

*"There's a right way and a wrong way to do things. Do the right way
and you're living—do the wrong and while you may be walking
around, you're as dead as the beaver hat."*

Davy Crockett

Common kitchen-variety Ohio Blue Tip Matches advertise they "strike
anywhere." That's what the customer wanted and that's what the customer got, and still gets today. The box labeled "Made in the U.S.A."
opens the question of how this product survived the onslaughts of time,
space, and matter: cheap Asian imports, the advent of butane lighters,
marked changes in the habits and lifestyles of the buying public, technological advances, and so forth. My twofold answer to this question is *they
did not ignore* that indelible reason that a business survives: It gives real
life in terms of buying power to its customers, and gives its customers
what they are *not* currently getting from markets. I'll expand on this—
no, actually focus on this almost entirely—as we go along since I believe
the talent issue, to include not judging the customer in a real-world sense,
is what we most miscalculated about dot-commers. But then, too, what
we most misjudged about ourselves is what we've always misjudged about
ourselves.

The vast majority of smaller businesses changing hands in the United
States are still like the examples presented elsewhere in the book. What we've

always differentiated in business valuation has been tangible asset value and intangible asset value as homogenous components of a collective value—to wit, hard assets as employed to produce cash flows producing total values. But as any small-business owner or serious-minded small-business buyer/seller can attest, that handy-dandy loan-to-value ratio of one's friendly banker does not get elevated much over collateralizing what can be touched and felt (tangible property). Fair market values of hard assets will continue for some time to call the shots in terms of borrowed capital from the host of banking institutions. But means for borrowing shifted. Why? The new kid on the block: *intellectual property*.

The online technology era has elevated Angels and Venture Capitalists (VC) into their full glory. Few traditional lending sources are incorporated to accept the high risks associated with lending on intangible assets, and the dreams of would-be entrepreneurs. Differing from traditional lenders, Angels and VCs often take ownership stakes in ventures funded. Holding these "equity" positions gives them the perfect right to get in one's face, even when things appear to be going well. The VC is commonly the highly educated and competent financial person, but tends to lack hands-on operating skill. On the other hand, the Angel is most apt to be the high-net-worth individual with direct hands-on management experience. Unlike traditional lenders, VC and Angel alike hasten for quick returns from their vested capital. The exit objective for both is generally five to seven years (i.e., *impatient* capital). Exit strategies target public offerings of stock (IPOs) or the enterprise's outright sale. From the date of birthing, the dot-com founder was forced into maintaining high focus on satisfying investors' short-term needs versus long-term operation—not that he or she hadn't been interested in the quick-buck-and-out all along, too. The arena is now full of the walking wounded—or the dead. Many remaining founders are disillusioned, disheartened, or downright discouraged. According to numerous articles, it seems those outfits faring best are the ones who self-funded or used other "patient" capital and stuck to old concepts of planned long-term growth. Venture Capitalist, Angel, and founder greed played a major role in launching a host of ill-conceived ideas. The teacher has taught.

Why so much failure cresting at once? Prosperous times, for one reason. Another, summed by something heard at an MIT Capital Forum near the peak of this period: "Too much money chasing too few good deals!" You don't experience such widespread business failure until two or more elements play in the game. Running a business becomes a financial matter only *after* you have gained sufficient customer-buying to cause sales to generate expenses, the need to pay the bills. During its launching stage, a potential business must remain steeped with marketing concentration. Pure financial people do poorly assessing this early stage development. In this instance, the right hand (entrepreneurs) and the left (investors) remained yards apart in their (mis)understanding of each other's skills. Investors trusted too much to the preexistence of entrepreneurial knowledge that did not exist. Entrepreneurs trusted too much that investors would provide links to gaps in essential knowledge. Financial people do far better at assessing the overall concept once businesses gain performance histories. Huge mistakes were made by valuation tacticians who had little or no hands-on experience with the general management scenario. "Comparable sale" comparison as the benchmark in the valuation model proved abysmally inadequate to estimating a dot-com business's worth. In fact, history now shows that the comparable sale method only multiplied upon the original error.

Thanks to information technology, this past decade has ushered in an explosion of new intellectual property. One of the fundamental changes wrought by information technology is the availability of data unprotected by the traditional barriers of time, space, and matter. This liberating effect also creates significant risks. If you can gain access to the information of others on computers all over the world, then so can others gain access to your information on your computer and in your communications. For aeons, key information of the successful business derived and held onto its value by that information not being widely known. Now, the new risk for getting into and staying in business is against the priority that everybody can know everything about everyone else. Copyright and patent laws go far toward guiding proprietary data, but once the cat is out of the bag and trade secrets are lost, they no longer provide the catalyst to the added-value once planned.

Highly suspect to any valuation undertaking must be a thorough questioning of the foundation on which all forecast financial data are based. *Of the six or seven major reasons attached to dot-com failures, overestimating consumer preference/demand and underestimating the cost of acquiring customers rank at least third and fourth.* We in the valuation trade always thought we had a good grasp on evaluating the marketing elements of new enterprise, but experience now reveals we didn't know nearly enough, or we didn't engage our knowledge. Thus, we, too, contributed to dot-com failures.

Of the six or seven major reasons attached to dot-com failures, the remainder cling tightly to human error, for example, clueless overspending done in unaffordable places, seeking to attract ill-defined customers; a failure to understand the industry in which the dot-commer chose to do business (in fact, a demonstrated blatant expectation they could compete against established brick-and-mortar players without needing in-depth knowledge about the industries they entered); a gross lack of real-world knowledge about how business works; abominable fiscal controls, or none at all; and just about every failed dot-com never really got to flight because they couldn't execute ideas even when concepts were generally good ones at the get-go. The one reason that sticks out foremost to me is the failure to ensoul business ambitions by surrounding their dreams and efforts with people who possess strengths greater than their own. The talent issue!

The methods for starting any new enterprise have not changed. The quality of its founder; the character of its customers and marketplace; the capital and environment to do what must be done—these are still the essential ingredients for moving any business idea forward. For a time, we (the host of us) all forgot these primary rules.

The Japanese way to learning: "If you want to know something, you must become one with it." My father captured it this way: "If you ever wannna learn about something—really learn about it—you have to commit something that makes you stay glued to the learning experience." In this case, I invested dollars in the dot-com arena and stuck around for what became a wild ride. Mesmerized like many, I, too, made pretty good bucks before being shaken back into reality. In time, I lost pretty much what I'd earned. With more time, I learned not to be stupid. What hasn't changed is the investor's eventual need for sanity at the bottom line, that tangible factor of quality returns for invested capital. Nature's law may be "what goes up must come down," but business investors follow the lateral law: "What goes in must come out (with greater value upon exit)."

Focus on Factors That Drive Markets to Know If You Have Any Business to Value at All

"Just about anyone you ask will give you just about any kind of answer. Ask the unqualified person and you're just about done."

"You cannot be conquered from without until you have destroyed yourself from within."

Rome

What Should My Business Be?

As simple as this question sounds, few people in business ask it. That's most unfortunate, because not knowing the answer is a major reason that businesses fail. Peter Drucker coined the phrase this way, "Indeed, the question looks so simple that it is seldom raised, the answer seems so obvious that it is seldom given." A real-estate business sells real estate. A furniture manufacturer sells furniture. A paint store sells paint. A dot-commer might operate via technology, but it *does not* sell technology. Most are either retailers or distributors, not too unlike brick-and-mortar competitors. Dot-commers are *not* invisible to competitors, and they certainly compete in the same arena for the very same consumer purchases.

Amazon.com is a giant distributor and retailer differing mainly by its lack of a traditional storefront. But its need for warehousing space, shipping and handling, and support staffing does not vary in cost structure from its brick-and-mortar cousins.

So really, what does Amazon.com sell? Books and their other product lines? I think almost definitely not. Sure, books and so forth are bought at Amazon.com, but most customers shop there for the simple *convenience*—avoiding the traffic and parking hassles common to visiting storefront shops. Thus, when building an Amazon.com-like customer model, one *must* segregate unto its own model only for those customers who might be most motivated to purchase for convenience reasons.

Anyone can buy books through one of hundreds of bookstores peppering the landscape, in nearly every town in the world. Talking face to face with dealers lulls us into believing that customer service in general will remain within our control. This is the shopping model most of us grew up using. Buying "blind" is still quite foreign to most shoppers, and although attitudes are changing, something extra must be provided to hook the new adventurer into online purchasing. Purchasing regularity is even more key to building the long-range sales model, but getting the customers is only one thing. Keeping them coming back is another. So the plan for customer retention must be reliable. Consistent and *exceptional* customer service is essential—actually, the unique handling of customer needs is more important still. And because nearly anyone can learn nearly everything about everyone else on the Internet, explicit assurance of the privacy of credit card numbers and other financial information used to make purchases must be given. Minimizing returned merchandise is key to the least-cost modeling. Examine most closely the *thought* behind the planning. Wrapped and tied-up-in-a-bow plans reflect merely the effect of whatever thoughts went into them. Evaluating "effect" is a meaningless wandering away from finding truth.

*"The thought behind all things . . . which is the **cause** of all things."*
Walter Russell

Not too many years ago nearly everyone in small and large towns and cities alike needed to schedule the purchase of almost every commodity around nine-to-five business hours. Today, nearly everything anyone could want is available at nearly any hour. Products and services have taken on so many added varieties, and new items being introduced every day make choice a complex and wearisome process for customers. Businesses that are formed today without the most clairvoyant of purposes simply get lost in the maze of brick-and-mortar enterprises. Information technology only layers another jungle on top of the maze for shopper confusion. So many available customers will only divide into so many competitor outfits so many times. Only founders unique in purpose and direction will find paths out of this jungle.

Generational Influences Affect Markets

Generational preferences, attitudes, and habits play a crucial role in shaping consumer trends. What's funny, what's stylish, what's status, what's taboo, what works, and what doesn't vary by generation. *The dot-com/ online buying arena is impacted more significantly than all other types of businesses by the generational split in buying habits.* Why?

First, 46 percent of U.S. households are *without computers.* Non-computerized households worldwide range downward from 86% to 29% as the average. Those who do not own a computer, or own a computer but are not connected to the Internet, are unlikely to be customers in the dot-com/online buying arena. We all know that computer ownership is more often found in younger family households. Much of the world's older population is not comfortable using this technology. Still, the world's older population may be among the most avid book consumers (sticking to Amazon.com-type purchases). It is important that the customer profile factor in the impact of unavailable technology on the overall business model.

The vast majority of buying online is done through credit card purchase. While these cards are relatively easy to obtain in this day and age, they are just as easy to lose. Prevailing economic status within age categories must be factored into the customer profile. Young people, who may be the most excessive and impulsive of all spenders, may also be unlikely to meet minimal financial standards for credit card ownership.

We've known for years that getting the customer model down pat is the critical basis for business forecasts—the crux for the long-term success of any enterprise. However, interpreting even well-assembled market research can be like reading tea leaves to the novice, and the dot-com arena oozed with its high share of untrained adventurers.

As co-founder and longtime advisor to a successful seed-capital investment exchange/technology forum, I've reviewed the business plans of hundreds of would-be owners. Some get funded—most do not. The following reflects the primary reasons why Angels might refuse to fund a business plan.

1. Failure to define customers clearly

2. Failure to reveal exciting management planning

3. Failure to define—clearly—the mission and product or service

4. Failure to include a plan to attract and hold employees whose satisfaction is measured in responsibility and accomplishment, not wages

5. Failure to display entrepreneurial smarts and ambition, not luck

6. Failure to identify and demonstrate how alternative opportunities might present themselves, and what plan of action would be contemplated

7. Lack of assessment of industry trends and the prognosis for sliding into niche markets

8. Lack of thorough assessment of competition as such plays into the proposer's plan for success

9. Failure to systematically identify horizontal trends affecting a product or service

10. Failure to systematically describe how marketing and sales will be accomplished. More specifically, a marketing plan without a description as to how $1 of sales in the financial plan has been expectantly achieved.

11. Failure to budget for costs of new infrastructure with growth

12. Too focused on overall profits, versus a budgeting of cash requirements on a daily and/or monthly period (unwillingness to recognize and accept that cash flow, rather than profit, matters most to enterprise)

13. Failure to reconcile monthly profit/loss forecasts with actual payable and receivable practice (commonly shows up in plans as out-of-control spending)

14. Lack of succession planning—particularly, step-aside strategy for if/when the business reaches beyond the capability, or interest, of the founder

Peter Drucker said, "So many new businesses start out with high promise. They do extremely well the first year or two and then suddenly, are up to their ears in trouble. If they survive at all, they are forever stunted." Big, small, tiny, or still the dream, there simply is no way to avoid the real world.

As we age, we carry yesteryear's comforts and thought patterns with us. These were inconsequential to the business environment until the exponential growth in communication and the advent of medical miracles gave each new generation a longer lifespan. The following section highlights specific differences between generations and why generational preference must be so thoughtfully considered when developing the customer profile.

Matures   Born 1909 to 1945   *Very slow at relating to new products and change*

Factors affecting: Great Depression, New Deal, WWII, GI Bill. Grew up during tough times. More constrained set of expectations—discipline, self-denial, hard work, obedience to authority, financial and social conservatism.

Example: With excessive talking, my dad used to say, "Son, you go on like a broken record. You sound like you were vaccinated with a phonograph needle." I understood this because I owned and played a phonograph. My children, on the other hand, grew up in an era where music is played from a CD burned on a computer. They have no concept of the phonograph; thus, will not really understand statements such as my dad used with me.

Example: (social conservatism) One of my sons, not married, lives with his girlfriend and they have a child—marriage is not being contemplated. To his grandparents that was a real taboo and purpose for outcast.

Baby Boomers   Born 1946 to 1964   *Born to prosperity—they take most things for granted.*

Factors affecting: A great society, general economic prosperity, expansion of suburbia, Nixon, color TV, sexual liberation. It's the "me" generation, built on the sense of entitlement. Most pursue personal goals with a vengeance and tolerate nothing short of instant gratification. Great customers to have!

Generation X-ers   Born 1965 to 1987   *Bore easily and will trek next door for products NOW!*

Factors affecting: Divorce, AIDS, Sesame Street, MTV, crack cocaine, Game-Boy, the PC. It's the "why me?" generation. Wary and uncertain, but savvy and enthusiastically ready, willing, and able to take on new challenges they face. Curiously, X-ers embrace some of the values of Maturers.

Generation To Be Named (Generation Y?)   Born 1988 to present

This generation's preferences cannot yet fully be known. The oldest member is perhaps aged 13. An important input to modeling, however, because this fledgling generation holds the tightest grip on longer-term future sales of any business just starting out today. The start-up, with no funds to spare, cannot misstep by not identifying this generation's reactions to product introductions.

Each generation's communication model varies with the conditions prevailing in the world around them as they grew up. 1987's Black Monday is significant to me, but to individuals entering college this fall (born 1980–1981), it's no more relevant than the Great Depression of 1929. These youngsters were 11 years old when the Soviet Union broke apart. They are too young to remember the Challenger space shuttle blowing up. Stamps have always cost 32/33/34 cents. The compact disc was introduced when they were 1 year old, and the expression "you sound like a broken record" means nothing because they have never operated a record player. The movie *Star Wars* looks very fake to them and the special effects are pathetic. Over half of this generation will complete college (in my era, the rate was around 15%).

And add these data to deliberations: By 2015, Matures will be aged 70 to 106; Baby Boomers, 51 to 69; and Generation X-ers, 32 to 50. The new segment (Generation Y?) will be between 20 and 31. The forecast is for roughly 63 million in this new generation—5.8 million more than in their mother's and father's Gen-X. This math doesn't compute. The birth rate was down in Gen-X. As of July 1, 1990, the median age was 32.8 years. By July 1, 2015, the median age is estimated to move up to 37.3. The total U.S. population is expected to grow from about 250 million to over 310 million in this period. On the one hand, our population is expected to live longer and include more of us; but on the other, the young population—having had fewer children—is expected to increase by nearly 20 million? How is that possible? Look closely at U.S. immigration plans. My guess is that we will import most of this growth. Serious discussions are already under way in D.C. The government has targeted mostly well-educated tech types—immediately job-capable folks who hit the U.S. streets bringing in good paychecks and paying taxes from day one.

Assuming that all customers behave in the same manner can be a serious mistake. We must always be on guard to avoid one-dimensional strategies. Marketers who pay close attention to generational marketing and consider all external changes to target-market populations usually thrive and grow.

How Would I Find You If I Didn't Know About You?

The key to drawing customers to a website is to give them a variety of options to access the site. To that end, one must utilize both online and offline marketing techniques, and also find ways to integrate the two so that they complement each other.

Off-site marketing is only marginally available for the start-up that has not acquired deep pocket resources. But even when given the resources, too many start-ups squander more than they can afford, and spend ineffectively. While off-site marketing can be quite effective, there is no real way to tell who is receiving the message, or if they are even active Internet participants. Each source for off-site marketing maintains demographics of their listening, viewing, or reading audiences. The dot-commer must target offline advertising dollars carefully and then only spend where advertising hits audiences that are most in line with its own customer profiles. My sampling size was too small to project meaningful statistical incidence, but overspending on off-site advertising prevailed in 19 of 21 online failures studied. At least eight recent articles on dot-com failure highlight overspending on offline advertising among major reasons for demise.

Eighty to 85 percent of traffic arrives at a website because an interested individual was able to locate the site online. Internet market research firms claim that 70 percent of all online traffic will arrive at the new site through major directories (e.g., Yahoo!, Look Smart, and The Mining Co.) or through search engines (e.g., Alta Vista, Excite, HotBot, InfoSeek, and Lycos). Unfortunately, it's not just as simple as connecting up with any directory or search engine. The web host-selection problem is not really different from radio stations and the music played to listening audiences. Individual stations take great effort to appeal largely to a specific listening group (country and western, blues, jazz, rock, etc.). Online directory and search engine hosts seek to minimize competition by appealing to defined segments of the market; therefore, situating the new website cannot be left to random positioning.

How consumers learn about a site or are directed to a site should be detailed through formidable architecture that shows alternative planning for the failure of original actions to target consumers effectively.

Who Is the Customer?

There is only one purpose for starting a business: to create customers! Are customers male, female, or taken from both sexes? Do customers come from the Mature, Baby Boomer, Gen-X, or Gen-Y demographic? What primary territory might draw the most customers? What features or benefits do customers expect in the product or service? Will they be repeating customers, and if so, how often will they buy? What buying motivations would cause them to buy from me (online)? Is there something I can do to my product or service or website that would stimulate increased buying (e.g., color and psychographic components of design or packaging)? Will this batch of customers be profitable? Dot-commers did far too much guesswork constructing customer profiles. They also expected too much draw from the techno curiosity factor, expecting customers to come shop at a website just for the technology reason alone. Inadequate thought was given to how the customer definition changes in the no-see-um environment of online marketing.

As the old saying goes, "Garbage in, garbage out." Reasonably predictable sales and expense forecasts have always hinged on some basic premise of truth. This should not have been news! This is elementary statistics—high school stuff—yet, they (and we) missed it! Vis-a-vis, a lack of talent issue. *Building a business plan is first the test of a hypothesis for its containment of customer reality.* And second, if passing on its fundamental principle, it is a projection outward from one source of truth. Sadly, with too much hope and idle prayer for an idea, the first step is too often skimmed over entirely. Only when the profile of the *most ideal* (and most likely) customer has been well framed can primary, secondary, and tertiary customer profiles be adequately developed. Sales forecast may then be extrapolated—one customer at a time—from each of these ranks. But these data remain characteristically unreliable until passing safely beyond bombardments from the realities found in market demographics, real-world competitions, factors of (or inhibiting) supply and demand, conditions of prevailing and future economies of scale, issues of production and/or distribution, and, undeniably, the reasonable availability of proper talent to execute plans for accomplishment.

Who Is the Competition?

There is only one proper and safe assumption to hold sacred about the competition: Great ideas attract vultures! Someone else will develop the better mousetrap the day after any new product goes into production. A competitor's ease of market entry is the cancer to launching and holding on to ideas. The only surefire defense lies in knowing more about them than they know about you. Once all is launched, the brass ring for success eventually goes to the one maintaining the most *unfair advantage* over all the other competition. There is no end to anxieties drafted from the competition unless one knows their strengths and weaknesses. It is careless to attack the greater strength. Niche market holders sift through competitor weaknesses to match against strengths in themselves for seizing upon the unfair market advantage.

What Makes the Customer Buy from One Business over Any Other?

Customer loyalty is a figment of the imagination for anyone who thinks such an animal exists. Customers are only loyal to the vision they see through their own eyes. Roadblocks to the mounting of sales come down to three generic essentials: price, quality, and service being offered. Rarely, if ever, will any business possess all three to advantage. The price advantage (mass merchandising, for example) usually gives up quality or service or both, the service advantage might give up price and possibly quality, and the quality advantage most likely gives up price and might give up service. These distinctions identify how consumers view dealing with any business through their eyes. Planned architecture that fails to realize how the consumer personally views the total shopping experience at a new enterprise also reveals the initiate's lack of thought about going into business.

Time, space, and matter *do* still apply at the point of purchase. Early in the dot-com buildup, founders learned that deeper discounts than anticipated were needed to jump-start consumer buying. They also gradually learned that discounted selling would remain the high need in the consumer model. Giving then reneging doesn't work. Thus, they should also have known that the most initial competition would come from the mass-merchandiser, the deep-pocket specialist in discounted merchandise. It's doubtful that a gnat on the back is worrisome to any elephant. Wal-Mart, for example, is the leader in wholesale leveraged buying. They can afford to discount and still maintain profitable margins. The dot-commer can neither buy nor sell on such competitive margins and stay whole. Attacking service or quality or both might have led to better choices.

SUMMARY

Time is the precious commodity that creates wealth. Time to make, to package, to deliver, to retool, and to repeat the processes over and over again pits every business owner against everyone else in the game. The more efficient they become with their time, the more they hold an advantage over everyone else. Milt Friedman said that inflation is too much money chasing too few goods. During past eras, inflation of this sort was more in evidence because of the time limitations on production. Today, information technology equals saving time, cutting costs, increasing profits, and decreasing error and waste.

Every corner of the globe is now the shopping haven for even the least-traveled among us. Click a mouse today and you are anywhere in the world you want to be. Computers are becoming as commonplace in the household as knives and forks. In a decade, nearly everyone will be using them more than the phone. In two decades, few people will remember when we didn't have them. *Space*, once the constraint of doing nearly everything, will only advocate definition for traveling outside our universe.

Teleporting *matter* becomes real. Products and services extended by a thread, through data bytes, will weave the new shopping interface into common habit. When we do go out to shop, it will be for the *antique* experience. Behemoth real-estate structures will not be needed to house the increasing thousands working from their homes. I know this last paragraph may sound a bit ridiculous, but the framework *is* already in place, and for even more unthinkable events to happen to life and the shopping experience.

If any great change occurs in the equation for how we value companies, it will lie in how we view present and future usages of time, space, and matter in business operation. It will lie in how we keep up with changes made possible through information technology for consumer purchasing. It will lie in how we view the impact of increasingly savvy tech-oriented competition. It will lie in how we as tacticians comprehend the growth of the New Era business enterprise. It will lie in how well we learn what we don't now know. The math for doing valuation work doesn't change, but the people doing the math must. I know we will both learn and make essential change.

THUS, ON A MINOR NOTE

Stock market activity has been a barometer on how well we have come to accept change. Values have risen from P/E ratios of 15 to as high as 40 in terms of safety margins investors will accept. What investors accept conditions what valuation tacticians do.

Louis Rukeyser's March 2001 "hype and buy-me newsletter" carried the headlining question, "Are Technology Stocks Dead?" I loved his response: "My Answer is 'BULL!' " He went on, "Anyone who hasn't noticed that Wall Street has a perennial penchant for panic clearly hasn't been paying attention. Tighten the screws for a few hours, and fear beats greed by a landslide." A new crop of better developed, better funded, and better managed online technology businesses will come out of the embers. However, I disagree with Mr. Rukeyser's thoughts about fear beating out greed (for too long), because the market-watchers and players were still plunking down cash in the NASDAQ as recently as just a few days ago. On March 12, 2001, fear hit again; it can't help but return. But greed only sleeps for a while. It, too, returns.

Case of Shot Myself in the Foot

In 1963 I came up with what ended in a bird-brained debacle—a "Pheasant Under Glass" restaurant/franchise concept. Chicken franchises were hot; pheasant, considered the meal of kings—this idea would certainly take a new business up and out of sight. I had even enlisted a top radio announcer to be partner and to lend the use of his name. We became excited: collected and analyzed tons of chicken data, had special under-glass-like containers designed, commissioned architectural renderings for buildings, designed a flexible distribution system, set standards for book-keeping—the whole nine yards! But the most important yard missing was the first yard. Production! How does one commercially grow a supply of pheasant sufficient to feed an army that might not stop growing? The U.S. Department of Agriculture pointed us to the nation's largest grower. For many years, he'd been in the business of supplying the U.S. Fish and Game people with ready-for-release birds to seed in places where populations of pheasant were dying out. Try as he may, and for over 10 years, he could never get his adult-bird production beyond 250,000 per year. We learned that pheasant is an incredibly complex and high-risk bird to raise. We also learned that 250,000 birds would be unlikely to supply more than 2.3 facilities in less than one year from opening. Breakeven on initial development costs could not occur until the sixth facility was up and running. $175,000 and much wasted time now foolishly out the window, I had spent less than $500 on phone calls and travel to learn from a professional grower that my original hypothesis was broken. I started out looking for answers in all the wrong places.

Appendix A

Valuation of a Marina

Author's Responses

Until a business actually sells, there are no right or wrong answers as to its value; there are only estimates as to what buyers and sellers *might* accomplish through *arm's-length* negotiations. For all practical purposes, arm's length simply means that a buyer and a seller are "free" to accept or reject any and all proposals made by each other. For example, in cases of divorce, death of owners, or impending bankruptcies, sellers may not have much choice and thus may not be as *freewheeling* in their negotiations as they might otherwise be without the influence of these external pressures.

Estimating fair market value of businesses assumes that the only *external influence* is one of supply and demand economics, which is traditionally rooted in a concept of scarcity. Asset values, cash flows, financing conditions, and freedom of choice for both parties set that stage. However, Alchemic* economics (belief that today's markets are no longer driven by scarcity but rather by a concept of *creating abundance*) offers that predicting *most-likely* selling prices may or may not entirely fit conditions based on scarcity. The issue of estimating fair market value has traditionally been scientific in nature, and the *process* has frequently been completed by an individual whose primary strengths lie in finance or accounting. In that respect, and at least on the small-company valuation scene, knowledge about the motivations (emotional makeup) of a *sole* decision maker in the closely held enterprise can be missing. Unless the value processor also possesses intimate marketplace awareness, these estimates for fair market value can quickly become ruled by the numbers game. As a rather too

---

*Alchemy—A medieval chemical science and speculative philosophy aiming to achieve the transmutation of the base metals into gold, the discovery of a universal cure for disease, and the discovery of a means of indefinitely prolonging life. In effect, a power or process of transforming something common into something special. C.G. Jung, in his 1944 book *Psychology and Alchemy*, offered that the aim for gold was the human wholeness of individualism (a process rather than a goal).

common practice, the prediction of most-likely prices under which businesses might elicit transfers of ownership is derived from the spectrum and wide use of *"comparable" sales techniques*. It is indeed hard to compare the educations, experiences, skills, and driving forces of individuals who presume to operate these so-called comparable businesses. Thus, small businesses can possess both fair market values forecast through the numbers game and most-likely values, which are largely an emotional game played out by buyers and sellers themselves (and measured best by the marketing representatives who sell these small businesses). If Alchemic economics plays any role in small-business purchase, and I strongly suspect that it does, then buyers might frequently enter negotiations with additional unmeasurable criteria that is not based in *any* past occurrence of comparability. Mix this well, as in our case example, with the ambiance of a body of navigable water, then even the skills of a rocket scientist may be unable to predict where the projectile of "price" will land.

OUR CASE

The owner of this marina has scraped out a living during the past 11 years of ownership. He has improved the business considerably during his tenure, but cash has always been in short supply. From a business standpoint, he is under no duress to sell; however, *he has an opportunity to manage an oceanfront complex at a very good salary.* I purposely left this vital detail out so that readers would view the practice exercise through an arm's-length window (which, incidentally, is the more traditional viewpoint assumed by a majority of players). The dilemma (emotional) faced by our seller could be assessed as follows:

1. Eleven years of ownership without much to show for it in the way of financial returns.
2. Time-fuse on a job opportunity that represents a better lifestyle and escape from financial struggle.

Do not be misguided by the "grass is greener on the other side of the fence" theory. Pride and self-esteem, contained in item 1, are major hurdles to overcome. Item 2 can conjure a sense of running away from the battle. The entrepreneurial nature of small-business owners is to fight with pride until the battle is over. For the benefit of readers, let me summarize what I believe this seller has been thinking: "I want as much cash from my sale as possible so that I can go on to the job with a sense of pride."

The *beginning* balance sheet 11 years ago reveals approximately what he paid for the business originally. With the exception of inventory ($148,790 at the time of his purchase), 1999 discloses the rest.

Inventory	$148,790
Land	30,000
Buildings/Docks	368,178
Vehicles	30,435
Furniture/Equipment	7,608
Tools	14,565
Signs	6,438
Goodwill	30,000
Less: Floor-Plan Interest	− 36,014
Approximate Price Originally Paid	$600,000

Why is this important to know? Psychologically (by reason of self-esteem), few sellers will part with their businesses *below this number,* unless "forced" to do so by external influences **beyond their control**. Compelling though it may seem, accepting or rejecting the "job" *is,* nevertheless, within the seller's control. This sets the stage for estimating a *most-likely* selling price. Will the fair market estimate accommodate at least $600,000, and, if not, what "sale features" can be included to arrest potential feelings of low self-esteem and still encourage sale?

Our first task is to review what is being held out for sale with the business:

Appraised Value of Assets Held Out For Sale

Land/Buildings/Docks (Includes Improvements)	$358,178
Vehicles	21,000
Furniture/Equipment	6,000
Tools	9,000
Other/Signs	5,000
"Owned" Inventory	212,385*
Total	$611,563

*$72,261 of the products are in "floor-plan" inventory at 2% per month carrying cost. For a properly qualified buyer, these may be *assumed* and thus do not require additional financing. However, bear in mind that a lender would add these costs to other debt-service payments as they consider the extent of other capital they might loan.

Based on the footnote above, total assets held out for sale could, subsequently, be reduced to $539,302. Floor-plan interest is already included in operating expenses.

At this stage, we must determine whether *cash flows* will support the purchase of assets ($539,302) plus the difference to $600,000 ($60,698) of goodwill . . . or even more in value. The balance sheets and income statements are repeated here for your convenience.

Practice Session—Marina
Balance Sheets

	1999	2000	2001
Assets			
Current Assets			
Cash	$ 5,049	$ 2,256	$ 2,307
Acct./Rec.	17,691	12,684	16,026
Inventory	215,814	204,300	212,385
Prepaid Expenses	8,733	6,933	
Total Current Assets	$247,287	$226,173	$230,718
Fixed			
Land	$ 30,000	$ 30,000	$ 30,000
Bldg./Docks	368,178	368,178	368,178
Improvements	42,537	46,785	46,785
Vehicles	30,435	30,435	30,435
Furn./Equip.	7,608	7,608	7,608
Tools	14,565	14,565	14,565
Signs	6,438	6,438	6,438
Less: Deprec.	− 125,328	− 142,398	− 148,242
Total Fixed	$374,433	$361,611	$355,767
Other			
Reorg. Exp.	$ 756	—	—
Goodwill	30,000	30,000	30,000
Total Other	$ 30,756	$ 30,000	$ 30,000
TOTAL ASSETS	$652,476	$617,784	$616,485
	1999	2000	2001
Liabilities			
Current			
Acc./Payable	$ 3,270	$ 1,647	$ 2,604
Deposits	4,293	828	1,074
Notes—Floor Plan	104,529	97,242	72,261
Mortgage	57,567	43,500	45,990
Total Current	$169,659	$143,217	$121,929
Long-Term Mortgage	$257,709	$246,381	$234,234
Total Long Term	$257,709	$246,381	$234,234
TOTAL LIABILITIES	$427,368	$389,598	$356,163
Equity	$225,108	$228,186	$260,322
TOTAL LIABILITIES & EQUITY	$652,476	$617,784	$616,485

Practice Session—Marina
Reconstructed Income Statements for Valuation

	1999	2000	2001
Sales	$550,521	$583,656	$538,776
Cost of Sales	357,387	345,201	314,811
Gross Profit	$193,134	$238,455	$223,965
% Gross Profit	35.1%	40.9%	41.6%
Expenses			
Advertising	$ 13,392	$ 7,893	$ 10,650
Vehicle Exp.	231	1,608	696
Prof. Fees	6,924	5,031	4,311
Insurance	22,743	19,023	29,979
Office Supplies	1,944	1,986	1,596
Repair/Maint.	3,450	3,252	7,707
Wages	17,832	23,331	17,895
Floor-Plan Int.	19,107	19,434	16,671
Shop Supplies	6,420	6,288	10,686
Taxes—Real Est.	3,351	6,660	6,660
Taxes—Payroll	5,517	6,999	3,669
Telephone	3,729	3,747	3,711
Travel	3,891	1,992	2,043
Uniforms	450	540	630
Utilities	4,578	4,350	3,138
Miscellaneous	6,435	10,938	4,938
Total Expenses	$119,994	$123,072	$124,980
Recast Income	$ 73,140	$115,383	$ 98,985
% Recast Income	13.3%	19.8%	18.4%

Ratio Study

Financial experts will not always agree as to which ratios are particularly germane to the small and privately owned enterprise. I feel that it is essential to examine the following:

$$\text{Ratio for Gross Margin} = \frac{\text{Gross Profit}}{\text{Sales}} \text{ or}$$

1999	2000	2001	Industry Median
35.1	40.9	41.6	**58.0**

This ratio measures the percentage of sales dollars left after goods are sold. Although gross margins have improved, they remain below the industry median. A number of potentially adverse conditions could be pulling these margins down in our target company. It may be in product "mix," due to poor buying decisions, low "quantity" buying, low profit-yield services offered, and so on. A prospective buyer might be advised to look into what effect unavailable cash has had on gross margins.

The current ratio provides a rough indication of a company's ability to service its obligations due within one year. Progressively higher ratios signify increasing ability to service short-term obligations. Bear in mind that liquidity in a specific business is a critical element of asset composition. Thus the acid test ratio that follows is perhaps a better indicator of liquidity overall.

$$\textbf{Current Ratio} \ = \ \frac{\text{Total Current Assets}}{\text{Total Current Liabilities}} \quad \text{or}$$

1999	2000	2001	Industry Median
1.5	1.6	1.9	.8

The quick, or acid test, ratio is a refinement of the current ratio and more thoroughly measures liquid assets of cash and accounts receivable in the sense of ability to pay off current obligations. Higher ratios indicate greater liquidity as a general rule. Our target company seems to be improving in this department.

$$\textbf{Quick Ratio} \ = \ \frac{\text{Cash and Equivalents} + \text{Receivables}}{\text{Total Current Liabilities}} \quad \text{or}$$

1999	2000	2001	Industry Median
.1	.1	.2	.2

A ratio of less than 1.0 can suggest a struggle to stay current with obligations. The median suggests that the industry as a whole may wrestle with liquidity problems by the nature of doing business and, even the top 25% of reported companies reflect only a ratio of .5. This comprises our third index signaling a "downside" nature.

$$\textbf{Sales/Receivable Ratio} \ = \ \frac{\text{(Income Statement)}}{\frac{\text{Sales}}{\text{Receivables}}} \quad \text{or}$$
$$\text{(Balance Sheet)}$$

1999	2000	2001	Industry Median
31.1	46.0	33.6	34.3–186.1

This is an important ratio and measures the number of times that receivables turn over during the year. While erratic in nature and about average in sense of the industry median, we cannot put much weight on this ratio, since receivables tend to be so small.

$$\text{Day's Receivable Ratio} = \frac{365}{\text{Sales/Receivable Ratio}} \quad \text{or}$$

1999	2000	2001	Industry Median
12	8	11	**11–2 days**

This highlights the average time in terms of days that receivables are outstanding. Generally, the longer that receivables are outstanding, the greater the chance that they may not be collectible. Slow-turnover accounts merit individual examination for conditions of cause. Turnover in our target seems acceptable by industry standards.

$$\text{Cost of Sales/Payables Ratio} = \frac{\text{Cost of Sales}}{\text{Payables}} \quad \text{or}$$

1999	2000	2001	Industry Median
109.3	209.6	120.9	**27.3**

Generally, the higher their turnover rate, the shorter the time between purchase and payment. Lower turnover suggests that companies may frequently pay bills from daily in-house cash receipts due to slower receivable collections. This practice may be somewhat misguided in light of investment principles whereby one normally attempts to match collections relatively close to payments so that more business income can be directed into the pockets of owners. Some businesses may, however, have little choice. Our target company is exceptionally attentive in paying bills. This raises a question of floor-plan management. For example, is there a good balance of cash being used to pay floor-plan interest, versus a better use toward purchased inventory? How might this play out in terms of increasing gross margins?

$$\text{Sales/Working Capital Ratio} = \frac{\text{Sales}}{\text{Working Capital*}} \quad \text{or}$$

1999	2000	2001	Industry Median
7.1	7.0	5.0	**−21.9**

*Working capital equals current assets less current liabilities.

A low ratio may indicate an inefficient use of working capital, whereas a very high ratio often signals a vulnerable position for creditors. This *minus* industry median indicates that working capital is quite regularly scarce or that inefficient uses of working capital prevail throughout this industry. The results of this ratio indicate positive signs. Though working capital increased in each of these years ($77,628 to $82,956 to $108,789), the ratio dropped off in 2001 because of the lowest sales performance during the three-year period. Ratios, by themselves, may not always tell the whole story.

To analyze how well inventory is being managed, the cost of sales to inventory ratio can identify important potential shortsightedness.

$$\text{Cost of Sales/Inventory Ratio} \;=\; \frac{\text{Cost of Sales}}{\text{Inventory}} \quad \text{or}$$

1999	2000	2001	Industry Median
1.7	1.7	1.5	**3.8**

A higher inventory turnover can signify a more liquid position and/or better skills at marketing, whereas a lower turnover of inventory may indicate shortages of merchandise for sale, overstocking, or obsolescence. These lower turnovers of inventory leave me skeptical about conditions in this asset. My first inclination would be to look, item by item, to determine what, if any, products could be changed from stock to "custom" order, or dropped entirely. $140,124 ($212,385 − $72,261 in floor plan) is a great deal of money to be turning over at less than twice per year.

THE VALUATION EXERCISE

Book Value Method

Total Assets at Year-End 2001	$ 616,485
Total Liabilities	356,163
Book Value at Year-End 2001	$ 260,322

Adjusted Book Value Method

Assets	Balance Sheet Cost	Fair Market Value
Cash	$ 2,307	$ 2,307
Acct./Rec.	16,026	16,026
Inventory	212,385	212,385
Prepaid Exp.		
Land	30,000	358,178
Real Estate/Docks	368,178	Included
Improvements	46,785	Included
Vehicles	30,435	21,000
Furniture/Equip.	7,608	6,000

Assets	Balance Sheet Cost	Fair Market Value
Tools	14,565	9,000
Signs	6,438	5,000
Other	30,000	Included
Accumulated Deprec.	− 148,242	N/A
Total Assets	$ 616,485	$ 629,896
Total Liabilities	$ − 356,163	$ − 356,163
	$ 260,322	

Adjusted Book Value at 2001		$ 273,733

Weighted Average Cash Flow

1999	$ 73,140	(1)	=	$ 73,140	
2000	115,383	(2)	=	230,766	
2001	98,985	(3)	=	296,955	
Totals		(6)	=	$ 600,861	
	Divided by			6	
Weighted Reconstructed Income				$ 100,144	

The flip-side nature of three years of sales and income suggests the possibility that revenues might have peaked and that income is now largely dependent upon each year's economy. However, to assure oneself of such assumptions, several other years' performances should be examined. You can take this assumption for granted in our case.

Hybrid Method

(This is a form of the capitalization method.)

1 = High amount of dollars in assets and low-risk business venture

2 = Medium amount of dollars in assets and medium-risk business venture

3 = Low amount of dollars in assets and high-risk business venture

	1	2	3
Yield on Risk-Free Investments Such as Government Bonds[a] (often 6%–9%)	8.0%	8.0%	8.0%
Risk Premium on Nonmanagerial Investments[a] (corporate bonds, utility stocks)	4.5%	4.5%	4.5%
Risk Premium on Personal Management[a]	7.5%	14.5%	22.5%
Capitalization Rate	*20.0%*	*27.0%*	*35.0%*
Earnings Multipliers	**5.0**	**3.7**	**2.9**

[a]These rates are revised periodically to reflect changing economies. They can be composed through the assistance of expert investment advisers if need be.

This particular version of a hybrid method tends to place 40% of business value in book values.

Book Value at Year-End 2001	$260,322	
Add: Appreciation in Assets	13,411	
Book Value as Adjusted	$273,733	
Weight to Adjusted Book Value	40%	$109,493
Weighted Reconstructed Income	$100,144	
Times Multiplier	×3.7	$370,533
Total Business Value		$480,026

Market Value of Assets Held Out for Sale

Inventory	$212,385
Less: Floor-Plan Inventory	− 72,261
Subtotal	$140,124
Land/Buildings/Docks	358,178
Vehicles	21,000
Furniture/Equipment	6,000
Tools	9,000
Signs	5,000
Total	$539,302

Excess Earnings Method

(This method considers cash flow and values in hard assets, estimates intangible values, and superimposes tax considerations and financing structures to prove the most-likely equation.)

Reconstructed Cash Flow	$ 100,144
Less: Comparable Salary (provided)	− 27,000
Less: Contingency Reserve	− 5,000
Net Cash Stream to Be Valued	$ 68,144

Cost of Money

Market Value of Tangible Assets	
(See reconstructed balance sheet)	$ 539,302
Times: Applied Lending Rate	×10%
Annual Cost of Money	$ 53,930

Excess of Cost of Earnings

Net Cash Stream to Be Valued	$ 68,144
Less: Annual Cost of Money	− 53,930
Excess of Cost of Earnings	$ 14,214

Intangible Business Value

Excess of Cost of Earnings	$ 14,214
Times: Intangible Net Multiplier Assigned	×2.0*
Intangible Business Value	$ 28,428
Add: Tangible Asset Value	539,302
TOTAL BUSINESS VALUE (Prior to Proof)	$ 567,730
	(Say $570,000)

Financing Rationale

Total Investment	$ 570,000
Less: Down Payment	− 142,500
Balance to Be Financed	$ 427,500

*Refer to Figure 9.1 in Chapter 9.

At this point, we must gauge the amount in prospective bank financing. It's important to use a good deal of logic at this stage of valuation or you will waste a lot of time coming up with reliable estimates. One can set up the financing scenario in any way appropriate to local conditions.

Real Estate ($358,178) at 65% of FMV	$232,816
Furniture/Equip. ($6,000) at 30% of FMV	1,800
Tools ($9,000) at 50% of FMV	4,500
Vehicles ($21,000) at 30% of FMV	6,300
Inventory ($140,124) at 50% of Book Value	70,062*
Estimated Bank Financing	$315,478
	(Say $315,000)

*While inventory is stated at $212,385, bear in mind that $72,261 of that inventory is already under floor-plan financing.

Bank (10% x 15 years)	
Amount	$315,000
Annual Principal/Interest Payment	40,620

Testing Estimated Business Value

Return: Net Cash Stream to Be Valued	$ 68,144
Less: Annual Bank Debt Service (P&I)	− 40,620
Pretax Cash Flow	$ 27,524
Add: Principal Reduction	11,655*
Pretax Equity Income	$ 39,179
Less: Est. Dep. & Amortization	− 14,150
Less: Estimated Income Taxes	− 2,006
Net Operating Income (NOI)	$ 23,023

*Debt service includes annual principal payments that are traditionally recorded on the balance sheet as a reduction in debt owed. (I use an average of the first five or six years.)

Return on Equity:

$$\frac{\text{Pretax Equity Income}}{\text{Down Payment}} = \frac{\$ 39,179}{\$142,500} = 27.5\%$$

Return on Total Investment:

$$\frac{\text{Net Operating Income}}{\text{Total Investment}} = \frac{\$ 23,023}{\$570,000} = 4.0\%$$

A Bit of Proof

Basic Salary	$27,000
Net Operating Income	23,023
Gain of Principal	11,655
Tax-Sheltered Income (Dep.)	14,150
Effective Income	$75,828*

*This number should not include dollars set aside in the contingency and replacement reserves.

At this time we have taken our first shot at estimating the marina's value using the excess earnings method. Although I said in the beginning that the seller would not provide owner financing (all sellers say that), this does not mean such should not be figured. A tip: Few businesses in America sell without it.

However, we have a very real problem in that we are *short* $112,500 (a selling price of $570,000 minus bank financing of $315,000, minus the down payment of $142,500 equals $112,500). Decrease selling price by that amount, or increase cash from the buyer by that amount, is the choice left. Increasing the down payment to $255,000 might be quite impractical, since this would represent nearly 45% of the selling price and be considered not prudent in the eyes of most buyers. A much more practical thought would be to approach the seller, present the facts, and let *him* choose.

Digressing for a moment, let's add one other bit of simple arithmetic: $570,000 plus $72,261 in floor-planned inventory equals $642,261 realized in sale. Framed in this light (and assuming the culprit self-esteem lurks about), the seller might be more inclined to provide financing for the cash shortfall.

Financing Rationale	
Total Investment	$ 570,000
Less: Down Payment	− 142,500
Less: Bank Financing	− 315,000
Balance to Be Financed by the Owner	$ 112,500

Bank (10% x 15 years)	
Amount	$315,000
Annual Principal/Interest Payment	40,620

Note: Deciding what structure can be offered to a seller is a linear problem to some extent. As payments are made on bank loans, the *principal amount* goes down while equity increases to the extent of those payments. Since *functional* obsolescence does generally occur in some of these assets, no one can precisely determine just where the lines of decreased debt and decreased asset value cross over such that refinancing might accommodate "balloon" payments often expected by sellers. For a plethora of both psychological and practical reasons, I prefer not to suggest balloon payments whenever they can be avoided. Thus, my first exploration or question revolves around how much additional burden existing cash flow can withstand. Past experience teaches me that about 8% and eight years "feels" reasonably correct in our target case. If my gut feeling is wrong, all I need do is reopen the experiment.

Seller (8% × 8 years)	
Amount	$112,500
Annual Principal/Interest Payment	19,085
Combined Annual Principal/Interest Payment	$ 59,705

Testing Estimated Business Value	
Return: Net Cash Stream to Be Valued	$ 68,144
Less: Annual Debt Service (P&I)	− 59,705
Pretax Cash Flow	$ 8,439
Add: Principal Reduction	25,561
Pretax Equity Income	$ 34,000
Less: Est. Dep. & Amortization (Let's Assume)	− 14,150
Less: Estimated Income Taxes (Let's Assume)	−0−*
Net Operating Income (NOI)	$ 19,850

*I have assumed that increased interest (an expense item on the income statment) paid on higher debt will eliminate profit and, therefore, business tax obligations.

Return on Equity:

$$\frac{\text{Pretax Equity Income}}{\text{Down Payment}} = \frac{\$\ 34,000}{\$142,500} = 23.9\%$$

Return on Total Investment:

$$\frac{\text{Net Operating Income}}{\text{Total Investment}} = \frac{\$\ 19,850}{\$570,000} = 3.5\%$$

Buyer's Potential Cash Benefit

Forecast Annual Salary	$ 27,000
Pretax Cash Flow (contingency not considered)	8,439
Income Sheltered by Depreciation	14,150
Less: Provision for Taxes	–0–
Discretionary Cash	$ 49,589
Add: Equity Buildup	25,561
Discretionary and Nondiscretionary Cash	$ 75,150

Seller's Potential Cash Benefit in Sale

Cash Down Payment	$142,500
Bank Financing Receipts	315,000
Gross Cash at Closing	$457,500*

*From which must be deducted capital gains and other taxes. Structured appropriately, the deal qualifies as an "installment" sale with the proceeds in seller financing taxed at a lower rate in later periods.

At this point, another critical question must be answered in terms of seller financing: Will $457,500 take care of existing debt? Returning to the balance sheet, we find that accounts payable ($2,604), current portion debt ($45,990), and long-term debt ($234,234) equal $282,828 ... or $174,672 over and above debt (bear in mind that floor-planned notes of $72,261 are presumed transferable to a buyer). Capital gains tax might not be a problem if the deal is structured right—book value at the time of the seller's purchase was $600,000, and we are proposing sale at $570,000.

Projected Cash to Seller by End of Eighth Year

Cash at Closing	$457,500
Add: Principal Payments	112,500
Add: Interest Payments	40,176
Pretax Eight-Year Proceeds	$610,176

$610,176 plus floor-plan transfer of $72,261 provides the seller the option of quoting $682,437 as the sale price for his marina. Taking this approach to convince the seller to provide some element of financing may not always work, but it did in this instance. Self-esteem was preserved to the extent that the seller felt comfortable in moving on to accept the job offered.

Results

Book Value Method	$260,322
Adjusted Book Value Method	273,733
Hybrid (capitalization) Method	480,026
Excess Earnings Method	570,000

I ask once again, how did you do?

Questions:

1. What should this business be listed for? *I recommended $645,000 on the basis of $72,261 in floor-plan debt being transferable to the buyer.*

2. What is the *most-likely* sale price? $570,000

3. Would **you** pay this amount? *Only you know the answer to this question.*

The marina sold for $570,000 less an adjustment for inventory taken three days before closing. A bank provided slightly more than our example in financing, and the buyer made a larger than presented down payment . . . seller financing ended up at $85,000 over seven years.

I want to point out an important feature not covered during our evaluation: In the opening remarks of the case exercise, I mentioned that the 2,000-square-foot building included the *owner's living quarters.* While the size of quarters and the location may not always be convenient for a new owner's family, there is, nevertheless, a value of substance in light of future rental income. Or the space provides temporary living arrangements that reduce personal expenses for family housing. I did not include rental income, since the nature of this facility makes rental to outsiders impractical, and possibly unsafe, in terms of the security of assets. I did, however, recognize that cash returns to a buyer could be *tighter* than customary, because living expenses could be "sheltered" within the business itself. Perhaps judgmental on my part, but I feel that sellers should not be penalized when living accommodations are available to new owners who might otherwise simply choose to live elsewhere. By the same token, unless the income offered from these quarters could potentially be significant, I will ignore this part of the equation but may arbitrarily "squeeze" cash flow harder than usual.

Appendix B

Yegge's Rules for Making Deals Work

1. When conditions warrant, become a deal killer yourself.

2. Run free when you see what appears to be a Trojan Horse.

3. Contrary to law of the land, all deals are "guilty" until proven innocent.

4. For a deal to be good, the deal must be good for *all* parties. When the proposed deal does not feel, sound, or act good, then quality suspicion should become replacement rule number four.

5. Be friendly with business brokers and listen to what they have to say, but double-check numbers using accountants, and double-check contracts with attorneys before signing.

6. The only thing urgent in life is life itself—everything else, given time, will fall into place. In the business setting, urgent actions can be prone to produce urgent and unsatisfactory results.

7. As buyer or seller, don't become a training ground for inexperienced brokers. Ask brokers up front about their personal experience handling business transactions.

8. Ask—listen, suggest—listen, cooperate in solving, look into a mirror, and then act.

9. When you can't also make a friend during negotiation, revisit and question merits in the overall deal. You can't negotiate with strangers.

10. You can't handle situations unless there is complete understanding between *all* parties.

11. Be optimistic—think positive! Assume the ball has already been carried to touchdown.

12. Never wait for something to happen. State personal needs early in the game, and make it happen!

13. While you must eventually dive way beneath the surface to get at the chest, the *promise* in any treasure can ordinarily be discovered on the surface. Decisions to buy and sell small businesses are made in stages, and receiving proper information is encouraged by growing levels of trust.

14. The only time to let the world know about any deal is when the i's are dotted, the t's are crossed . . . and the deal has "cleared" the bank.

15. Price it and leave it, or take it and price downward accordingly what remains.

16. Sell, don't tell. The silent majority are the significant majority, because actions speak louder than words.

About the Author

Two thousand and one marks the passage of 16 years in the field of small-business consulting, and 21 years in other small-business ownership for me. This, I believe, is a relatively long time for a man to survive without the trappings and, yes, the safety of the corporate cocoon, where I spent the previous years of my business life. Somewhere along the line, I found time to acquire graduate degrees in both psychology and business. Without the blending of these two disciplines, I might still be in the corporate environment.

A first taste of small-business ownership came during my final tour with Navy Recruiting in Boston, where I founded an automatic letter writing and data processing business to supplement the cost of higher education. I sold this business in 1968, left the Navy, and joined a consulting firm part-time. A combination of consulting and academic networking thrust me into my own consulting business, but an uncontainable yearning grew in me in graduate school. My bright, shiny master's in business told me to move on when I was invited into the exciting prospect described through my education for the large, multinational corporate life.

Six-plus years in a large corporation introduced me to many wonderful experiences, among which was working in the mergers and acquisitions department, where I had the toughest boss in my career. He was also the best of all those before and after him. Much of my current entrepreneurial belief system was molded during these "high-flying," leveraged buyout times of the late 1960s and early 1970s. This corporation was acquired by still a larger giant, and this, too, was a valuable education, but one best left to tell at another time. When my boss fell under the proverbial ax customarily wielded on those at the top of acquired companies, I realized that it was time to move on again. Considered a "young Turk" (term of the times), I clearly had paths awaiting me in the "500" business world.

However, an old saying goes, "You can take the boy out of the country, but not the country out of the boy." I was born and raised in economically poor Huron, South Dakota, where the vast majority of businesses are relatively small. Missouri may be considered the "show-me" state, but South Dakota has produced more than its share of "I can do it myself" native sons. Thus, a return to the drawing board for small business.

Between then and now, I have purchased and sold 5 small businesses, brokered 300 plus, and presently own or co-own 4, including a start-up entrepreneurial online service. I have been a receiver in several businesses, including an agricultural operation, and have owned or operated manufacturing, retail, and service businesses. I am currently a consultant to two local universities in the development of formal small-business degree programs.

It is my hope that this book brings credible logic to the arduous *process* that some of us go through while deciphering various elements of small-business purchase and sale. It is also my hope that the suggestions offered herein will lend strength to negotiations between parties when confronted by the opinions of accountants, lawyers, buyers, sellers, business brokers, mothers, fathers, mothers-in-law, and fathers-in-law. I add the last four categories to emphasize the very real possibility in small business for the "blue-sky" dilemma presented in an old real estate story to occur—the one where a consulted father-in-law, a self-ordained expert, kills the proposed deal. After all, many of us finance some of our ventures with family-owned capital. However, a little help from your friends can be important. I've not forgotten important boyhood lessons in communication learned from informal gatherings around a rather courtly potbelly stove in the old corner store. As grandfather once asked the group, "What's better than psychotherapy, lasts longer, and costs a lot less?" Help from your friends; talk things over—open up. Their common sense and concern for you may be better than all the technical training in the world.

It is my further hope that you will send comments, thoughts, constructive criticisms, or other ideas that may improve the quality of this book for future editions. In addition, I would like to hear about your experiences in using this book.

> *"If a man does not keep pace with his companions, perhaps it is because he hears a different drummer. Let him step to the music he hears, however measured or far away."*
>
> Henry David Thoreau

Index